Oliver GOLDSMITH

a reference guide

SAMUEL H. WOODS, JR.

G.K.HALL&CO.

70 LINC

Library of Congress Cataloging in Publication Data

Woods, Samuel H.
  Oliver Goldsmith, a reference guide.

  (A Reference guide to literature)
  Includes index.
  1. Goldsmith, Oliver, 1728-1774—Bibliography.
I. Title. II. Series.
Z8353.W65   [PR3493]   016.828'609   81-23734
ISBN 0-8161-8339-2   AACR2

This publication is printed on permanent/durable acid-free paper
MANUFACTURED IN THE UNITED STATES OF AMERICA

To Clara Belle

Contents

The Author viii

Preface ix

Introduction xiii

Journal Abbreviations xxi

Goldsmith's Major Works xxiii

Writings about Oliver Goldsmith 1

Index 189

The Author

Samuel H. Woods, Jr., received his A.B. cum laude and his M.A. from Harvard, and his Ph.D. from Yale, with a dissertation on Goldsmith's essays and The Vicar of Wakefield. He has taught at the University of Colorado, Duke University, and is now a professor of English at Oklahoma State University.

His publications include Introduction to Literature, with Mary Rohrberger and Bernard Dukore; Reading and Writing about Literature, with Mary Rohrberger; essays on John Crowe Ransom in College English and PMLA; and essays on Goldsmith in Eighteenth-Century Studies and Studies in Burke and His Time.

Preface

This book provides an annotated list of writing about Oliver
Goldsmith and his works from the beginning of his literary career
through 1978. However, because Goldsmith was such a voluminous and
versatile writer, I have not tried to include comments about all his
works, but have generally limited the listings to the writing about
those pieces commonly considered belles-lettres or "literary," and
omitted comment about his many pieces of what is usually called his
"hack writing," such as his prefaces and introductions, his histories
of England, Greece, and Rome, and his History of the Earth and
Animated Nature, though in many cases, the literary quality of these
works raises them considerably above the level usually assigned to
hack writing. I have, however, included some pieces dealing with
this body of work when they shed light on Goldsmith's thinking, but
generally I have limited the material I have included to that which
sheds light on those pieces included in Arthur Friedman's monumental
Collected Works of Oliver Goldsmith (Oxford: Oxford University
Press, 1966, 6 vols.). Thus most of the material listed here deals
with Goldsmith's life and, of his works, his essays, including The
Citizen of the World; his poems, especially The Traveller, The
Deserted Village, and Retaliation; his novel, The Vicar of Wakefield;
and his two plays, The Good Natur'd Man and She Stoops to Conquer.

Since for much more than two hundred years after his death,
Goldsmith's essays, poems, novel, and plays have been almost continu-
ously in print, I have not attempted to list every edition of his
individual works, although I have listed the major collected editions,
partly because their editors' comments have considerable importance
and partly because each major collected edition has added or sub-
tracted works from the Goldsmith canon, until with Friedman's
edition we now have a fairly reliable idea of most of those pieces
which Goldsmith did indeed write, although hardly a year passes that
claims are not put forward in behalf of an addition or two to his
writings. It is always possible that some major new addition to the
canon may be discovered, but it now seems improbable. Editions of
Goldsmith's works and Introductions to various editions are cited by
the name of the editor or author of the Introduction.

Preface

I have not attempted to list all the trade printings of individual works by Goldsmith, because while the large number of these shows that he has continued to be a popular author for most of the past two hundred years, few if any of these printings contain edited texts and thus have no particular interest for the serious student of Goldsmith. However, the splendidly detailed bibliographies of Goldsmith in both the Cambridge Bibliography of English Literature by Ronald S. Crane and in the New Cambridge Bibliography of English Literature by Arthur Friedman provide more specific information about separate issues of individual works.

I have not sought to trace the translations of Goldsmith's works, since these are recorded in Crane's and Friedman's bibliographies, though I have tried to include all significant scholarly works in languages other than English, especially those in French and German. Similarly, I have not included imitations of Goldsmith's works such as Timothy Dwight's "Greenfield Hill," in which the language directly recalls The Deserted Village. With other writers the problem of determining influence is far more difficult and beyond the scope of this collection. As my listing will show, Washington Irving was clearly attracted to Goldsmith's personality and his writing, yet the extent to which Goldsmith's style or thinking influenced Irving's own writings is much harder to determine. Irving's three biographies of Goldsmith certainly contributed to Goldsmith's popularity among nineteenth-century American readers, but a careful assessment of Goldsmith's literary reputation in America will require more detailed study than my listings can provide, though I have tried to indicate important American reprintings of English works. However, for detailed listings of separate American editions, I refer the reader to Crane's and Friedman's bibliographies.

While I have tried to include all important editions of Goldsmith's works and of writings about him and his works, I have made no effort to treat the innumerable school-text editions of his individual writings. All these I have examined, especially those published in the nineteenth and early twentieth centuries, are of no consequence textually or critically, since the biographical and critical introductions derive from editions I have described and the texts have no real authority, reflecting at best the state of Goldsmith scholarship at the time.

I have indicated items I was not able to examine personally with an asterisk preceding the entry number. Also asterisked are items for which the annotation is based on a later edition than the one cited; I indicate the text used at the end of the annotation.

In compiling my finding lists, I have depended heavily on the MLA International Bibliography, the Annual Bibliography of English Language and Literature of the Modern Humanities Research Association, Ronald S. Crane's Goldsmith bibliography in The Cambridge Bibliography of English Literature, Arthur Friedman's Goldsmith bibliography in The New Cambridge Bibliography of English Literature, "English Literature, 1660-1800, A Bibliography of Modern Studies," published from 1926 to 1974 in Philological Quarterly, and now published as The Eighteenth Century: A Current Bibliography by the American Society for Eighteenth-Century Studies, and The Year's Work in English Studies. To the compilers and annotators of these invaluable works, I express my heartfelt gratitude for their careful efforts, without which this book could never have been written.

I have done most of the research for this book in two libraries, the British Library, London, and the Edmon Low Library of Oklahoma State University. To D. T. Richnell, Director-General of the Reference Division, and the staffs of the North Library and the Reading Room of the British Library, I should like to express my deep thanks for their helpfulness, courtesy, and kindness to me. I am especially grateful to my home library, the Edmon Low Library of Oklahoma State University, especially to Roscoe Rouse, Librarian; Heather M. Lloyd, Lorna Ruesink, and Terry Basford, Research Librarians, for their extraordinary skill and speed in securing interlibrary loans for me; and to Carol Ahmad, former Humanities Librarian, Gerald Newman, Acting Humanities Librarian, and Terry Basford, Assistant Humanities Librarian, for help in innumerable miscellaneous ways. I also want to thank Joseph Moldenhauer, Chairman of the Department of English, University of Texas-Austin, for arranging my appointment as a Visiting Scholar, so that I might examine several eighteenth-century periodicals not otherwise available in the Library of the University of Texas-Austin.

Although I have been studying Oliver Goldsmith and his writings for more years than I now like to think, I have compiled and written this book only during the last three years, although I have drawn upon my review essay "The Vicar of Wakefield and Recent Goldsmith Scholarship," which originally appeared in Eighteenth-Century Studies 9 (Spring 1976):429-43; and "The Goldsmith 'Problem,'" Studies in Burke and His Times 19 (Winter 1978):47-60, and express my gratitude to the editors of these journals for permission to do so. I take great pleasure in acknowledging the help and encouragement of the following people:

Arthur Weitzman of Northeastern University, who asked me to undertake the book and who has shown great patience and tact in helping me see the book through the press; Janice Meagher, Associate Editor, G. K. Hall & Company, for smoothing out many rough places for me; Richard Quintana of the University of Wisconsin-Madison, who encouraged me from the beginning of this project and made so many helpful suggestions that I cannot begin to specify them. I am especially grateful to him for his critical reading of the Introduction and correcting several of my errors; he bears no responsibility for those that may remain. He has also called my attention to several Goldsmith items I should otherwise have missed; Gordon Weaver of Oklahoma State University for calling my attention to John

Ginger's <u>The Notable Man</u>, a book I might otherwise have missed; Charlene Fries, who prepared the typescript for the publisher and endured my vagaries and absentmindedness with never-failing, cheerful patience; my wife, who encouraged and helped me from the beginning in many ways that she will never know. The dedication is meager thanks for all she has done.

Introduction

The reader of this book may form an opinion of the nature and range
of interest in Oliver Goldsmith and his writings from the material
contained here. I have begun by providing examples of contemporary
English reviews of Goldsmith's major writings, at least in part to
show the frequent division of critics' opinions. The division--or
uncertainty--is particularly striking in the reviews of The Vicar,
where early reviewers clearly did not understand the book or at any
rate had a hard time making clear to their readers what they thought
of it. Since sharp differences of opinion about the novel exist
among twentieth-century critics, perhaps we should not be surprised.
In somewhat similar fashion, the audiences of Goldsmith's plays had
difficulty deciding what to make of his first play, The Good Natur'd
Man, and though the reviewers of the second, She Stoops to Conquer,
were delighted and amused, the reviewers of the printed play differed
sharply and found its plot improbable. Contemporary audiences still
delight in the play, and now even readers and critics of the printed
text seem less troubled than pleased.

Goldsmith's poems today are to be found in nearly all high school
and college anthologies of English literature, but almost certainly
do not arouse the same enthusiasm among their readers that they did
with Johnson or Hawkesworth, their eighteenth-century reviewers. For
one thing, involuntary readers, as most students are, seldom respond
with enthusiasm, but the general decrease in the poetry-reading
public is almost certainly important in this change, too, though
sometimes one suspects that the poetry-reading public may well be a
constant, small proportion of the population.

In some ways, Goldsmith's personality has from his own lifetime
been a puzzle. To their contemporaries, such major personalities as
Swift, Pope, or Johnson had broadly some kind of particular character,
though it might or might not be one that was admired or disliked.
But even during his own lifetime, Goldsmith the man was hard for many
of his contemporaries to understand. Sir Joshua Reynolds seems to
have understood him best, though Johnson considered him a man of
talent very early in his career, when Goldsmith had published nothing
signed with his own name, and Johnson insisted that he be one of the
original members of the Club when it was organized in 1764. But the

more usual opinion was Horace Walpole's description of him as "inspired idiot" or Garrick's somewhat snide mock epitaph that he "wrote like an angel but talked like poor Poll," similar opinions stressing the gap between Goldsmith's skill with his pen and his notoriously inept social behavior. Boswell clearly had trouble understanding both Goldsmith and Johnson's recognition of his talents. Thus, during his own lifetime, Goldsmith did not make sense to most of his contemporaries as a coherent personality, and anecdotes of his strange behavior circulated widely and of course on his death more were recollected.

When Goldsmith died, some of those who knew him best like Reynolds, Percy, and Johnson did not know how old he was and did not know exactly where he had been born. It is true that these men came of a generation to whom personal revelation was abhorrent and the details of a man's inner life were certainly not matters for public discussion, and often not even for very private conversation with one's very best friends. Goldsmith was certainly a major literary figure in English life when he died, even though most of his income derived from his compilations rather than from those relatively few works upon which his literary reputation has rested during the past two hundred years. Because of his public reputation for bizarre behavior, there was curiosity about his life--in present day terms he was a celebrity and the object of public interest. Almost immediately following his death, collections of anecdotes began to appear, and those by Glover, a casual Irish acquaintance of some years' standing, set the tone for most of these early short biographical sketches based on the writers' personal recollections and literary gossip. They are frequently inaccurate in detail, and succeeding ones almost always repeat the earlier, with the general outlines traceable back to Glover's account, three versions of which appeared in the year of Goldsmith's death. None of Goldsmith's close friends like Reynolds, Johnson, or Percy published any account with claims to being definitive soon after his death. As is well known, copyright problems had prevented Johnson from including Goldsmith among the poets he wrote about in the preface to the booksellers' collection of English poets, a fact that virtually everyone regretted and still regrets. Percy, not yet elevated to the dignity of an Irish bishopric, planned a collected edition of Goldsmith's works for the benefit of the poet's poor Irish relatives and gave the materials he had collected to Johnson, who was balked in his efforts by the copyright problem, as Katherine C. Balderston has shown in her History and Sources of Percy's Memoir of Goldsmith (Cambridge: Cambridge University Press, 1926). On Johnson's death the materials returned to Percy's keeping and various problems delayed the projected edition and Percy's authoritative but brief life prefacing it until 1801. Thus for twenty-five years after Goldsmith's death, no reliable account of his life was available, and valuable as Percy's account is, in its brief space of 118 pages it does not provide a detailed account and certainly is by no means comparable to Boswell's Life of Johnson in scope. One result of this fact is that during the first half of the nineteenth century, a major thrust in the writing about Goldsmith is biographical, resulting in three major efforts. After Percy's brief life, Irving's 1825 short life, like Percy's prefaced to a collected edition, reflected a conscientious effort to provide a brief biographical and critical account of Goldsmith's work, using the most reliable printed sources but not attempting to go beyond these; Irving's 1840 and 1849 expansions reflect little essential change in attitude or interpretation and neither shows original research. In each case Irving probably deserves greater credit than he has usually been given for the quality of his work, although his interpretation of Goldsmith's personality is not one finding many supporters today. He was by no means the first to present "poor Goldsmith," the gentle genius underpaid by the publishers, but he certainly did much to set this image, which others continued to stress until quite recent times.

Sir James Prior's two-volume Life, published in 1837, was the first full-scale biography produced. Prior went as far as he could beyond printed sources, interviewing those people in Ireland he could find with some memories of Goldsmith and collecting letters from others who had had some direct knowledge of him. Prior's life reflects his diligence in accumulating minute information, and while he is unremarkable as a stylist, he is among the most objective early full-scale biographers and least prone to give us the "poor Goldsmith" of Irving. As such, his biography remains of great value.

Goldsmith's next major biographer, John Forster, though he did a good bit of original research, drew enough on Prior's work to an extent that it aroused Prior's resentment. Forster and Irving between them probably fixed the legend of "poor Goldsmith," the lovable but childlike writer exploited by the booksellers and forced to unpalatable hack writing by these greedy businessmen--a legend that hardly squares with Goldsmith's own remarks that the booksellers and the public are an author's best friends. Unfortunately, this legend informs most Victorian writing about Goldsmith with a few exceptions like William Black, and even affected the view of him taken by Austin Dobson, probably the best-informed late nineteenth-century writer about Goldsmith and usually level-headed in his judgment.

As this summary shows, from the appearance of Percy's Life in 1801 through Forster's 1854 revision of his biography, much of the writing about Goldsmith and interest in him was biographical, at least partly because of the nineteenth century confusion of biography and literary criticism. This confusion led to a strong emphasis on biographical writing and often only a fairly sketchy interest in Goldsmith's writing, or at least the sense that his writing was of secondary importance to his life. The "poor Goldsmith" legend at any rate suited the nineteenth-century truism that writers are creatures misunderstood by their societies, usually exploited, and almost always alienated.

Introduction

During his own lifetime Goldsmith had practiced virtually every major literary form that period considered important, and at his death, Johnson expressed the consensus of that generation in his epitaph when he wrote <u>nullum</u>, <u>quod</u> <u>tetegit</u>, <u>non</u> <u>ornavit</u>. However, Johnson's taste and Goldsmith's too was quite conservative, with little sympathy for the rising tide of what would become Romanticism, beginning to make itself felt in the poetry of Gray, Collins, and Cowper and in the sentimental novels and plays. As a literary form, the essay periodical scarcely survived the mid-eighteenth-century revival of which <u>The Citizen of the World</u> was a late example. The collected editions of the <u>Spectator</u>, <u>Rambler</u>, and even <u>The Citizen of the World</u> might continue to be published, bought, and read, but few if any later series were even written.

Thus, at the time of Goldsmith's death, the shifting from the Augustan sensibility to what would emerge as Romanticism was evident in the writers' groping toward a new idiom, even though something like general public acceptance of the new mode would not occur until around 1830. This shift in literary taste may help account for the mixed reception of Goldsmith's writing by major nineteenth-century critics. Except for Scott, Goethe, Hazlitt, Thackeray, George Eliot, and Henry James, the major figures among the Romantics and Victorians showed little interest in or enthusiasm for him, though some of this absence of comment can be explained by the general nineteenth-century dislike of the eighteenth, perhaps best summed up in Matthew Arnold's description of Dryden and Pope as "classics of our prose."

Despite this antipathy, though, Goldsmith was apparently more popular than Johnson with the reading public, since after Percy's collection, itself going through six editions, the nineteenth century saw six separate major collected editions of Goldsmith's works: Irving's, Prior's, Bohn's, Cunningham's, and Gibbs's extensive revision of Bohn's, while after the 1825 Oxford edition of Johnson's works, only the 1850 Bohn edition appeared. How much those library editions were actually read and how much they served as furniture in Victorian middle-class libraries is, of course, hard to tell, but the constant issuing of individual works or one-volume collections by Goldsmith during this period does suggest that nineteenth-century Englishmen and Americans did read Goldsmith and not just fill their bookshelves with neat, uniformly bound sets of his works.

During the later nineteenth century and the twentieth century, as English literature came to be a part of the university curriculum and Goldsmith was commonly accepted and assigned as a standard eighteenth-century author, estimates of his popularity became distorted by the very fact that a considerable number of his readers were no longer voluntary. As the study of English literature became professionalized, the number of dissertations and journal articles devoted to his work provides some index of scholarly and critical

interest, and the interest of the general public becomes much
harder to estimate. However, even here scholarly publication is
not always a very valid index to professionals' opinion of literary
importance. Scholars, of course, publish newly discovered information and edit manuscripts and texts that need editing. The successive
recovery of Boswell manuscripts has provided a vast amount of material
to be classified, catalogued, and edited, and has obviously shed
much new light not only on Boswell but on most other members of the
Johnson circle, including Goldsmith. In recent years, a large number
of scholars have been engaged in and are engaged in bringing these
papers to publication. Certainly, Macaulay's ideas about Boswell
have long been exploded among the informed, but whether or not the
present general scholarly consensus about Boswell will change very
greatly because of all this recent scholarship is a question only
time itself can answer. Thus, the number of scholarly titles
published over a given period may provide a kind of very rough idea
of critical opinion about an author among academic professionals,
but it may also reflect merely fortunate accidents like the recovery
of the Boswell papers. The fact that we have had few if any
Goldsmith manuscripts to be edited in this century tells us almost
nothing about what professionals think of Goldsmith the writer.

Beyond question, the single piece of Goldsmith's writing that has
claimed the most enduring popularity has been The Vicar of Wakefield.
This fact may be partly explained by the shift from poetry to prose
fiction as the form of literature most popular with the general
reader, a shift occurring during the nineteenth century. Another
reason for this novel's popularity during the nineteenth century lies
in its greater observation of propriety than is to be found in
Fielding, Smollett, or Sterne, and even its avoiding the preoccupation
with sexual problems, however properly treated, found in Richardson's
novels. A frequent reason for praising the book among Victorian
critics is its sweetness of tone and its pure morality as well as
the pathos in the suffering of its characters. Another element that
contributed to its popularity is its rural setting, certainly an
added attraction in an increasingly industrialized, urbanized
England. Although its original reviewers were puzzled by it, they
do not describe the book as satirical and even shy away from considering it comedy. Throughout the nineteenth century, the general
antipathy to irony worked against the idea that the novel could
contain these elements, and such a view continues among a significant
number of important Goldsmith scholars today, although another
considerable group of present day eighteenth-century scholars believe
the comic-satirical view of the novel may be closer than the other to
Goldsmith's own intentions. A somewhat smaller group, not always
thoroughgoing admirers of the book's artistry, believe that Goldsmith
did not provide clear enough signals to the reader if he wanted the
book to be read as comic satire and that, for all its charm, the
novel is not completely successful, but too ambiguous for completely
clear interpretation.

Introduction

During his own lifetime, Goldsmith was probably most admired for his poetry, especially his heroic couplet poems, and described as a follower of Pope and Dryden. Certainly in his lifetime a writer did more to establish a serious literary reputation by writing a successful poem than any other form of literature, and Goldsmith solidified himself as a writer to be taken seriously rather than a mere bookseller's drudge with The Traveller and again with The Deserted Village. However, in considering his contemporary and early critics' tendency to praise him first of all as a "poet," we need to bear in mind that they frequently used the word to mean any writer of literary merit. Goldsmith himself uses the word in this way in his Enquiry into the Present State of Public Learning in Europe, and Johnson has Imlac use the word in this broad, generic sense in Chapter 10 of Rasselas and almost certainly used the word in this broad, generic sense in the epitaph he wrote for Goldsmith's memorial tablet in Westminster Abbey. Thus, almost certainly a considerable amount of the early praise for "Goldsmith the poet" includes his writing in other forms besides verse. But also until relatively late in the nineteenth century, being a poet carried more cultural prestige and status than did being any other kind of writer, though, of course, throughout the nineteenth century until the present time, the writer of prose fiction, especially the novelist, had gradually been displacing the poet as the main kind of literary personality. Beyond this problem, even though Goldsmith was considered a follower of Pope and thus writing in a poetic form with few attractions for the nineteenth-century reader, the subject matter of his poetry--description of foreign and English landscape--appears to have preserved him a considerable number of readers. The same rural setting that attracted readers to the Vicar also drew them to The Traveller and The Deserted Village, especially the second poem, where the pastoral elements and the nostalgic lament for the loss of rural innocence to city-bred corruption undoubtedly attracted readers. The philosophical strain that led Johnson to prefer The Traveller seems to have had less appeal than the pastoral and nostalgic elements during this period dominated by a Romantic sensibility. In more recent times, Goldsmith's poems have generally had fewer admirers than his prose or his second play, apparently because those very elements that helped maintain his popularity through the nineteenth century appear to have little or no appeal to more recent tastes in poetry for wit and irony, tastes that have helped rehabilitate Pope, Swift, and even Johnson as poets.

The fortunes of Goldsmith's plays have pretty much followed their original records. The Good Natur'd Man has been seldom revived on the stage, but She Stoops to Conquer has become part of the classic repertory, frequently revived by both amateur and professional companies and received with the same kind of delight by audiences ever since its first production.

The inclusion of Goldsmith as a standard author in the university English literature curriculum occasioned professional study of

his works by scholars. Just as a great deal of writing about
Goldsmith in the first hundred years after his death concentrated
on his life rather than on his writing, the problem of identifying
what he did write, especially during his early, unknown years, has
occupied the energy of not only early biographers like Prior but also
such twentieth-century scholars as Ronald Crane, Arthur Friedman,
and others. Balderston's edition of the letters and her studies of
the Percy memoir and of Goldsmith manuscripts are also landmark
studies. Much twentieth-century scholarship has been taken up with
Goldsmith's sources, sometimes in the tedious work of early twentieth-
century German scholars, and far more profitably in the work of
Crane, Lytton Sells, Friedman, and others in identifying particular
sources Goldsmith used, so that we know how heavily he drew upon
French literature. This identification of his debt to French
literature, location of his genuine writing, and the rejection by
Crane and Friedman of spurious pieces especially culminated in 1966
in the publication of Friedman's magnificent critical edition of the
Collected Works. The absence of any better text than Gibbs's late
nineteenth-century one for more than half of the twentieth century
almost certainly discouraged the quantity of Goldsmith scholarship.

Since 1966 and the appearance of Friedman's critical text,
Goldsmith scholarship has become much livelier than it was for a
long time. Ricardo Quintana's very well balanced study in 1967
shed fresh light on Goldsmith as a Georgian writer, not an Augustan
or pre-Romantic, to be understood in the special context of his own
times. In 1969, Robert Hopkins's True Genius of Oliver Goldsmith
stimulated considerable controversy, with most reviewers rejecting
Hopkins's thesis that Goldsmith's true genius is his comic satire,
especially that his prose works like The Citizen of the World, The
Life of Richard Nash, and the Vicar are consistently satiric, though
comically so, rather than with Swift's saeva indignatio. Since
then, Hopkins's thesis has been argued about considerably, with
most of the argument centering on whether or not the Vicar is
consistently satirical. The argument has by no means ceased, but the
writing about Goldsmith that goes on now more than two hundred years
after his death has changed a great deal. We still do not have a
fully satisfactory biography, but since Wardle's 1957 life, we have
had a reasonably good factual account of what Goldsmith the man did,
and though gaps in our knowledge remain, they are likely to remain
unfilled, so that for some parts of Goldsmith's life we shall
probably never have accurate information. What all the facts mean
is not completely agreed upon by those scholars to whom Goldsmith is
a major interest, and such argument is almost certainly not entirely
undesirable, since through the difference of opinion comes new
thinking as well as reconsideration of old.

Goldsmith's literary reputation probably reached its highwater
mark, as George Rousseau has noted, during the nineteenth century,
when Samuel Johnson's, Alexander Pope's, and Jonathan Swift's
several literary reputations were probably at their lowest ebb.

Today we recognize that the Goldsmith that Irving, and more especially
Forster presented was a misinterpretation of Goldsmith as both man
and writer. We also recognize that Swift and Pope were almost certainly the giants of the early eighteenth century. For a number of
years now, we have been reading Johnson and recognize his greatness
not only as a man but as a writer, too. Surely we are not far from
the day when we shall recognize that Goldsmith is Johnson's fitting
companion as the second great writer of the later eighteenth
century--certainly not Johnson's equal in the force and range of
his mind, but perhaps in a kind of intuitive way, a finer artist
than Johnson, beyond a doubt in the drama, almost certainly a better
novelist, and an essayist of perhaps not better but certainly
different quality. Johnson remains the masterly serious writer of
the Georgian period though not without his touches of wry, ironic
humor. Goldsmith is surely the master comedian of the mid-eighteenth
century, but a comedian behind whose mask lies his own special irony,
too, one that is hard to define but which Goethe described as
"benevolent." Surely George Rousseau is right in his optimism that
we have finally begun to ask the right questions about Goldsmith
after being long distracted. The answers we have been getting in
recent years are often better, and we are moving toward a clearer
understanding of the Oliver Goldsmith that Johnson correctly
described to Boswell as "a very great man."

Journal Abbreviations

BNYPL   Bulletin of the New York Public Library

CE   College English

ELN   English Language Notes

HLQ   Huntington Library Quarterly

JEPG   Journal of English and Germanic Philology

JHI   Journal of the History of Ideas

L&P   Literature and Psychology

MLN   Modern Language Notes

MLQ   Modern Language Quarterly

MLR   Modern Language Review

MP   Modern Philology

N&Q   Notes & Queries

PQ   Philological Quarterly

RES   Review of English Studies

SAQ   South Atlantic Quarterly

SB   Studies in Bibliography

SEL   Studies in English Literature, 1500-1900

TLS   London Times Literary Supplement

UTQ   University of Toronto Quarterly

Goldsmith's Major Works

An Enquiry into the Present State of Polite Learning in Europe, 1759

The Citizen of the World, 1762

The Life of Richard Nash, of Bath, Esq., 1762

The Traveller, 1764

Essays, 1765

The Vicar of Wakefield, 1766

The Good Natur'd Man, 1768

The Deserted Village, 1770

She Stoops to Conquer, 1773

Retaliation, 1774

Writings about Oliver Goldsmith

<u>1759</u>

A. Books--None

B. Shorter Writings

1   A.B. [pseud.?]. Review of <u>An Enquiry into the Present State</u>
    <u>of Polite Learning in Europe</u>. <u>Gentleman's Magazine</u> 29
    (April):169-71.
         Concerned almost totally with critics and criticism and
    with making distinctions about taste he thinks Goldsmith
    should have realized. Does not judge other parts of the
    book.

2   ANON. Review of <u>An Enquiry into the Present State of Polite</u>
    <u>Learning in Europe</u>. <u>Critical Review</u> 7 (April):369-72.
         Mainly a summary of what the reviewer considers the
    author's errors of argument. With more attention to
    science, he would have been more precise, and with less
    attention to the arts, he might have written with less
    elegance but more strength.

3   ANON. Review of the <u>Bee</u>. <u>Critical Review</u> 8 (December):499.
         Two sentences comment that the collection is not equal
    to the "honied lucubrations" of Addison or Johnson, but
    find it greatly preferable to many similar collections.

4   [KENRICK, WILLIAM.] Review of <u>An Enquiry into the Present</u>
    <u>State of Polite Learning in Europe</u>. <u>Monthly Review</u> 21
    (November):381-89.
         Reflects directly on the author's character and finds
    little original in the book, instead trite opinions that
    have been repeated from author to author. Friedman,
    <u>Works</u> 1:247, believes Kenrick's attack reflects Griffiths's
    quarrel with Goldsmith over his pawning a suit for which
    Griffiths had advanced Goldsmith the money.

1760

1760

A. Books--None

B. Shorter Writings

   1   [KENRICK, WILLIAM.] Review of The Bee. Monthly Review 22
       (January):38-45.
            Mainly quotations. Somewhat favorable and patronizing.
       Finds the style agreeable but not exciting and most of the
       subjects already somewhat worn, and to overcome these
       disadvantages, the author would have to show more talent,
       humor, and variety of style.

1762

A. Books--None

B. Shorter Writings

   1   ANON. Review of The Citizen of the World. Critical Review 13
       (May):397-400.
            Favorable if not enthusiastic, discounting the original-
       ity, though finding the letters superior to other similar
       series published in newspapers. Does find Lien Chi
       Altangi's comments generally agreeable in his, but occa-
       sionally making comments inconsistent with his being
       Chinese. Praises his good sense and occasional genius, as
       well as his humor. Finds many skillful comments on books
       and men and recommends the series.

   2   ANON. "Monthly Catalogue." Monthly Review 26 (June):477.
            A brief review of The Citizen of the World, criticizing
       the Chinese philosopher as having nothing Asiatic about
       him, but making sensible remarks on men, manners, and
       things. Notes that the book is said to be the work of the
       author of An Enquiry and apologizes for the adverse remarks
       in the review of that work (1759.B3) as not intended to
       reflect personally on the author.

   3   ANON. Review of The Life of Richard Nash. London Chronicle,
       12-14 October.
            The most favorable of the reviews, arguing the anonymous
       author seems to have known Nash personally and to have been
       furnished with authentic memoirs of him, and his skillful
       use of them shows they were properly placed. Praises the
       book for being entertaining and perhaps even more

instructive, but criticizes Goldsmith's treatment of James
Quin, the actor.

4   ANON. Review of The Life of Richard Nash. St. James Magazine
     1 (October):124-29.
          Attacks the triviality of the subject and the tendency
     of the editor to swell the size of the book, and also
     attacks Goldsmith's treatment of Quin.

5   ANON. Review of The Life of Richard Nash. Critical Review 14
     (October):270-76.
          Mainly a long extract, but the brief critical remarks
     are kinder to the writer than the book, seeing the author's
     talents as capable of a greater subject, but "We cannot,
     however, but take pity on a writer of genius, thus tortured
     to give substance to inanity" (p. 276).

6   ANON. Review of The Life of Richard Nash. Monthly Review 27
     (November):38-39.
          Only two sentences: "A trivial subject, treated for the
     most part in a lively, ingenious, and entertaining manner.
     Mr. Samuel Johnson's admirable life of Savage seems to have
     been chosen as the model of this performance."

7   [RIDER, WILLIAM.] "Dr. Goldsmith." In An Historical and
     Critical Account of the Living Writers of Great-Britain
     wherein their Respective Merits are Discussed with the
     Utmost Candour and Impartiality. London: printed for the
     author, pp. 13-14.
          Goldsmith is credited with the doctor's degree from
     Edinburgh and praised for his Essay on the present State
     of polite Learning in all Parts of Europe [sic], The Bee,
     but especially The Citizen of the World. "He is superior
     to most of them [his contemporaries] in Style, having
     found out the Secret to unite Elevation with Ease, a
     perfection in Language, which few Writers of our Nation
     have attained to . . ." (p. 13). Reprinted in 1974.A6.

                    1764

A. Books--None

B. Shorter Writings

     1   ANON. Review of The Traveller. London Chronicle 18-20
         (December):564.
              Praises the poem, the first piece published

1764

with Goldsmith's name, highly for poetic merit surpassing what has been seen for several years and for strength of thought.

2   ANON. Review of The Traveller. Gentleman's Magazine 34 (December):594.
    Very favorable. The first paragraph is typical: "We congratulate our poetical readers on the appearance of a new poet so able to afford refined pleasure to true taste as the writer of the Traveller: After the crude and virulent rhapsodies upon which caprice and faction have lavished an unbounded praise, that if known to any future time will disgrace the present, it is hoped this poem will come with some advantage, and that a general encouragement of real merit will shew, that we have not lost the power to distinguish it" (p. 594). Praises Goldsmith's patriotism and quotes the section of the poem describing Britain. Reprinted: 1974.A6.

3   [JOHNSON, SAMUEL.] Review of The Traveller. Critical Review 18 (December):458-62.
    Very high praise with considerable summary and quotation. Praises the didacticism, the main position, and the versification of the poem. The last sentence summarizes the high praise of the review: "Such is the poem, on which we now congratulate the public, as a production to which, since the death of Pope, it will not be easy to find anything equal" (p. 462). Reprinted: 1974.A6.

1765

A. Books--None

B. Shorter Writings

1   ANON. Review of The Traveller. St. James's Chronicle, 7-9 February.
    The reviewer expresses some surprise at apparent public neglect [a second edition was not needed for almost three months]. Praises the poem's beauties and the variety, imagination, and finish shown in the description of the various countries. The reviewer also sees the next to the last paragraph of the dedication as referring to Charles Churchill, who had died 4 November 1764, and finds it ample testimony to the merit of this poem that it ranks as highly as it does with Churchill dead.

2   [LANGHORNE, JOHN.] Review of The Traveller. Monthly Review
     32 (January):47-55.
          A mixed review, critical of details and the general
     conception, especially the author's political philosophy,
     but praising Goldsmith's descriptive passages for their
     sentiment and happy expression. The final sentence, after
     quoting the lines devoted to France, concludes: "We must
     now refer the Reader to the poem itself, which we cannot
     but recommend to him as a work of very considerable merit"
     (p. 55). Reprinted: 1974.A6.

                            1766

A. Books--None

B. Shorter Writings

1   ANON. Review of The Vicar of Wakefield. Monthly Review 34
     (May):407.
          A very mixed review, as the opening sentence indicates:
     "Through the whole course of our travels in the wild regions
     of romance, we have never met with anything more difficult
     to characterize, than the Vicar of Wakefield; a performance
     which contains beauties sufficient to entitle it to almost
     the highest applause, and defects enough to put the
     discerning reader out of all patience with an author
     capable of so strangely under-writing himself." Criticized
     for "his limited knowledge of men, manners, and characters,
     as they really appear in the living world.--In brief, with
     all its faults, there is much rational entertainment to be
     met with in this very singular tale: But it deserves our
     warmer approbation, for its moral tendency; particularly
     for the exemplary manner in which it recommends and
     enforces the great obligations of universal BENEVOLENCE.
     . . ." (Reprinted: 1974.A6.

2   ANON. Review of The Vicar of Wakefield. Critical Review 21
     (June):439-41.
          A very mixed review, but finding more to praise than to
     blame. "The author seems to us to possess a manner
     peculiar to himself; it is what the French would term
     naiveté. . . . He appears to tell his story with so much
     ease and artlessness, that one is almost tempted to think,
     one could have told it every bit as well without the least
     study; yet so difficult is it to hit off this mode of
     composition with any degree of mastery, that he who should
     try would probably find himself deceived . . . " (p. 439).

1768

The reviewer reminds us that the novel is supposed to have been written by the Vicar himself and finds the rather unworldly attitude aptly reflects his character. Generally, praises the characterization, restating admiration for Primrose's characterization, and concludes: "But, pray, Dr. Goldsmith, was it necessary to bring the concluding calamities so thick upon your old venerable friend; or in your impatience to get to the end of your task, was you not rather disposed to hurry the catastrophe?--Be this as it may, we cannot but wish you success, being of opinion, upon the whole, that your tale does no little honour to your head, and what is still better, that it does yet more to your heart" (p. 441). Reprinted: 1974.A6.

1768

A. Books--None

B. Shorter Writings

1   ANON. Review of The Good Natur'd Man [performance]. Lloyd's Evening Post, 29 January-1 February.
    Primarily a summary of the action, but comments on the Bailiff Scene: "This whole scene, in which those fellows perpetually joined conversation, in language uncommonly low, gave some offense the first night of its being acted."

2   ANON. Review of The Good Natur'd Man [performance]. Theatrical Monitor, no. 9 (6 February):1-4.
    Mechanically discusses fable, characters, moral, sentiments, and diction, and finds the play lacking in fine sentiments, but Goldsmith has also "been guilty of improprieties of expression."

3   ANON. Review of The Good Natur'd Man [printed play]. Gentleman's Magazine 38 (February):78-80.
    Mainly summary with many quotations. The characters are well drawn and contrasted, particularly Croker and his wife, Lofty, and young Honeywood. The Bailiff Scene is "infinitely ridiculous" but it depends on the kind of manners which contemporary taste will hardly admit even in farce.

4   ANON. Review of The Good Natur'd Man [printed play]. Critical Review 25 (February):147-48.
    A mixed review, criticizing both the characterization, especially of Honeywood, and the plot. Praises Croker, but

1770

Honeywood is not a strong enough character, considering he is the hero. Lofty is a promising character, but it is improbable that the Crokers would be imposed upon by him. "The scene of the bailiffs, retrenched in the representation, and here restored by the author, in deference to the judgment of a few friends, who think in a particular way, we neither wholly approve nor condemn. Coarse characters should be touched by a delicate pencil, and forcible situations should be rather softened than aggravated" (p. 148). Reprinted: 1974.A6.

5   ANON. Review of The Good Natur'd Man [printed play]. Monthly Review 38 (February):159-60.
        "A pleasant play to read" (p. 159). Croker's characterization praised. The bailiffs seemed impossible in performance but are acceptable in reading. The play has several problems, but parts are genuinely comic and show Goldsmith a writer of genius though not yet skilled enough in the difficult business of writing drama. Finds it more promising than Dryden's first comedy, The Wild Gallant.

6   Q. IN THE CORNER [pseud.]. Review of The Good Natur'd Man [performance]. St. James's Chronicle, 28-30 (January).
        A fairly detailed review of the first performance, urging that the Bailiff Scene be shortened or completely dropped and that the actors should speak louder. The Bailiff Scene was omitted after the first night.

1770

A. Books--None

B. Shorter Writings

1   ANON. Review of The Deserted Village. London Magazine 39 (June):318.
        "A very elegant poem written with great pains, yet bearing every possible mark of felicity."

2   ANON. Review of The Deserted Village. Critical Review 29 (June):435-43.
        Begins favorably, praising both the sentiment and the rhymed couplets, but disagrees with the thesis of the poem, that luxury is as productive of happiness as of misery, but believes a good poem can be written based on a false hypothesis. Several passages quoted, and the apostrophe to Poetry near the end characterized as beautiful but

1770

imaginative. Attacks Goldsmith's opinion that the present
times are unfavorable to literary merit, concluding: "Dr.
Goldsmith deserves the highest applause for employing his
poetical talents in the support of humanity and virtue, in
an age when sentimental instruction will have more powerful
influence upon our conduct than any other; when abstruse
systems of morality, and dry exhortations from the pulpit,
if attended to for a while, make no durable impression"
(p. 443). Reprinted 1974.A6.

3   HAWKESWORTH, JOHN [X, pseud.]. Review of The Deserted Village.
Gentleman's Magazine 40 (June):271-73.
Acts "as Moderator between Dr. Goldsmith and modern
politicians, by shewing that luxury, in different stages,
is first the support, and then the ruin of a commercial
state" (p. 271). Then praises the poem for avoiding
obsolete words and phrases, affected terms; for not adopting
the prosody of early poets, excessive epithets, and strained
metaphorical language [all criteria Goldsmith himself had
used in criticizing contemporary poetry, as in his review
of Gray's Odes (Works 1:112-17)]. After several long
quotations, tells the reader that in the poem, "if he has
not vitiated his taste, till like a sick girl, he prefers
ashes and chalk to beef and mutton, we can promise him more
pleasure than he has received from poetry since the days of
Pope" (p. 273).

4   [HAWKESWORTH, JOHN.] Review of The Deserted Village.   Monthly
Review 42 (June):440-45.
Very favorable and very similar to 1770.B2. Agrees with
Goldsmith's condemnation of luxury but not with his ideas
that it is causing depopulation, especially emigration.
Frequent quotations, especially praising the style for
avoiding archaic phrases and forced constructions now
popular, concluding "We hope that, for the honour of the
Art, and the pleasure of the Public, Dr. Goldsmith will
retract his farewel to poetry, and give us other opportuni-
ties of doing justice to his merit" (p. 445). Reprinted:
1974.A6.

1773

A.   Books--None

B.   Shorter Writings

1   ANON. Review of She Stoops to Conquer [performance].   Morning

Chronicle, 16 March.
   Quite favorable: praises the poet as "exceedingly
probable and fertile," with good stage business and
incident, original characters drawn well, highly finished,
and well supported from first to last; full of real wit
and humour without absurdities. Praised as the best
comedy since Colman and Garrick's Clandestine Marriage,
1766, and Hardcastle and Marlow singled out for praise as
characters, with Marlow's praised for originality. "The
engine of the plot, and the source of infinite mirth and a
variety of very laughable mistakes, which arise in a simple,
artless manner, and which the author has taken an admirable
advantage of, and produced a very comic effect from,
without exceeding the line of probability. . . ." The rest
of the review praises the principal actors: Lewes as
Marlow, Mrs. Bulkeley as Kate, Shuter as Hardcastle, Mrs.
Green as Mrs. Hardcastle, and Quick as Tony Lumpkin. Also
describes most of the troubles the play had encountered:
production at the end of the season, the difficulties of
casting the play, and rumors that the play's humor was
"exceedingly low."

2   ANON. Review of She Stoops to Conquer [performance]. Lloyd's
    Evening Post, 15-17 March.
       Mainly a reprint of 1773.B1, but with most of the
    criticism left out.

3   ANON. Review of She Stoops to Conquer [performance]. Public
    Advertiser, 18 March.
       After discussion of the play's action, the reviewer
    keenly points out that the play's virtue lies not in
    forced opposition of characters or in exchange of fine
    sentiments, "but in a Disposition of Things uncommon and
    unexpected, but very artfully made credible; in a rapid
    Succession of diverting Incidents, from which the Attention
    can never be disengaged, and in a Train of lively
    Dialogues, in which, by a perpetual Mistake of his own
    Situation, every Speaker thinks justly, and yet thinks
    wrong."

4   ANON. Notice of the 25 March performance of She Stoops to
    Conquer. Morning Chronicle, 26 March.
       Reports that almost all the audience had copies of the
    play in hand [F. Newbery published it 25 March], and the
    orange-women reported extremely heavy sales, which
    continued. Friedman reports, Works 5:93, n. 1, "advertise-
    ments and paragraphs in the London newspapers announcing
    new publications of the comedy, each designated merely as

1773

'A New Edition.' There are Dublin, Belfast, and Philadelphia editions dated 1773."

5 ANON. Review of She Stoops to Conquer [printed play].
Critical Review 35 (March):229-30.
Follows ideas similar to those Goldsmith had used in his
"Essay on the Theatre" (Works 3:209-13): Among the
ancients, Aristotle defined comedy as "an exhibition of
human manners in low life" (p. 229); of the moderns, the
Italians have done poorly in comedy, the French better, and
the English even better. However, recently weeping comedy
has prevailed in France and had great popularity in England,
though this play tries to revive laughing comedy. "To
conclude; the utmost severity of criticism could detract
but little from the uncommon merit of this performance; and
the most labored encomiums could add as little to the
general and judicious applause with which it still continues
to be received" (p. 230). Reprinted: 1974.A6.

6 ANON. Review of She Stoops to Conquer [printed play]. London
Magazine 42 (March):144-46.
Unfavorable, primarily summary of the action, with one
paragraph of criticism: "This comedy is not ill calculated
to give pleasure in the representation; but when we regard
it with a critical eye, we find it to abound with numerous
inaccuracies. The fable . . . is twisted into incidents
not naturally arising from the subject, in order to make
things meet; and consistency is repeatedly violated for the
sake of humour" (p. 146). Might praise Goldsmith for
writing an anti-Sentimental Comedy, but he erred too far in
the other direction and produced a farce. "A stricter
consistency in the fable, and a better attention to the
unity of time in particular, would have exalted the comedy
to a good and just reputation" (p. 146). Reprinted:
1974.A6.

7 ANON. Notice about She Stoops to Conquer [performance].
Morning Chronicle, 8 September.
Reports performances of the play in most towns in
England with theaters and many villages with theatrical
barns. "In our American plantations also, has this mirth
exciting comedy been performed. The New York papers,
brought by Monday's mail, inform that 'She Stoops to
Conquer' was performed at the theatre in John-street, New
York, by the American company, on the 2d of August last."

8 [WOODFALL, WILLIAM.] Review of She Stoops to Conquer [printed
play]. Monthly Review 48 (March):309-14.

Unfavorable, since Woodfall defines comedy as "a dramatic representation of the prevailing manners of people not in very high or very low life" (p. 309), and thus comedy has changed: "Some of our late writers have therefore very judiciously had recourse to what is called Sentimental Comedy, as better suited to the principles and manners of the age. A general politeness has given a sameness to our external appearances; and great degrees of knowledge are every where diffused" (p. 309). Accuses Goldsmith of having read more about his fellow men than he has seen of them. Attacks the blunders of the characters as not credible or probable. Conceded some skill in dialogue, particularly the kind that arouses laughter when heard, but not when read. Recommends Goldsmith take a story, set in the past, when manners were similar to those he presents here, and the audience then could imagine itself back in time and thus derive the same kind of enjoyment it receives from the best old comedies. Reprinted: 1974.A6.

1774

A. Books--None

B. Shorter Writings

1 ANON. Review of Retaliation. Monthly Review 50 (April):313-14.
    Praised for its wit and freedom from ill-nature, and the pointed-justness of the characters, quoting the epitaph on Burke as a sample and praising the lines on Garrick as "the most masterly part" (p. 314).

2 ANON. Review of Retaliation. Critical Review 37 (May):392.
    Describes the occasion of the poem, with quotations, and concludes: "The members of the club are characterized in a potential strain of panegyric or delicate satire, in which good humour, and a facetious turn of thought are equally conspicuous. However frivolous the occasion and nature of this jeu d'esprit may be, it is a production which will reflect no discredit on the genius of the author" (p. 392).

3 [GLOVER, ?SAMUEL.] "Authentic Anecdotes of the Late Dr. Goldsmith." Universal Magazine 54 (May):252-55.
    Glover knew Goldsmith as a fellow Irishman and provides a biographical summary, with numerous errors: "was, with his brother the Rev. Henry Goldsmith, placed in Trinity-

1774

College, Dublin, about the latter end of the year 1749"
(p. 252), then to study medicine at Edinburgh, then to
Rotterdam, Brussels, Flanders, Strasbourg, and Louvain,
where he obtained a medical degree, and to Bern and Geneva,
accompanying an English gentleman. At Geneva became tutor
to a pawnbroker's heir. Dates the inception of The
Traveller from his visit in Switzerland, and quotes specimen
passages. His pupil paid him off at Marseilles and
Goldsmith made his way through France with difficulty to
Dover in 1758. Summarizes his known literary career with
general accuracy. "He was a studious and correct observer
of nature, happy in his selection of images, in the choice
of his subjects, and in the harmony of his versification,
and though his embarrassed situation prevented him from
putting the last hand to many of his productions, his
Hermit, his Traveller, and his Deserted Village, bid fair
to claim a place among the most finished pieces in the
English language" (p. 255). The author claims his
anecdotes "are all founded on facts, and collected by one
who lived with him upon the most friendly footing for a
great number of years, and who never felt any sorrow more
sensibly than that which was occasioned by his death"
(p. 255).

4   _____. The Life of Dr. Oliver Goldsmith written from
Personal Knowledge, Authentic Papers, and Other Indubitable
Authorities. London: J. Swan, 46 pp.
     Largely a reprint of 1774.B3. Glover established the
tradition of using passages from Goldsmith's writings as
literal accurate biographical accounts: "Presuming that
the best use to which biography can be applied is to profit
by the amiable part of the author's character, I shall
extract, for the entertainment and instruction of my
readers, such passages of Dr. Goldsmith's works, as mark
in a striking manner the unbounded benevolence of his
temper, or the elegant simplicity of his mind. That he
thought justly on most occasions is a fact that will
appear incontestible from the perusal of many of the
following observations . . ." (p. 15). Extensive passages
from The Vicar of Wakefield, The Traveller, The Deserted
Village, "The Hermit," and Retaliation follow.

5   _____. "Characters--Dr. Goldsmith." Annual Register.
London: P. & J. Doddsley, pp. 29-34.
     Largely a reprint of 1774.B3.

6   [GOOD, ?]. A Catalogue of the Household Furniture, with the
Select Collection of Scarce, Curious, and Valuable Books

in English, Latin, Greek, French, Italian, and Other
Languages, Late the Library of Dr. Goldsmith, Deceased.
[London: n.p.], 12 pp.
   Good, whose first name has not survived, auctioned off
Goldsmith's furniture and library. Reprinted: 1837.A1,
Appendix, 2: 575-84; 1854.A1, Appendix 2, 2: 494-500;
1973.B10.

7   [HAWES, WILLIAM.] An Account of the Late Dr. Goldsmith's
      Illness, so far as Relates to the EXHIBITION of Dr. James's
      Powders, together with Remarks on the Use and Abuse of
      Powerful Medicines in the Beginning of Fevers and Other
      Acute Diseases. London: W. Brown & H. Gardner.
      Dedicated to Reynolds and Burke. Hawes, an apothecary,
had attended Goldsmith in his last illness and defends his
professional conduct. He tried to dissuade him from
overdosing himself with Dr. James's Powders, brought in two
physicians as consultants, Drs. Fordyce and Turton, who
gave the same advice, which Goldsmith refused to follow.
Much of the pamphlet urges caution in taking this medicine,
as Dr. James himself did. In the third edition, an
appendix contains statements by servants and nurses that
the medicine Goldsmith took was genuine and not any form of
imitation.

8   PRATT, SAMUEL JACKSON [Courtney Melmoth]. The Tears of Genius,
      Occasioned by the Death of Dr. Goldsmith. London: T.
      Becket, 13 pp.
      Dedicated to Reynolds. An elegy in a mixture of meters,
but chiefly blank verse with some heroic couplet and prose
sections: "I resolved to set out upon an irregular
principle, that without enchaining myself to any critical
uniformity, I might have scope and lattitude for whatever
varieties of versification should fall in my way" (Dedication, p. i). Personified Genius mourns Goldsmith, and
sections following mourn Gray, using heroic quatrain; young;
Sterne, using prose; Shenstone; Lyttelton; and Hawkesworth,
using prose. Reprinted: 1774.A4.

9   [TAIT, JOHN, and WOTY, WILLIAM.] The Druid's Monument.
      London: T. Davies.
      Dedicated to Burke. Written in 32 ballad-like stanzas
like "Edwin and Angelina," with references to that poem,
The Deserted Village, and The Traveller. The speaker
encounters a druid who laments "'a fav'rite son of fame'"
(1.44), followed by fourteen lines of "The Inscription," in
heroic couplets by William Woty. Reprinted: 1974.A6.

1776

1776

A. Books--None

B. Shorter Writings

1   ANON. Review of The Haunch of Venison, a Poetical Epistle to
     Lord Clare. Critical Review 41 (June):479-90.
         Begins with a complaint about spurious works being
     passed off as genuine writings by Goldsmith during the
     period following his death in 1774. However, this poem
     shows Goldsmith's genuine touch and would not be considered
     fraudulent even if there were not other evidence it is
     genuine. Ends with three sentences summarizing the content
     and a brief quotation.

2   ANON. Untitled essay on The Vicar of Wakefield. The Babbler
     77 (10 July):55-59.
         Some specific comment on the novel, but primarily
     attacks the novel's idea that the poor are happier than the
     rich and argues that both groups are about equally
     contented or discontented with their lots. Men should
     thank God for the blessings they have here and not complain
     they do not have more. Reprinted: 1974.A6.

3   [LANGHORNE, JOHN.] Review of The Haunch of Venison, a Poetical
     Epistle to Lord Clare. Monthly Review 55 (August):157.
         Complete notice: "In the true style of familiar Humour."

4   [SPILSBURY, FRANCIS.] Preface to Free Thoughts on Quacks and
     their Medicines Occasioned by the Death of Dr. Goldsmith
     and Mr. Scawen. London: J. Wilkie, pp. xvii-xxx, xxxv-
     xxxvi.
         An answer to Hawes, 1774.B7, by the maker of a rival
     patent medicine, Spilsbury's Drops. Concludes that Hawes's
     motive was probably not primarily to give information of
     Goldsmith's death as an important man, that Hawes has not
     shown sufficient concern about the dangers of strong
     medicines like James's Powders, and concludes that irre-
     sponsible people like Goldsmith may indeed harm themselves
     with such medicines, but that any harm is their responsi-
     bility and not that of the medicine maker or seller.
     Concludes with testimonials to his medicine and a list of
     sellers. Partially reprinted: 1974.A6.

<u>1777</u>

A. Books--None

B. Shorter Writings

   1   [CAMPBELL, THOMAS.] [Brief comment.] In <u>A Philosophical</u>
       <u>Survey of the South of Ireland in a Series of Letters to</u>
       <u>John Watkinson, M.D.</u> London: W. Trahan & T. Cadell,
       p. 437.
           Perhaps harmful to Goldsmith's memory to draw his
       "poetical character" from his plays, though they are truly
       comic. "His fame must be founded on his <u>Traveller</u>,
       <u>Deserted Village</u>, and <u>Vicar of Wakefield</u>." His epitaph is
       being written by Johnson, "which is more honorable to the
       bard than if his ashes had been deposited in the cemetary
       of kings." Johnson's epitaph quoted from copy furnished
       from the publisher, though not yet finished because of
       uncertainty about Goldsmith's exact birthplace.

   2   [MALONE, EDMOND.] "The Life of Oliver Goldsmith, M.B." In
       <u>Poems and Plays</u>. Dublin: Price et al., pp. iii-xi.
           Reprints Glover's "Anecdotes," 1774.B3, with corrections
       and additions, for example, Malone reports 1729 as birthdate,
       not 1731; corrects the dates of Goldsmith's years at
       Trinity College; and provides the correct date of 1749 for
       his receiving the B.A. "The writer of these memoirs is
       indebted for the principal anecdotes contained in them to
       a Gentleman who well knows their authenticity, and who long
       lived with Dr. Goldsmith on the most friendly terms, and
       never felt any sorrow more sincerely than that which was
       occasioned by his death" (p. 31n).
       Also contains 1774.B7 and Woty's "Inscription" from 1774.B10.
       [Reprinted in <u>Poems and Plays</u> (London: B. Newbery & T.
       Johnson, 1780); <u>The Poetical and Dramatic Works</u> (London:
       B. Newbery & T. Johnson, 1780), pp. iii-x; and <u>Miscellane-</u>
       <u>ous Works</u> (Perth: R. Morison & Son, 1792), pp. v-xi.] Reprinted
       partially: 1974.A6.

<u>1780</u>

A. Books--None

B. Shorter Writings

   1   ANON. "Anecdotes of the Late Dr. Goldsmith." <u>Universal</u>
       <u>Magazine</u> 67 (August):82-85.

1780

Mentions 1774.B3 and quotes from 1780.B2, p. 141, and is a condensation and selection from the latter. Reprinted: 1974.A6.

2   DAVIES, THOMAS. [Anecdotes of Goldsmith.] In <u>Memoirs of the Life of David Garrick</u>. 2 vols. London: Thomas Davies, passim but especially 1:141-62, 277-78.

Describes Goldsmith: "An inexplicable existence in creation; such a compound of absurdity, envy, and malice, contrasted with the opposite virtues of kindness, generosity, and benevolence, that he might be said to consist of two distinct souls, and to be influenced by the agency of a good and bad spirit" (p. 141). Draws heavily on Glover, Malone, and personal knowledge, stressing the inconsistencies of Goldsmith's behavior and personality. The account of the inception of <u>Retaliation</u> quite naturally appears more sympathetic to Garrick than to Goldsmith.

<u>1785</u>

A. Books--None

B. Shorter Writings

1   SCOTT, JOHN. "On Goldsmith's <u>Deserted Village</u>." In <u>Critical Essays on Some of the Poems of Several English Poets</u>. London: James Phillips, pp. 247-94.

One of the first detailed criticisms of the poem. Would have liked the poem better if all the material about inhabited Auburn and all the material about deserted Auburn had been grouped together; thinks the description of village diversions are too prolix and general; believes the adjective "sweet" is properly used but "displeases by perpetual repetition" (p. 279); praises the portraits of the preacher and schoolmaster and the description of the alehouse: "we have here no imaginary Arcadia, but the real country; no poetical swains, but the men who actually drive the plough, or wield the scythe, the sickle, the hammer, or the hedging bill . . ." (p. 271); and summarizes: "The Deserted Village . . . is on the whole, a performance of great merit; it has numerous excellencies, and numerous faults, and while we are charmed with the former, we cannot but regret that more pains were not taken to avoid the latter" (p. 294). Reprinted: 1974.A6.

*2   PIOZZI, HESTER LYNCH THRALE. [Anecdotes of Goldsmith.] In <u>Anecdotes of the late Samuel Johnson, LL.D. during the</u>

Last Twenty Years of His Life. London: T. Cadell.
   Primary source material of great value, though not
always accurate in detail. Of particular interest:
Johnson and Mrs. Thrale discuss Goldsmith as Johnson's
biographer (18 June 1773) (p. 23); her version of the sale
of The Vicar of Wakefield, which she dates 1765 or 1766,
but Johnson did not identify the author and book until "ten
years after, I dare say" (p. 78); "[Johnson's] vein of
humour was inexhaustible; though Dr. Goldsmith said once to
him, We should change companions oftener, we exhaust one
another and soon be both of us worn out. Poor Goldsmith
was to him indeed like the earthen pot to the iron one in
Fontaine's Fables; it had been better for him perhaps, that
they had changed companions oftener yet no experience of
his antagonist's strength hindered him from continuing the
contest" (p. 117). Johnson generally concealed behavior
by Goldsmith his other friends considered foolish. Sources
are 1861.B1 and 1942.B4. [Annotation based on S. C.
Roberts, ed., Anecdotes of the late Samuel Johnson, LL.D.
during the last Twenty Years of his Life (Cambridge:
University Press, 1925), 255 pp., passim.]

                        1787

A. Books--None

B. Shorter Writings

   1   HAWKINS, Sir JOHN. [Anecdotes of Goldsmith.] In The Life of
       Samuel Johnson, LL.D. London: T. Cadell, passim.
          As a member of the Club, much of Hawkins's knowledge of
       Goldsmith was firsthand, but according to Percy, Hawkins
       stopped coming to the Club in 1768 (Boswell, Hill-Powell,
       ed., 1:478, n. 2). Praises his writings generally, but
       finds his personality and behavior flawed: "to the graces
       of urbanity he was a stranger. With the greatest pretensions
       to polished manners he was rude, and, when he most meant the
       contrary, absurd" (p. 416). "He that can account for the
       inconsistencies of character . . . otherwise than by
       shewing, that wit and wisdom are seldom found to meet in
       the same mind, will do more than any of Goldsmith's
       friends were able to do" (p. 420). "As he wrote for the
       booksellers, we, at the club, looked upon him as a mere
       literary drudge, equal to the task of compiling and
       translating, but little capable of original, and still less
       of poetical composition: . . . [he] surprised us with 'The
       Traveller'. . . . The favorable reception which this essay

1791

of his poetical talent met with, soon after tempted
Goldsmith to the publication of his 'Deserted Village,' the
merits whereof, consisting in local particularities and
beautiful descriptions of rural manners, are sufficiently
known" (p. 420). Partially reprinted: 1974.A6; abridged:
1961.A2.

1791

A. Books--None

B. Shorter Writings

1   BOSWELL, JAMES. [Anecdotes of Goldsmith.] In The Life of
     Samuel Johnson, LL.D. 2 vols. London: Charles Dilly.
        Together with Percy's Life (1801.B2) and Prior's Life
     (1837.A1) and Collected Letters, ed., Balderston (1928.A1)
     and Reynold's "Portrait" (1972.B4), one of the absolutely
     essential sources for biographical and early critical
     comment on Goldsmith's life, personality, and works by
     Johnson, Boswell, and others. The Hill-Powell edition is
     especially useful because of the extensive annotation and
     the invaluable index. Boswell's presentation of Goldsmith
     has been much argued, especially as biased against
     Goldsmith, but aside from Johnson, more space is devoted to
     Goldsmith than any other writer (references in the Hill-
     Powell index occupy ten columns). [Text used: Life,
     edited by George Birkbeck Hill, revised by L. F. Powell,
     2d ed., 6 vols. (Oxford: Clarendon Press, 1964), passim.]
     For recent views of Boswell's interpretation of Goldsmith,
     see 1961.B4 and 1970.B6. See also 1928.B1, 1950.B1,
     1955.B1, 1956.B2, 1959.B1.

1792

A. Books--None

B. Shorter Writings

1   ANON. "Anecdotes of Dr. Goldsmith." European Magazine 21
     (February):88.
        Short items: credited with predicting the French
     Revolution in the Citizen of the World [Letter 56]; wished
     to buy the MS. copy of [Chatterton's] Rowley poems but could
     only offer a note of hand and so was refused by the owner,
     George Catcott of Bristol. Repeats Johnson's praise of The

1798

Traveller, Goldsmith's social ineptness and writing skill.

1793

A. Books--None

B. Shorter Writings

    1   [COOKE, WILLIAM.] "Table Talk." European Magazine 24
        (August):91-95; 24 (September):170-74; 24 (October):258-64.
        Miscellaneous anecdotes by a contemporary acquaintance.
        Account of the first night of She Stoops to Conquer
        (p. 173), the fullest to appear in print thus far; records
        Goldsmith's unsuccessful attempt to drop the title "Doctor"
        in favor of "Mister." A valuable early source generally
        accepted as reliable. See also 1805.B1.

1796

A. Books--None

B. Shorter Writings

    *1   AIKEN, J[OHN, M.D.] "A Critical Dissertation." In The
        Poetical Works of Oliver Goldsmith, M.B. London.
        The "Life" repeats material from Glover, Malone, Boswell,
        and Cooke. The "Critical Dissertation" ranks Goldsmith's
        verse as very close to Dryden and Pope's in quality; sees
        simplicity as his prime virtue; calls it a master of
        descriptive poetry because of his using particular images
        instead of general ones, combining and contrasting
        materials effectively with great force and clarity. Aiken
        was Mrs. Anna Barbauld's brother: see 1810.B1. [Text used:
        Oliver Goldsmith, Poems, Plays & Essays with an Account of
        his Life and Writings, to which is added a Critical
        Dissertation on his Poetry (London: Scott, Webster, &
        Geary, 1835), pp. i-xlvi.] Reprinted: 1974.A6.

1798

A. Books

    1   GOLDSMITH, OLIVER. Essays and Criticisms, with an Account of
        the Author. 3 vols. London: J. Johnson, 1:240 pp.;
        2:262 pp.; 3:276 pp.

1798

The first serious attempt to identify and collect
Goldsmith's shorter periodical publications. The "Account
of the Author," 2:xi-xxiv, is a reprint of Malone's "Life"
(1777.B2). Volume 1 reprints Essays, 1766, but 2 and 3
contain the first effort at collecting Goldsmith's shorter,
anonymously published magazine and newspaper pieces. The
identifications were made by Thomas Wright, "a man of
literary observation and experience, [who] had, during his
connection with those periodical publications, in which the
early works of Dr. Goldsmith were originally contained,
carefully marked the several compositions of the different
writers, as they were delivered to him to print. . . . Mr.
Wright was therefore prevailed upon to print the present
Selection, which he had just compleated at the time of his
death" (pp. viii-ix). Friedman (Works. 2, passim)
discusses the authenticity of the pieces.

B. Shorter Writings--None

1801

A. Books--None

B. Shorter Writings

1   D'ISRAELI, ISAAC. Literary Miscellanies, Including a Disserta-
    tion on Anecdotes. New ed. rev., enl. London: Murray &
    Highley, pp. 83-84.
        A set comparison between Goldsmith's genius and Johnson's,
    with D'Israeli giving the palm to Goldsmith's writing for
    its "felicity and vivacity" rather than to "that Art, that
    habitual pomp, and that ostentatious eloquence which
    prevails in the operose labours of Johnson" (p. 84).
    Goldsmith's reputation for vanity and jealousy often sneered
    at, despite the "aimiableness of his heart" (p. 84). Clear
    preferences for Goldsmith's writing over Johnson's "heavier"
    prose, indicating some shift in taste from the period when
    both writers were alive.

2   [PERCY, THOMAS et al.] "Life of Dr. Oliver Goldsmith." In
    The Miscellaneous Works of Oliver Goldsmith, M.B. 4 vols.
    London: J. Johnson: G. & J. Robinson; W. J. & J. Richard-
    son; W. Othridge & Son; F. & C. Rivington; J. Matthews;
    J. Walker; W. Lowndes; J. Sacherd; G. Wilkie; P. McQueen;
    Longman & Rees; Vernor & Hood; Cadell, Jun. & Davies; Murrah
    & Highley; E. Newbery, 1:1-118.

An essential source. The first really carefully written
life of Goldsmith, containing original letters and documents
and based on Percy's close friendship with Goldsmith.
Authorship and composition, see 1926.A1, 1974.A2, and
1976.A1. Brief selection reprinted in 1974.A6. Critical
edition, 1974.A2 and 1976.A1.

1804

A. Books--None

B. Shorter Writings

1   EVANS, JOHN. "Original Anecdotes of Goldsmith." In The
    Poetical Works of Oliver Goldsmith. London: Thomas Hurst,
    pp. vi-xlvi.
        Goldsmith's teaching at Dr. Milner's school, including
    his reply to Miss Milner's question what commentator on
    Scripture he would recommend; Goldsmith, after a pause,
    replied, "Common Sense is the best interpreter of the
    sacred writings."

2   MUDFORD, WILLIAM. "Life and Critique." In Oliver Goldsmith,
    Essays on Men and Manners, with a Life and Critique on the
    Writings and Genius of the author by William Mudford.
    London: M. Jones, pp. vi-xviii.
        "Life" contains nothing new and owes a heavy debt to
    1801.B1. The "Critique" apparently reflects the general
    view that Goldsmith wrote well and pleasantly whatever his
    subject, and concludes: "As a poet, he probably stands in
    the first class; but in the other departments of literature,
    he has many equals, and many superiors" (p. xviii). The
    book is a reprint of Goldsmith's Essays, 1765. The
    "Critique" is reprinted: 1974.A6.

1805

A. Books--None

B. Shorter Writings

1   COOKE, WILLIAM. [Anecdotes of Goldsmith.] In Memoirs of
    Samuel Foote. 3 vols. London: Richard Phillips, 1:184-86;
    3:77-78.
        The first passage stresses Goldsmith as the first to

1806-1807

attack sentimental comedy; the second the disparity
between his distinction as a writer and his "vain and
humble, coarse and refined, judicious and credulous"
manners (3:78). Reprinted: 1974.A6.

1806-1807

A. Books--None

B. Shorter Writings

1   CUMBERLAND, RICHARD. Memoirs. 2 vols. London: Lackington,
    Allen & Co., 1, passim.
       Despite his own sentimental comedies, Cumberland enjoyed
    a warm friendship with Goldsmith. Does not believe
    Goldsmith wrote enough poetry to be counted a first-rate
    poet, but of his dramas: "it is to be lamented he did not
    begin at an earlier time to turn his genius to dramatic
    compositions, and much more to be lamented that after he
    had begun, the succeeding period of his life was so soon
    cut off" (p. 276). Cumberland met him c. 1773, and
    supported Johnson in urging Colman to produce She Stoops
    to Conquer. Cumberland provides an account of the selling
    of the Vicar, p. 273, some details of which differ from
    Boswell's and Mrs. Thrale's. Partially reprinted: 1974.A6.

1808

A. Books--None

B. Shorter Writings

1   EVANS, JOHN. "Anecdotes of Goldsmith." European Magazine 53
    (May):373-75.
       A fuller account of 1804.B1, chiefly dealing with
    Goldsmith's life at Dr. Milner's school in 1756, and
    containing the anecdote of Goldsmith, the servant William,
    and the cheese candle. Anecdotes are well authenticated,
    based on Miss Milner's recollections recorded by Evans.

2   MANGIN, EDWARD. An Essay on Light Reading, As It May Be
    Supposed to Influence Moral Conduct and Literary Taste.
    London: James Carpenter, pp. 129-52.
       After attacking Fielding and Smollett as morally
    corrupting compared with Richardson, moves on to Goldsmith,
    and can shed some light on his exact birthplace because of

letter from the Rev. Annesley Strean, pp. 136-50, offering
evidence, mainly a letter from Robert Jones Lloyd, that
Goldsmith was born at his grandmother's house at Smith-Hill,
not Pallas, as Johnson's epitaph states. Mangin's
justification: "it is desirable to know even the most
trivial circumstance connected with the life of one whose
writings are destined to delight and improve mankind
hereafter, and whose private history will probably form
an object of eager inquiry to generations yet unborn"
(p. 152). Partially reprinted: 1974.A6.

<u>1810</u>

A. Books--None

B. Shorter Writings

 1   BARBAULD, ANNA. [Brief Life of Goldsmith.] In <u>The British</u>
      <u>Novelists with an Essay, and Prefaces, Biographical and</u>
      <u>Critical</u>. Vol. 23. London: F. C. & J. Rivington et al.,
      pp. i-xx. [Contains Coventry's <u>History of Pompey the</u>
      <u>Little</u> and <u>The Vicar of Wakefield</u>.
         One of many popular collections of fiction. Biography
      depends chiefly on Glover, 1774.B3. Critical comments on
      all Goldsmith's works and points out morals in poems but,
      surprisingly, not in the <u>Vicar</u>, where she praises his
      humour: "The plot of this piece is full of improbabilities,
      but whatever its faults, we easily forgive the author, who
      has made us laugh, and has made us cry" (pp. xi-xii).

 2   CHALMERS, ALEXANDER. "Life of Goldsmith." In <u>Works of the</u>
      <u>British Poets</u>. Vol. 16. London: J. Johnson et al.,
      pp. 479-87. [The series uses Johnson's <u>Lives of the Poets</u>,
      with additional lives by Chalmers.]
         "Life" largely based on 1801.B1 with many quotations.
      Critical summary: "In description, pathos, and even
      sublimity, he has not been exceeded by any of the poets of
      his age, except that in the latter quality he must yield to
      Gray" (16:486).

<u>1811</u>

A. Books--None

B. Shorter Writings

 1   MUDFORD, WILLIAM. "Critical Observations [on <u>The Vicar of</u>

1813

Wakefield]." In The British Novelists, Comprising Every
Work of Acknowledged Merit Which Is Usually Classed Under
the Denomination of Novels. Accompanied with Biographical
Sketches of the Authors and a Critical Preface to Each
Work. London: W. Clarke; Goddard, Taylor & Hessey; J. M.
Richardson; Sherwood, Necky, & Jones, 3:i-iv [Also
contains Tristram Shandy, A Sentimental Journey, and
Gulliver's Travels; each work is paged separately.].
    Another popular collection like 1810.B1 and 1810.B2.
The biographical sketch reprints 1804.B2. The "Critical
Observations" find little to criticize: the plot is
probable, but does find the Vicar's loss of fortune
displeases, and the incidents of the conclusion "are heaped
together with too much rapidity, with too little attention
to probability, and into too profuse a display of human
calamity" (p. iv) and speculates this ending may have been
caused by Johnson's hasty sale of the novel. Concludes
with praise of the "fine strain of pious and Christian
morality which pervades every part of it . . ." (p. iv).

1813

A. Books--None

B. Shorter Writings

  1   NORTHCOTE, JAMES. [Anecdote of Goldsmith.] In Memoirs of Sir
      Joshua Reynolds, Kt, Comprising Original Anecdotes of Many
      Distinguished Persons, his Contemporaries and a Brief
      Analysis of his Discourses to Which Are Added Varieties on
      Art. London: Henry Colburn. [Revised as The Life of Sir
      Joshua Reynolds, 2 vols (London: Henry Colburn, 1818).
      Extensive material, some drawn from Percy, but much on
Northcote's personal friendship with Reynolds, with Percy
perhaps Goldsmith's closest friend. Perhaps because of his
close friendship with Reynolds, Northcote shows considerable
insight into Goldsmith's personality. As Reynolds's pupil,
Northcote came to know Goldsmith well, and his views of
Goldsmith's personality were undoubtedly influenced by
Reynolds, best expressed in 1952.B4. [References are to
the 1st ed., passim, and include the 1815 Supplement,
passim.] Reprinted, much condensed: 1974.A6.

A. Books--None

B. Shorter Writings

   *1   HAZLITT, WILLIAM. [General comment on Goldsmith's work.] In
      Lectures on the English Poets. London: Taylor & Hessey.
         Praises poetry, Vicar, plays, Citizen of the World, and
      notes almost universal popularity. [Text from Works,
      edited by P. P. Howe, after the edition of A. R. Waller &
      Arnold Glover, Centenary edition. (London: Dent, 1924)
      5:119-20.]

A. Books--None

B. Shorter Writings

   *1   HAZLITT, WILLIAM. [Comments on various writings.] In
      Lectures on the English Comic Writers. London: Taylor &
      Hessey.
         Mrs. Hardcastle and Tony seen as indebted to Mrs.
      Blackacre and son in Wycherley's Plain Dealer; Citizen of
      the World "more original, more natural, and more
      picturesque than Johnson"; latter part of the Vicar heavily
      indebted to Wilson's account and Adams's domestic life in
      Joseph Andrews; Good Natur'd Man inferior to She Stoops to
      Conquer. [Text from Works, edited by P. P. Howe, after the
      edition of A. R. Waller & Arnold Glover, Centenary edition
      (London: Dent, 1924) 6:70, 104-14, 115, 164.]

A. Books--None

B. Shorter Writings

   1   COLMAN, GEORGE, The Younger, ed. Posthumous Letters from
      Various Celebrated Men; Addressed to Francis Colman, and
      George Colman the Elder. London: T. Cadell & W. Davis,
      pp. 180-81.
         Letter 28 requests Colman [the elder] to make up his
      mind about changes he may want in the play [She Stoops to
      Conquer] and Goldsmith will try his best; "For God sake
      take the play and let us make the best of it, and let me

1820

have the same measure at least which you have given as bad
plays as mine" (p. 181). Reprinted: 1928.A1.

2   NEWELL, R. H. "Remarks." In The Poetical Works of Oliver
     Goldsmith, with Remarks Attempting to Ascertain, Chiefly
     from Local Observation, the Actual Scene of "The Deserted
     Village." London: Suttaby, Evance, & Co., pp. 61-81.
         Believes Goldsmith used memories of Lishoy, County
     Westmeath, where he spent his early years. First formed
     this belief in 1806 during a visit to Ireland, and later
     visits and closer inspection confirms his belief. Quotes
     from Gold smith's letters published in Percy's "Life" (1801.B1)
     to support "a probabliity that his poetical expression
     of affection might be sincere. . . . At the same time, it is
     not intended to deny, that much of the description may be
     applicable to England; but rather to suggest whether the
     Poet may not very ingeniously have contrived to give an
     English character to circumstances and objects plainly and
     originally, Irish" (p. 64). Some details do not fit:
     Kilkenny-West Church was probably substituted. Appends
     sketches of Lishoy Mill, Kilkenny-West Church, Hawthorn
     Tree, South View from Goldsmith's Mount, Parsonage, School
     House, and a Vignette: the Mount and the Copse.

1822

A. Books--None

B. Shorter Writings

1   GOETHE, JOHANN WOLFGANG VON. [Comments on Goldsmith.] In
     Autobiography [Dictung und Wahrheit, 1822]. 2 vols.
     Translated by John Oxenford, 1846-1848. Bohns's Standard
     Library. London: George Bell & Sons, passim.
         Goethe's Autobiography had been translated into English
     in 1824 from a French translation by Aubert de Vitry, but
     did not have wide circulation until Oxenford's more complete
     translation was published. In 2:208-11, describes how
     through Herder he came to know the Vicar and was impressed
     by Goldsmith's presentation of the Vicar as priest and
     farmer: "a man, with feelings of pure humanity, strong
     enough not to deviate from them under any circumstances,
     and by this already elevated above the many . . ." (p. 209),
     and by Goldsmith's attitude: "it represents the reward of
     good and intentions and perseverance in the right, it
     strengthens an unconditional confidence in God, and
     asserts the final triumph of good over evil, and all this
     without a trace of cant or pedantry. The author was

preserved from both of these by an elevation of mind that
shows itself throughout in the form of irony, by reason of
which this little work must appear to us as wise as it is
amiable" (p. 210). The lasting impression left on him:
"The above work had produced a great impression upon me,
for which I could not account. Properly speaking, I felt
myself in unison with that ironical tone of mind which
elevates itself above every object, above fortune and
misfortune, good and evil, death and life, and thus attains
to the possession of a truly poetic world. I could not,
indeed become conscious of this until much later: it was
enough that it gave me much to do at the moment; but I
could by no means have expected to be so soon transposed
from this fictitious world into a similar real one"
(p. 211). Reprinted: 1974.A6.

2   HAZLITT, WILLIAM. Table-Talk; or Original Essays. 2 vols.
London: John Warren.
     Goldsmith would survive as a classic on the basis of a
few chapters of the Vicar and the portrait of the schoolmaster in The Deserted Village; Jenkinson's cosmogony
jargon as an illustration of people with one idea;
Goldsmith jealous of women's beauty--the episode with the
Horneck sisters in their trip to France; unidentified
quotation used as epigraph for a chapter. [Text from Works,
edited by P. P. Howe, after the edition of A. R. Waller &
Arnold Glover, Centenary edition (London: Dent, 1924)
8:47, 60, 93, 226.]

1823

A. Books--None

B. Shorter Writings

1   [SCOTT, Sir WALTER.] "Memoir of Goldsmith." In Ballantyne's
Novelists' Library, to which are prefixed Memoirs of the
Lives of the Authors. London: Hurst Robinson, 5:xxii-
xxix.
     Outlines biography, comments briefly on his other major
literary works, and praises the novel for its "simplicity,"
the characterization; Goldsmith "wrote to exalt virtue and
expose vice; and he accomplished the task in a manner which
raises him to the highest rank among British authors"
(p. xxix).

1825

1825

A. Books--None

B. Shorter Writings

    1   IRVING, WASHINGTON. "Life of Goldsmith." In <u>Miscellaneous</u>
        <u>Writings of Oliver Goldsmith</u>. 4 vols. Paris: A. & W.
        Galignani & Jules Didot.
           "Life" occupies 1:i-cxxvii. Irving identified as editor
        but not author of life. Stanley T. Williams, <u>Life of</u>
        <u>Washington Irving</u> (Oxford: Oxford University Press, 1935),
        2:221, n. 14, believes "Irving's source was probably the
        'Prefatory Memoir' to Goldsmith in 'Ballantyne's Novelists'
        Library,'" but this first version by Irving contains
        material from Percy, Boswell, Hawkins, Cumberland, and
        other reliable sources. Stresses jealousy and gambling,
        and does sentimentalize Goldsmith, as Williams notes and
        the conclusion indicates: "The epithet so often heard, and
        in such kindly terms, of 'poor Goldsmith,' speaks volumes.
        Few who consider the rich compound of admirable and
        whimsical qualities which form his character, would wish to
        prune away its eccentricities, trim its grotesque luxuriance,
        or clip it down to the decent formalities of rigid virtue.
        . . . We question whether he himself would not feel
        gratified on the proofs of his greatness, . . . with the
        kindhearted phrase, so fondly and familiarly ejaculated, of
        'Poor Goldsmith!'" (p. cxxviii). Irving may be among the
        first to use the phrase "poor Goldsmith" sentimentally,
        which Johnson certainly does not do in Boswell, meaning
        only Goldsmith is dead. See 1840.A1, 1849.A1, A2, A3, and
        1850.A1. For bibliographical details see 1978.A1,
        p. xxiii, and Stanley T. Williams and Mary Allen Edge,
        compilers, <u>A Bibliography of the Writings of Washington</u>
        <u>Irving: A Checklist</u> (New York: Oxford University Press,
        1936), pp. 88-93.

    2   SCOTT, [Sir] WALTER. <u>Lives of the Novelists</u>. 2 vols. Paris:
        A. & W. Galignani, 2:91-117.
           A reprint of 1823.B1. Usually reprinted with this
        title. Reprinted with the title <u>Biographical and Critical</u>
        <u>Notes of Eminent Novelists</u>: 1974.A6.

1826

A. Books--None

B. Shorter Writings

1   CRADDOCK, JOSEPH. [Anecdotes of Goldsmith.] In Literary and
    Miscellaneous Memoirs. 4 vols. London: J. B. Nichols,
    passim.
        A friend of Goldsmith's who provided the epilogue printed
    with She Stoops to Conquer, and Goldsmith wrote the
    prologue to his tragedy Zobeide, 1771. Some repetition
    from Boswell, Percy, etc., but important for circumstances
    related to She Stoops to Conquer. "Dr. Goldsmith and I
    never quarrelled; for he was convinced I had a real regard
    for him; but a kind of civil sparring continually took
    place between us" (1:230). Condensed selection reprinted:
    1974.A6.

1829

A. Books--None

B. Shorter Writings

1   GOETHE, JOHANN WOLFGANG von. [Comments on The Vicar of
    Wakefield in a letter dated 25 December 1829.] In
    Goethe's Letters to Zelter. Translated by A. D. Coleridge.
    London: H. G. Bohn, p. 381.
        Goethe read the Vicar in his youth and continued to
    admire it throughout his life. He mentions having come
    across the book again and having reread it, recalling its
    profound influence on him as a young writer: "This high,
    benevolent irony, this just and comprehensive way of
    viewing things, this gentleness to all opposition, this
    equanimity under every change, and whatever else the
    kindred virtues may be termed--such things were a most
    admirable training for me, and surely these are the
    sentiments, which in the end lead us back from all the
    mistaken paths of life" (p. 381). Reprinted: 1974.A6.

1830

A. Books--None

B. Shorter Writings

   1   COLMAN, GEORGE the Younger. [Anecdotes of Goldsmith.] In
        Random Records. 2 vols. London: Henry Colburn & Richard
        Bentley, 1:110-13.
          Records being dandled on Goldsmith's knee, slapping him
        spitefully, and being put in a dark room as punishment,
        with Goldsmith coming shortly afterwards to play games with
        him, calm his fears, and restore his good humour.

 *2   HAZLITT, WILLIAM. Conversations with James Northcote, R.A.
        London: Henry Colburn & Richard Bentley.
          Northcote was eighty-four when Hazlitt published these
        conversations, and chiefly repeats material available in
        his own earlier Memoirs of Reynolds, 1813.B1, but does
        remark, "These men were not looked upon in their day as at
        present: Johnson had his Lexiphanes and Goldsmith was
        laughed at--their merits were to the full as much called in
        question, more so, than those of the author of Waverly . . ."
        (p. 275). [Text from Works, edited by P. P. Howe, after
        the edition of A. R. Waller & Richard Bentley, Centenary
        edition (London: Dent, 1924) 5:passim.]

1831

A. Books--None

B. Shorter Writings

   1   [GARRICK, DAVID.] [Letters relating to Goldsmtih.] In The
        Private Correspondence of David Garrick with the Most
        Celebrated Persons of his Time. 2 vols. London: Henry
        Colburn & Richard Bentley, passim.
          Three letters: (1) Dr. J. Hoadley to Mr. G[arrick].
        1773 [otherwise no date]. On Goldsmith's new farce, which
        Hoadley has not yet seen: "In his first play the town
        would not bear his low humour, and justly, as he degraded
        his 'Good-Natur'd Man,' whom they were taught to pity and
        have a sort of respect for, into a low buffoon, and what is
        worse, into a falsifier, a character unbecoming a
        gentleman" (1:506). (2) Goldsmith's letter to Garrick of
        6 February 1773, requesting Garrick return the MS. of She
        Stoops to Conquer (1:527). Reprinted: 1928.A1. (3) Mme.

Marie Jeanne Riccoboni, a novelist, had been sent a copy of
The Vicar by Richard Burke, Edmund Burke's younger brother,
who admired Goldsmith's novel. She disagrees and gives
her reasons to Garrick (2:492-94): the rapid movement from
happiness to misery is improbable; the moral lessons are
inapplicable to life; and experience proves that those who
are reduced to misery generally turn their ideas towards
baseness and crime rather than honesty and virtue, and she
wouldn't like to meet his prison congregation in a wood if
she had a thousand louis in her pocket. (3) is reprinted:
1974.A6.

1832

A. Books--None

B. Shorter Writings

1   TAYLOR, JOHN. [Anecdotes of Goldsmith.] In Records of My
    Life. 2 vols. London: Edward Bull, 1:107-9.
        Mostly devoted to the story of Cooke's borrowing a
    guinea, which Goldsmith had wrapped in paper and slipped
    under the door rather than leaving in the letterbox. When
    he teases Miss Clara Brooke too hard, she quotes from The
    Deserted Village, "And the loud laugh which spoke the
    vacant mind," and Goldsmith is quite abashed.

2   WELD, ISAAC. Statistical Survey of the County of Roscommon.
    Dublin: R. Graisberry, pp. 362-70.
        Includes material relating to "Oliver Goldsmith, the
    poet of Ireland, excellence" (p. 362). Discusses
    birthplace problem, citing Johnson's epitaph, Trinity
    College records (believed incorrect); Aiken's belief in
    Elphin (1796.B1); the Strean letter in Mangin (1808.B1),
    and quotes Lloyd letter from Strean, and moves on to
    summarize Goldsmith's education, his failure to be
    ordained, but his hard work as a writer, and his morality,
    especially in the Vicar, "in which true and genuine piety
    and humble resignation to the divine will, under the
    adversities of life, and the visitations of providence, are
    described in the most attractive colors . . ." (p. 370), a
    work with probably more moral influence than all the
    writings of the theologians of the diocese of Elphin since
    the time of St. Patrick.

1833

1833

A. Books--None

B. Shorter Writings

 *1 IRVING, WASHINGTON. "Life of Goldsmith." In <u>Miscellaneous</u>
   <u>Writings of Oliver Goldsmith</u>. 4 vols. Philadelphia:
   J. Crissy & J. Grigg.
    American edition of 1825.B1. For bibliographical
   details, see 1978.A1, p. xxiii, and Stanley T. Williams
   and Mary Allen Edge, compilers, <u>A Bibliography of the</u>
   <u>Writings of Washington Irving: A Checklist</u> (New York:
   Oxford University Press, 1936), pp. 88-93.

1835

A. Books--None

B. Shorter Writings

 *1 IRVING, WASHINGTON. "Life of Goldsmith." In <u>Miscellaneous</u>
   <u>Writings of Oliver Goldsmith</u>. 4 vols. Philadelphia:
   J. Crissy & J. Grigg.
    Reprint of 1833.B1. For bibliographical details, see
   1978.A1, p. xxiii, and Stanley T. Williams and Mary Allen
   Edge, compilers, <u>A Bibliography of the Writings of</u>
   <u>Washington Irving: A Checklist</u> (New York: Oxford
   University Press, 1936), pp. 88-93.

1836

A. Books--None

B. Shorter Writings

 1 [BUTLER, WILLIAM A.] "Gallery of Illustrious Irishmen: I.
   Goldsmith." <u>Dublin University Magazine</u> 7 (January):30-54.
    Introduction to the series, pp. 26-30, explains the
   scope and subsequent numbers present biographical sketches
   of Grattan, Berkeley [two parts], Boyle, and Flood.
   Goldsmith chosen for the versatility of his powers;
   discusses problem of his birthplace; uses Mrs. Hodson's
   "Narrative" from Percy's Life (1801.B1) heavily; considerable critical opinion: prefers <u>Good Natur'd Man</u> to <u>She</u>
   <u>Stoops to Conquer</u>, believing it like Molière; high praise

for <u>Citizen of the World</u>; believes Goldsmith most often thought of as a poet.

*2   IRVING, WASHINGTON. "Life of Goldsmith." In <u>Miscellaneous Writings of Oliver Goldsmith</u>. 4 vols. Philadelphia: J. Crissy & J. Grigg.
    Reprint of 1833.B1. For bibliographical details, see 1978.A1, p. xxiii, and Stanley T. Williams and Mary Allen Edge, compilers, <u>A Bibliography of the Writings of Washington Irving: A Checklist</u> (New York: Oxford University Press, 1936), pp. 88-93.

<u>1837</u>

A. Books

1   PRIOR, [Sir] JAMES. <u>The Life of Oliver Goldsmith, M.B., from a Variety of Original Sources</u>. 2 vols. London: John Murray, 1:534 pp., 2:593 pp.
    The first full length biography, undertaken because "To the list of writers of whom we know less than their reputation deserves, must be added Goldsmith. A biographical preface is all that has been hitherto awarded him, and it will scarcely be contended that he is unworthy of any thing more. Such sketch outlines of a life, much of it marked by daily struggles for daily bread, and part of it by the imprudences common to such a state of existence, can never be satisfactory, because they must inevitably omit all, or nearly all, that we wish to know. Biography to be useful must be minute; to be entertaining also it must be minute" (pp. viii-ix). Prior interviewed such surviving relatives and friends of Goldsmith as he could find living near Lishoy and Elphin, examined Trinity College records, wrote many letters to those who had known Goldsmith in England, drew on Percy's papers and materials from William Newbery, and Maj. General Sir Henry Bunbury, Bart., who had married one of the Horneck sisters. In addition, surveyed Goldsmith's life and writings as no biographer had to this time, and made new attributions of anonymously published writings. In addition, provides extensive commentary on all the major works and most of the minor ones, though viewing them from an early Victorian perspective rather than the Georgian one in which written. One of the sources essential to the student of Goldsmith's life and work. Unfortunately, no index. Reprints as appendix to Volume 2 the sale catalogue of Goldsmith's household furniture and of his library, 1774.B6. Brief selections on <u>Traveller</u>,

1837

Vicar, Deserted Village, and She Stoops to Conquer
reprinted in 1974.A6.

2   ., ed. The Miscellaneous Works of Oliver Goldsmith,
M.B., including a Variety of Pieces now first collected.
4 vols. London: John Murray.
  Published shortly after 1832.A1, as a result of
discoveries Prior made in writing the biography. The
second major edition, Percy's being the first. Remained
definitive until superseded by Bohn's, 1848.A2.

B. Shorter Writings

1   ANON. "Review of Prior's Life of Goldsmith." Gentleman's
Magazine, n.s. 7 (March):227-42.
  The leading review article and highly favorable, though
regrets Johnson could not include Goldsmith's life in the
Lives of the Poets. Much discussion of the poems,
indicating early Victorian interest in Goldsmith primarily
as a poet, and conventions of the images Goldsmith used are
traced. Believes theses of Traveller and Deserted Village
factually unsound.

*2   IRVING, WASHINGTON. "Life of Goldsmith." In Miscellaneous
Writings of Oliver Goldsmith. 4 vols. Philadelphia:
J. Crissy & J. Grigg.
  Reprint of 1833.B1. For bibliographical details, see
1978.A1, p. xxiii, and Stanley T. Williams and Mary Allen
Edge, compilers, A Bibliography of the Writings of
Washington Irving: A Checklist (New York: Oxford
University Press, 1936), pp. 88-93.

3   [WILMOTT, R. A.] "Review of Prior's Life of Goldsmith and
J. Mitford's Works of Gray." Church of England Quarterly
Review 1 (April):360-89. [Goldsmith discussion, pp. 360-
81.]
  Extremely favorable, both to Prior's work and
Goldsmith's: of the Vicar: "the unanimous opinion seems
to be, that no composition in any European language
possesses an equal charm . . . nor ought we to forget the
high praise due to the author [Goldsmith] for the moral
courage with which he abandoned the fashionable indecencies
of the age. Fielding and Smollett presided over Romance;
but Goldsmith shook off at once all the influence of
example and of reputation, and determined to adhere to
Nature" (p. 361). Versification of Traveller is more like
Dryden's than Deserted Village, "masculine, free, and
energetic; the pauses are happily placed; the diction

remarkably select, pure and expressive. In this poem the
excellencies of Dryden and Pope seem to be combined; it is
more polished than the first, more natural than the
second" (p. 367). "As a poem, it [the Deserted Village] is
generally deemed inferior to the Traveller, although
enjoying a wider popularity, and, in our opinion,
containing more poetical beauty" (p. 373)--evidence of
opinion shifting from Johnson's preference for Traveller.
Quotes anecdotes from Boswell to show Boswell used
Goldsmith as a foil to Johnson.

1840

A. Books

1   IRVING, WASHINGTON. Life of Oliver Goldsmith, with Selections
    from his Writings. 2 vols. Harper's Family Library. New
    York: Harper & Brothers, 1:331 pp., 2:318 pp.
        Revision and enlargement of 1825.B1, drawing heavily upon
    Prior (1837.A1) plus additional material from Boswell
    (1791.B1). Omits much of the 1825 critical evaluation of
    Goldsmith's writings. Plays down accounts of Goldsmith's
    jealousy and softens his accounts of his gambling. Presents
    Boswell as jealous of Goldsmith rather than Johnson hostile
    to him. Still uses accounts in writings as basis for
    biographical information. For bibliographical details, see
    1978.A1, and Stanley T. Williams and Mary Allen Edge,
    compilers, A Bibliography of the Writings of Washington
    Irving: A Checklist (New York: Oxford University Press,
    1936), pp. 88-93.

B. Shorter Writings

*1 IRVING, WASHINGTON, ed. "Life of Goldsmith." In Miscellaneous
    Writings, by Goldsmith. Philadelphila: J. Crissy & J.
    Grigg.
        Reprint of 1833.B1. For bibliographical details, see
    1978.A1, p. xxiii, and Stanley T. Williams and Mary Allen
    Edge, compilers, A Bibliography of the Writings of
    Washington Irving: A Checklist (New York: Oxford
    University Press, 1936), pp. 88-93.

1842

1842

A. Books--None

B. Shorter Writings

1   [D'Arblay, Frances Burney.] The Diary and Letters of Madame
    D'Arblay. Edited by Charlotte Barrett. London: Henry
    Colburn, pp. 38-39.
        After finding the Vicar inferior to other sentimental
    novels at age sixteen (see 1889.B1), Fanny Burney later
    came to admire it. Diary entry for August 1778 reports her
    disappointment in learning Goldsmith had based Croaker in
    the Good Natur'd Man on Johnson's Suspirus from the Rambler.
    "While we were yet reading this Rambler Dr. Johnson came in:
    we told him what we were about. 'Ah, madam!' cried he,
    'Goldsmith was not scrupulous; but he would have been a
    great man had he known the real value of his own internal
    resources.' 'Miss Burney,' said Mrs. Thrale, 'is fond of
    his Vicar of Wakefield: and so am I;--don't you like it,
    sir?' 'No, madam, it is very faulty; there is nothing of
    real life in it, and very little of nature. It is a mere
    fanciful performance'" (p. 39). Reprinted: 1974.A6.

1848

A. Books

1   BOHN, H. G., Ed. The Works of Oliver Goldsmith, with a Life
    and Notes. 4 vols. Bohn's Standard Library. London:
    George Bell & Sons.
        "Life" much concerned with Goldsmith's personal moral
    character and its connection with his works: "As the
    generality of men are more wicked than they appear, so, on
    the other hand, it may be suspected of Goldsmith, that he
    appears more faulty than he really was; at least it may be
    surmised that his vices were not so much worse, or more
    numerous, than those of many who left a better character,
    as that he had less art to conceal them. His simplicity in
    this respect does, however, form no proper justification of
    his conduct; and it cannot be sufficiently lamented that he
    who shewed himself so capable of appreciating the beauty of
    a virtuous life, should have indulged in irregularities
    which every good man must condemn" (p. 51). Considers his
    character as compounded of contradictions. Finds Goldsmith
    generally acknowledged as ranking among the foremost prose
    writers. "As a poet, Goldsmith ranks higher than any other
    English author who has written so little, with the exception,

perhaps, of Gray" (p. 53). Finds She Stoops to Conquer
more popular than The Good Natur'd Man, though critics will
like the second better.

    Through the wide currency of Bohn's cheap editions, his
"Life" undoubtedly exerted great influence; he almost
certainly drew upon Prior (1837.A1), and cites the best
available sources, especially Percy (1801.B1) and Boswell
(1791.B1). [Text of "Life" used: 1892 reprint of 1884
revision, 1:1-59.] A short selection reprinted: 1974.A6.

2   FORSTER, JOHN. The Life and Adventures of Oliver Goldsmith.
    London: Bradbury & Evans, Chapman & Hall, 698 pp.
        Draws heavily on Prior's research (1837.A1), but also
incorporated some original research. Primarily a compre-
hensive biographical account, but presents something of
Irving's "poor Goldsmith," but with much more insistence
that Goldsmith was swindled and oppressed by booksellers,
insulted and ridiculed by his friends, and generally
unappreciated during his lifetime. Offers little analysis
of Goldsmith's character or of his writing. Often tells us
more about Forster's own Victorian preoccupations than
about Goldsmith's life, continuing the tradition of
Goldsmith as the elegant writer who was a social buffoon,
though now we are asked to pity him as misunderstood. Very
little mention of Goldsmith's gambling.

B. Shorter Writings

1   ANON. "Goldsmith and his Biographers." Dublin University
    Magazine 32 (September):315-37.
        An incisive and acute review of Forster's life (1848.A1),
noting that his Goldsmith is not essentially different from
Scott's, and that both Forster and Prior "have formed a
strange ideal of the man--forgetting that in this, as in
other cases, the poet lives two distinct and wholly
disparate lives--that his world of imagination is more
often one entirely in contrast with that forced on him by
the realities of the world; that his walk upon earth is not
among the scenes which his fancy creates; that anything more
prosaic, more inconsistent with truth and nature, than the
effort, which some persons have been engaged in, to re-
create what they call his 'Auburn,' by clipping hawthorns.
. . . In short, we are inclined to think that when the life
of Goldsmith is hereafter written, the biographer's task
will be omission, not addition. . . . Both Mr. Prior and
Mr. Forster have, we think, something to answer for in
confusing matter so entirely distinct, as the poet's actual
life among men, and the fictitious, though no less real

1848

life, which he grew to the creations of his imagination.
. . . This effort to present before us, as the hero of a
romance, the Oliver Goldsmith of real life, is a violation
of the first considerations of art" (pp. 317-18).

2   [BULWER-LYTTON, EDWARD.] Review of John Forster's Life and
     Adventures of Oliver Goldsmith. Edinburgh Review 88 (July):
     193-225.
        Largely a biographical summary based on Forster, with
     some critical comments: "Goldsmith was emphatically a
     writer from experience. What he had seen what he had felt,
     that he reproduced. Comparatively with his other gifts,
     his imagination was not vivid or comprehensive" (p. 202).
     Believes Goldsmith repeats images, ideas, thoughts, and
     character types in closely similar language: "most of them
     [his characters], indeed, are but likenesses of the author
     himself in different positions" (p. 202). He has no
     understanding of Goldsmith's joking Irish humor; praises
     Forster, arguing he has full right to draw on Prior's
     scholarship. Believes Goldsmith would have profited from
     marriage. A fairly typical Victorian review, finding few
     problems with Forster's work and praising it for better
     writing and organization than Prior's.

3   C., S. P. "Memorials of Literary Characters, No. XVIII:
     Pedigree of the Poet Goldsmith." Gentleman's Magazine
     n.s. 7 (March):242.
        Brief note disagreeing with Prior on pedigree, arguing
     family came from Penshurst, Kent, with details about
     landholdings there in early seventeenth century; Prior had
     placed family in Crayford, Kent, but in Galway in 1541.

4   [LEWES, GEORGE.] Review of John Forster's Life and Adventures
     of Oliver Goldsmith. British Quarterly 8 (August):1-25.
        Criticizes Forster for stressing Goldsmith's times and
     neglecting Goldsmith, particularly the analysis of his
     character. Finds Forster pictorial, neglecting Goldsmith's
     character problems, treating him too tenderly, and not
     distinguishing sufficiently between his personal life and
     his imaginative life. Argues Forster sees Goldsmith's whole
     era from a nineteenth-century perspective, ignoring its own
     social and cultural assumptions.

1849

A. Books

1 IRVING, WASHINGTON. Oliver Goldsmith. New York: G. P.
   Putnam, 382 pp.
       Expansion of 1840.Al for inclusion in Putnam's first
   collected edition of his own works, and subsequently
   reprinted in these collected editions, 1864, 1868, and 1897.
   Preface acknowledges his debts to Prior and Forster and
   makes no claims for original scholarship. Expanding a hint
   from Forster (1848.Al) that Goldsmith might have been
   romantically attracted to Mary Horneck, Irving much more
   strongly speculates on the possibility of his romantic
   feelings for her. Greatly expands the amount and number of
   anti-Boswell references from 1840.Al, perhaps because of
   the large number of these in Forster, 1848.Al. Lacks
   Prior's detail and greater objectivity, Forster's concen-
   tration on milieu often to the neglect of Goldsmith, and
   apparently aimed at being a popularization for a more
   general reading public than either. None of Irving's
   three lives shows any specially "American" insights into
   Goldsmith's personality or writing, and, as noted, reflect
   prevailing interpretations found in most of the British
   writers. For bibliographical details, see 1978.Al, and
   Stanley T. Williams and Mary Allen Edge, compilers, A
   Bibliography of the Writings of Washington Irving: A
   Checklist (New York: Oxford University Press, 1936),
   pp. 88-93.

2 _____. Oliver Goldsmith. London: John Murray, 382 pp.
       English edition of 1849.Al, probably printed from the
   same plates. For bibliographical details, see 1978.Al,
   pp. xxxvi-xxxvii, and Stanley T. Williams and Mary Allen
   Edge, compilers, A Bibliography of the Writings of
   Washington Irving: A Checklist (New York: Oxford
   University Press, 1936), pp. 88-93.

B. Shorter Writings

*1 IRVING, WASHINGTON, ed. "Life of Goldsmith." In Miscellaneous
   Writings, by Goldsmith. Philadelphia: Crissy & Markley.
       Reprint of 1833.B1. For bibliographical details, see
   1978.Al, p. xxiii, and Stanley T. Williams and Mary Allen
   Edge, A Bibliography of the Writings of Washington Irving:
   A Checklist (New York: Oxford University Press, 1936),
   pp. 88-93.

1850

1850

A. Books

1   IRVING, WASHINGTON. Oliver Goldsmith. London: G. Routledge,
        224 pp.
            Pirated reprint of 1849.A1. For bibliographical details
        see 1978.A1, and Stanley T. Williams and Mary Allen Edge,
        compilers, A Bibliography of the Writings of Washington
        Irving: A Checklist (New York: Oxford University Press,
        1936), pp. 88-93.

1853

A. Books--None

B. Shorter Writings

1   THACKERAY, WILLIAM MAKEPEACE. The English Humourists of the
        Eighteenth Century. London: Smith, Elder & Co., pp. 248-
        71.
            Probably the most extreme example of sentimentalizing
        Goldsmith among Victorian writers, somewhat astonishing in
        view of Thackeray's own considerable knowledge of the
        eighteenth century, perhaps because Thackeray says almost
        nothing about his work but a great deal about his
        personality: "What is the charm of his verse, of his style,
        and humour? His sweet regrets, his delicate compassion,
        his soft smile, his tremulous sympathy, his weakness which
        he owns? Your love for him is half pity. You come hot and
        tired from the day's battle, and this sweet minstrel sings
        to you. Who could harm the kind vagrant harper? Whom did
        he ever hurt?" (p. 248). "Ah! if we pity the good and weak
        man who suffers undeservedly, let us deal very gently with
        him from whom misery extorts not only tears, but shame; let
        us think humbly and charitably of the human nature that
        suffers so sadly and falls so low. Whose turn may it be
        tomorrow: What weak heart, confident before trial, may not
        succumb under temptation invincible?   Cover the good man
        who has been vanquished--cover his face and pass on"
        (p. 252). Reprinted, with some deletions: 1974.A4.

1854

A. Books

1   CUNNINGHAM, PETER, ed. The Works of Oliver Goldsmith.
       4 vols.   London: John Murray, 1:480 pp., 2:487 pp.,
       3:447 pp., 4:450 pp.
          First published as part of "Murray's British Classics,"
       but then separately. A major edition, incorporating some
       newly ascribed essays. American edition, 1881.A1.

2   FORSTER, JOHN. The Life and Times of Oliver Goldsmith.
       2 vols. London: Bradbury & Evans, and Chapman & Hall,
       1:499 pp., 2:560 pp.
          A revision and enlargement with notes of 1848.A1, in
       which the emphasis on Goldsmith's times and contemporaries
       becomes even stronger, and Forster's pictorial method of
       presenting Goldsmith with little or no analysis of his
       personality remains.

B. Shorter Writings

1   [CAMPBELL, THOMAS.] Diary of a Visit to England in 1775 by an
       Irishman (the Reverend Thomas Campbell, Author of 'A
       Philosophical Survey of the South of Ireland') and Other
       Papers by the Same Hand. With Notes by Samuel Raymond,
       M.A., Prothonotary of the Supreme Court of New South Wales.
       Sidney: David Lovett Welsh, Atlas Office, 167 pp.
          Campbell became acquainted with Percy after Goldsmith's
       death and more or less took over the task of writing
       Goldsmith's biography from Percy, but died before the
       edition Percy had been superintending could be published.
       Campbell's manuscript biography is in the British Museum.
       See 1947.B2.

1856

A. Books--None

B. Shorter Writings

1   MACAULAY, THOMAS BABINGTON. "Goldsmith." Encyclopedia
       Britannica. 8th ed., 10:705-9.
          Biographical summary, based primarily on Prior and
       Forster. Frequently adverse comments on particular works:
       "In the Traveller, the execution, though deserving much

1861

praise, is far inferior to the design" (p. 706). The <u>Vicar</u> "rapidly obtained a popularity which has lasted down to our time, and which is likely to last as long as our language. The fable is indeed one of the worst that ever was constructed. It wants . . . probability . . . and consistency . . ." (p. 706). <u>The Deserted Village</u> "is made up of incongruous parts. The village in its happy days is a true English village. The village in its decay is an Irish village. . . . By joining the two, he has produced something which never was and never will be seen in any part of the world" (p. 707).

"Goldsmith has sometimes been represented as a man of genius, cruelly treated by the world, and doomed to struggle with difficulties which at last broke his heart. But no representation can be more remote from the truth. . . . He had none but himself to blame for his distresses. . . . It was not in dress or feasting or primiscuous amours or promiscuous charities that his chief expense lay. He had been from boyhood a gambler, and at once one of the most sanguine and the most unskillful gamblers" (p. 708).

Frequently reprinted as a school text separately or with other essays. Partly reprinted: 1974.A6.

1861

A. Books--None

B. Shorter Writings

1 [PIOZZI, HESTER LYNCH THRALE.] [Anecdotes of Goldsmith.] In <u>Autobiography, Letters and Literary Remains of Mrs. Piozzi</u>. Edited with notes and an Introductory Account of Her Life and Writings by A. Hayward. 2 vols. London: Longman, Green, Longman, & Roberts, passim.
    Raw materials from which 1786.B1 was quarried, with comments by Hayward, often drawing on Forster, 1848.A1. Most of this material came from 1942.B4

1865

A. Books--None

B. Shorter Writings

1 LESLIE, CHARLES ROBERT, and TAYLOR, TOM. [Anecdotes of Goldsmith.] In <u>The Life and Times of Sir Joshua Reynolds</u>,

<u>with Notices of Some of his Contemporaries</u>. 2 vols.
London: John Murray, passim.
    Mainly drawn from previous memoirs of Reynolds but uses
Reynolds's pocket-book memoranda to show Reynolds's
sympathetic friendship for Goldsmith, though Goldsmith is
sentimentalized in the usual Victorian fashion. Of
Reynolds's portrait [now at Woburn Abbey]: "This head of
Goldsmith is to me the most pathetic picture Reynolds ever
painted: not only because in looking at it, I think of the
'Deserted Village,' but for more because the sufferings of
a whole life and of the tenderest of hearts are written in
it" (1:361). His general treatment of Goldsmith: "Reynolds,
at all events, appreciated the beautiful, tender genius
which worked below that crust of awkwardness, uncouthness,
and childish vanity. He never started the laugh against
poor Goldy's innocent pleasure in his fine clothes, or
snubbed his sometimes ineffectual joke; never 'smoked' or
'hummed' or 'bit' him, as the slang of the time ran. He
seems at this time [c. 1770] to have dined oftener with
Goldsmith than any one else. They were often seen together
at Vauxhall and Ranelagh; the thickset little poet in
butterfly brilliance of colours, and the quiet painter in
sober black or brown" (1:363).

<u>1869</u>

A. Books--None

B. Shorter Writings

    1   MASSON, DAVID. Biographical Introduction to <u>The Miscellaneous</u>
        <u>Works of Oliver Goldsmith</u>. London: Macmillan, pp. ix-x.
        Uses the obvious sources--Percy, Prior, Forster, and
Boswell, and as in his <u>Life of Milton</u> he tends to treat
creative work as literal autobiography, but comments
directly on Goldsmith's use of his own experience: "All
Goldsmith's phantasies, whether in verse or prose . . . are
phantasies of what may be called <u>reminiscence</u>. Less than
even Smollett, did Goldsmith <u>invent</u>, if by invention we
mean a projection of the imagination into vacant space, and
a filling of portion, after portion of that space, as by
sheer bold dreaming, with scenery, events, and beings,
never known before. He drew on the recollections of his
own life, on the history of his own family, on the
characters of his relatives, on whimsical incidents that
happened to him in his Irish youth or during his continental
wanderings, on his experience as a literary drudge in London"

1878

(p. lix). Also argues that Goldsmith "discharged all
special Irish colour out of . . . [his] reminiscence. . . .
Goldsmith's heart and genius were Irish; his wanderings
about in the world had given him a touch of cosmopolitan
ease in his judgment of things and opinions, and especially,
what was rare among Englishmen then, a great liking for the
French; but in the form and matter of his writings he was
purposely English" (p. lx).

1878

A. Books

   *1   BLACK, WILLIAM. Oliver Goldsmith. English Men of Letters.
         London: Macmillan.
              Rejects Forster's view of Goldsmith as the unrecognized,
         underpaid, unappreciated genius, pointing out his financial
         improvidence and happy-go-lucky habits. Unusual for the
         period, rejects the view that the Man in Black's background
         and George's account of his adventures in Chapter 20 of the
         Vicar are reliable autobiographical accounts of Goldsmith's
         own adventures. Reports Goldsmith received medical degree
         during 1755-56 travels in Europe, but offers no specific
         evidence. Dates sale of the Vicar about the end of 1764,
         rather than the usual date of 1762, though does base his
         account of the sale on Boswell rather than Mrs. Thrale.
         Perceptive summary of personality: "The fact is this, that
         Goldsmith was possessed of a very subtle quality of humor,
         which is at all times rare, but which is perhaps more
         frequently to be found in Irishmen than among other folks.
         It consists in the satire of the pretence and pomposities
         of others by means of a sort of exaggerated and playful
         self-depreciation. It is a most delicate and most
         delightful form of humor; but it is very apt to be miscon-
         strued by the dull" (pp. 43-44). [Text used: New York:
         Harper & Brothers, 1879, 152 pp.]

B. Shorter Writings

    1   DURRAND, EDMUND. "The Deserted Village." N&Q, 5th ser. 10
         (3 August):p. 88.
              Citing Excursions through Essex, 1818, reports under
         heading "Springfield," legend that Goldsmith wrote the
         poem in a farmhouse opposite the church and that an old
         farmhouse still stands. Inquires if the house is the one
         of local legend and any good reason for thinking Springfield
         was the village Goldsmith was writing about in the poem?

2   REDWAY, GEORGE.   "The Deserted Village."   N&Q 5th ser. 10
     (12 October):p. 294.
        Most works Redway consulted do not mention Springfield,
     Essex, as scene of poem, but "agree with the general
     opinion that the scene . . . is taken from Lissoy"; notes
     that J. Cronin, Antiquarian Handbook to England and Wales,
     1849, and Lewis, Topographical Dictionary of England, 1831,
     both accept belief Goldsmith wrote the poem at Springfield.

1879

A. Books

1   BLACK, WILLIAM.   Oliver Goldsmith.   New York: Harper &
     Brothers, 152 pp.
        The American edition of 1878.A1. In both English and
     American editions this book continued to be reissued as
     demand warranted until the twentieth century, with many of
     these reissues undated, but the book remained available
     continuously throughout this period.

B. Shorter Writings

1   KELLY, J. J.   "The Early Haunts of Oliver Goldsmith."   Irish
     Monthly Magazine 7:194-205.
        Gives brief genealogical account, argues that Smith-Hill,
     Elphin, was Goldsmith's true birthplace, not Pallas, using
     Strean and Jones Lloyd letters (1808.B2). Sentimentalizes
     and identifies Lissoy as literal scene of Deserted Village
     and Vicar. Cites the Man in Black's reasons for not being
     ordained, given in letter 27, as those of Goldsmith. No
     original work here, but compilation from printed sources.
     Reprinted: 1905.A1.

1881

A. Books

1   CUNNINGHAM, PETER, ed.   The Works of Oliver Goldsmith.   4 vols.
     New York: Harper & Brothers.
        An American edition of 1854.A1.

<u>1883</u>

A. Books--None

B. Shorter Writings

1 FORD, EDWARD. "Names and Characters in <u>The Vicar of Wakefield</u>."
   <u>National Review</u> 1 (May):387-94.
   Mainly concerned with dating sale of <u>Vicar</u> manuscript,
   follows Boswell. Then tries to identify actual places with
   settings in the novel, and argues from the amount of
   specific detail, "it seems difficult to avoid the conclusion
   that Goldsmith must himself have walked over the whole
   country which he describes" (p. 387). Cites a letter from
   a Miss Bewick, remembering such a stranger and in later
   life identifying the stranger from a portrait of Goldsmith.
   Cites Craddock (1826.B1) remembering Goldsmith telling he
   made a journey to Wakefield then. "It is admitted that
   Goldsmith narrates his continental wanderings under the
   name of George Primrose; can anything be more probable than
   that he should have used his Yorkshire note-book in
   describing the journey of the Vicar himself, that he really
   did come across some of the scenes and incidents which he
   so graphically describes, and that from such mental
   sketches . . . perhaps more or less accurate, and blended
   with his own artless nature, he composed his charming
   picture?" (pp. 391-92). Quotes Irving (1849.A1) to support
   his approach: "'An acquaintance with the private biography
   of Goldsmith . . . lets us into the secret of his gifted
   pages; we there discover them to be little more than
   transcripts of his own heart, and picturings of his fortunes.
   Scarcely any adventure or character is given in his works
   that may not be traced to his own many-coloured story.
   "'There are few writers for whom the reader feels such
   personal kindness, for few have so eminently possessed the
   magic gift of identifying themselves with their writings'"
   (p. 394).

2 G[IBBS, J. W. M.]. "A Plagiarism of Goldsmith's." <u>Athenaeum</u>,
   no. 2910 (4 August):145.
   Goldsmith's use of the material in Letter 62 of the
   <u>Citizen of the World</u> "would even now be no bad excuse for
   a writer quoting somebody else's remark without further
   reference, while a hundred and twenty years ago such a
   method of quotation was so general as to be scarcely
   faulty at all.
   "The appearance of the essay entitled 'Female Characters'
   in Goldsmith's works is another matter. This, however,

46

is clearly, and upon W.H.O.'s own showing, no 'plagiarism' or fault or even act of Goldsmith's. Prior, who first, on the suggestion of T. Wright [a printer], included this essay in Goldsmith's works, and Cunningham, who all too unguardedly followed Prior, are the persons responsible for the inclusion, and not the sixty years before dead and gone Goldsmith."

3   O., W. H. "A Plagiarism of Goldsmith's." <u>Athenaeum</u> no. 2908 (21 July):81.
        Cunningham in his edition (1854.A1) lists among "Unacknowledged Essays" the paper "Female Characters" from the <u>Lady's Magazine</u> on the authority of Isaac Reed, Percy, and James Prior, the evidence largely being verbal similarities to Letter 62 of the <u>Citizen of the World</u>. W.H.O. identifies it as a paper by Lord Chesterfield in <u>Common Sense</u>, 10 September 1737, and reprinted in the Dublin 1777 edition of Chesterfield's <u>Miscellaneous Works</u>.

                              1884

A. Books

1   GIBBS, J. W. M., ed. <u>The Works of Oliver Goldsmith</u>. A New <u>Edition, Containing Pieces Hitherto Uncollected, and a Life</u> <u>of the Author</u>. With Notes from Various Sources by J. W. M. <u>Gibbs</u>. 5 vols. Bohn's Standard Library. London: George Bell & Sons, 1884-86. 1:491 pp. (1884), 2:486 pp. (1884), 3:540 pp. (1885), 4:522 pp. (1885), 5:539 pp. (1886).
        The "Life of Goldsmith" is H. G. Bohn's (1848.A1). Gibbs's edition was the best available collected edition until Friedman's (1966.A1) and marked an improvement on Bohn's (1848.A1) and Cunningham's (1854.A1). Frequently reprinted into the early twentieth century.

B. Shorter Writings

1   CROSS, MARIAN EVANS [George Eliot]. <u>Essays and Leaves from a</u> <u>Notebook</u>. [Edited by C. L. Lowes.] Edinburgh: W. Blackwood & Sons, pp. 286-87.
        Discusses different ways of story telling, from the kind that emphasizes an important event, an heroic deed, without worrying about what preceded, which she considers a more primitive narrative mode than the orderly presentation of events, though these are likely to be overcome by the

"sequence of associations" (p. 286). "But the simple
opening of a story with a date and necessary account of
places and people, passing on quietly towards the more
rousing elements of narrative and dramatic presentation,
without need of retrospect, has its advantages, which have
to be measured by the nature of the story. Spirited
narrative, without more than a touch of dialogue here and
there, may be made eminently interesting, and is suited to
the novelette. . . . But the opening chapters of the Vicar
of Wakefield are as fine as anything that can be done in
this way" (pp. 286-87). Reprinted: 1974.A6.

1885

A. Books

   1   GOLDSMITH, OLIVER. The Vicar of Wakefield. Being a Facsimile
Reproduction of the First Edition Published in 1766, with
an Introduction by Austin Dobson, and a Bibliographical
List of Editions of "The Vicar of Wakefield" Published in
England and Abroad. 2 vols. London: Elliot Stock.
     The introduction, called the "Preface," discusses the
problems involved in the sale of the manuscript and the
delay in publishing the book, with some discussion of
whether or not Wakefield, Yorkshire, is the actual setting
of the novel. Most of the editions listed in the bibliography Dobson examined personally and were in the British
Museum. Gibbs records (3:38, 236-37) seven variations
from the text of early editions, having used "mainly that
of the fifth London edition, 1773" (3:83). Friedman used
(Works 4:3-184) the first edition as his copy text,
incorporating the extensive revisions of the second edition
into his textual notes, not believing Goldsmith made any
major revisions after the second edition. Dobson's
facsimile is valuable for seeing the text upon which the
earliest reviewers of the novel base their comments.

B. Shorter Writings

   1   WELSH, CHARLES A. A Bookseller of the Last Century. Being
Some Account of the Life of John Newbery, and of the Books
He Published with a Notice of the Later Newberys. London:
Griffith, Farran, Okeden & Welsh, 383 pp., passim.
     Most of the extended references or discussions of
Goldsmith are directly quoted from Prior (1837.A1) and
Forster (1854.A1). Of particular interest concerning
composition of Vicar and the delay in publishing it

from 1762 to 1766: Welsh accepts Johnson's version in
Boswell, 1791.B1, as probably more accurate than Mrs.
Thrale's (1785.B2), p. 72. Believes Francis Newbery,
John Newbery's nephew, who bought the manuscript was
financed by his uncle. Thomas Carnan, owner of the copyright of the Traveller, opposed republication of Goldsmith's
poems in the booksellers' collective edition of English
poets, for which Johnson wrote the prefatory Lives. Carnan
was at odds with the other booksellers over the Stationers'
Company's legal right to exclusive publication of almanacs.
Francis Newbery's "relations with Oliver Goldsmith seem to
have been of a friendly and intimate nature" (p. 157),
since, on Prior's authority, reports Newbery advanced
Goldsmith money for another novel, and the plot which
Goldsmith offered was essentially that of the Good Natur'd
Man, which Newbery refused, but the debt was cleared when
Goldsmith offered the publication rights to She Stoops to
Conquer.

1888

A. Books

1   DOBSON, AUSTIN. Life of Oliver Goldsmith. Great Writers
    Series. London: Walter Scott, 214 pp. [Appendix:
    Bibliography by John P. Anderson, 24 pp.]
       Primary emphasis is biographical rather than critical
    and suffers from the condensation. Attitude is sympathetic
    yet somewhat cool, lacking the enthusiasm of Black (1878.A1)
    but avoiding the sentimentality of Forster (1848.A2).
    Draws heavily on Welsh (1885.B1) for a detailed and
    plausible account of the sale of the Vicar, arguing for
    1762 as the probable date. A useful corrective to Forster
    and Irving in assessing Goldsmith's personality: he
    managed money badly, spent lavishly on clothes, and almost
    certainly gambled heavily and unsuccessfully. "Born a
    gentleman, he had, nevertheless, started life with few
    temporal or personal advantages, and with a morbid
    susceptibility that accentuated his defects" (p. 195). "To
    men like Johnson, who had been intimate with him long, and
    recognized his genius, his attitude presented no difficulty,
    but to the ordinary spectator he seemed awkward and ill at
    ease, prompting once more the comment, that genius and
    knowledge of the world are seldom fellowlodgers" (p. 196).
    "In the fifteen years over which his literary activity
    extended, he managed to produce a record which has given
    him an unassailable position in English letters. . . .

1888

> he wrote some of the best familiar verse in the language,
> . . . two didactic poems, which are still among the
> memories of the old, as they are among the first lessons
> of the young" (p. 201). Stresses versatility and quality
> in poetry, essay series, novel, and drama, as well as real
> literary quality of his compilations.

B. Shorter Writings--None

1889

A. Books--None

B. Shorter Writings

1   D'ARBLAY, FRANCES BURNEY. The Early Diary of Frances Burney,
    1768-1778. 2 vols. Edited by Annie Raine Ellis. London:
    George Bell Sons, passim, but especially 1:13-14.
        Writing at sixteen in 1768, compares the Vicar unfavorably
    with the contemporary sentimental novel Henry and Francis:
    "The description of his rural felicity, his simple,
    unaffected contentment--and family domestic happiness, gave
    me much pleasure--but still, I was not satisfied, a something
    wanting to make the whole book satisfy me. . . . There
    really is but very little story, the plot is thin, the
    incidents very rare, the sentiments uncommon, the vicar is
    contented, humble, pious, virtuous . . ." (pp. 13-14), but
    she really prefers Henry and Francis. Selection reprinted:
    1974.A6.

1890

A. Books--None

B. Shorter Writings

1   S[TEPHEN[, [Sir] L[ESLIE). "Oliver Goldsmith." In The
    Dictionary of National Biography. Edited by Sidney Lee.
    London: Smith, Elder & Co., 22:86-95.
        A standard reference account skillfully synthesizing
    available knowledge and reflecting Stephen's great
    knowledge of the period. Balances ample eighteenth-
    century evidence of Goldsmith's foibles against "his having
    made the excellent hits reported by Boswell" (p. 93). Still
    valuable as a brief biographical account and for the
    sensible assessment of Goldsmith's character.

1891

A. Books--None

B. Shorter Writings

1   CAULFIELD, JAMES, First Earl of Charlemont. [Letters about
    Goldsmith.] In <u>Manuscripts and Correspondence</u>. Vol. 1,
    Twelfth Report, Appendix 10. London: Her Majesty's
    Stationer's Office, 1:317-19.
       The first a letter from Topham Beauclerk to Charlemont,
    24 December 1773, citing Goldsmith's idea that all forms of
    government are much the same; the second, Beauclerk to
    Charlemont, 12 February 1774, mentions that Goldsmith and
    Reynolds are on a round of pleasures and attendance at the
    Club has dwindled; the third, Charlemont to Edmond Malone,
    18 August 1777, asks he be remembered to Steevens as one
    who dined with him at "poor Goldsmith's."

1892

A. Books--None

B. Shorter Writings

1   DOBSON, AUSTIN. "The Citizen of the World" and "Goldsmith's
    Library." In <u>Eighteenth Century Vignettes</u>. London:
    Chatto & Windus, pp. 115-24; 167-75.
       First essay considers various predecessors of Goldsmith
    in the pseudo-letter genre, all well known. Believes "it
    is not too much to suppose that Walpole's jeu d'esprit
    supplied just that opportune suggestion which produced the
    remarkable and now too-much neglected series of letters
    . . ." (p. 116). Chief virtues of the series: "It is
    Goldsmith under the transparent disguise of Lien Chi--
    Goldsmith commenting after the manner of Addison and Steele,
    upon Georgian England, that attracts and interests the
    modern reader" (p. 117), and "the author's innate but
    hitherto undisclosed gift for the delineation of character"
    (p. 120) as seen in the Man in Black and Beau Tibbs that
    the modern reader likes. The second essay comments on the
    books listed in Good's sale catalogue (1774.B6), chiefly
    noting that no copies of Goldsmith's own writings are
    listed. Mentions Prior's (1837.A1) reprinting the
    catalogue.

1894

<u>1894</u>

A. Books--None

B. Shorter Writings

1   CAULFIELD, JAMES, First Earl of Charlemont. <u>Manuscripts and</u>
<u>Correspondence</u>. Vol. 2, Thirteenth Report, Appendix 8.
London: Her Majesty's Stationer's Office, 2:359-60, 363.
The first, an undated letter from Topham Beauclerk to
Charlemont with some minor anecdotes of Goldsmith; the
second, a letter from the Rev. Robert Burrowes, Secretary
of the Royal Irish Academy, letter 21 December [no year
given], asking information about Goldsmith.

<u>1898</u>

A. Books--None

B. Shorter Writings

*1   DOBSON, AUSTIN. "Goldsmith's Poems and Plays." In <u>Miscel-</u>
<u>lanies</u>. New York: Dodd, Mead.
A balanced account of the poems and plays by Goldsmith's
best known late nineteenth-century interpreter. [Text used:
Oxford World's Classics edition (London: Oxford University
Press, 1925), pp. 33-61.]

<u>1899</u>

A. Books--None

B. Shorter Writings

1   DOBSON, AUSTIN. "Goldsmith's Poems and Plays." In <u>A Paladin</u>
<u>of Philanthropy and Other Papers</u>. London: Chatto &
Windus, pp. 33-60.
A reprint of 1898.B1 with the change of title. Reprinted:
1924.B2, 1925.B3.

1900

A. Books--None

B. Shorter Writings

1   JAMES, HENRY. Introduction to The Vicar of Wakefield, by
        Goldsmith. Century Classics Edition. New York: Century
        Co., pp. xx.
            Comments on the book's amazing popularity, yet
        "Goldsmith's story still fails, somehow, on its face, to
        account for its great position and its remarkable career"
        (p. v). Argues that a book may have its luck in addition
        to its merit: "These various fates of books are to some
        extent a mystery and a riddle, but what is most striking in
        the fortune of Goldsmith's story is that, though we fail to
        explain it completely, we grudge it perhaps less than in
        any other case. The thing has succeeded by its incomparable
        amenity" (p. xvi). Believes the best parts are nearly all
        found in the first half of the novel: "the second half of
        the tale, dropping altogether, becomes almost infantine in
        its awkwardness, its funny coincidences, and big stitches
        of white thread" (p. xviii). But these elements not seen
        as criticism: "Thus it is that the book converts everything
        into a happy case of exemption and fascination--a case of
        imperturbable and inscrutable classicism. It is a question
        of tone. The tone is exquisite, and that's the end of it.
        . . . This comes, doubtless, to saying that the Vicar
        himself is, and that the book has flourished through having
        so much of him. It is he who is the success of his story;
        he is always kept true, is what we call to-day 'sustained,'
        without becoming pompous or hollow" (p. xix). Reprinted:
        1974.A6.

1901

A. Books--None

B. Shorter Writings

1   HENDERSON, W. A. "Birthplace of Oliver Goldsmith." N&Q, 9th
        ser. 8 (19 October):330.
            Favors the tradition of Smith-Hill, Elphin, as Goldsmith's
        birthplace over Pallas.

1902

1902

A. Books--None

B. Shorter Writings

1 DOBSON, AUSTIN. "The Vicar of Wakefield and its Illustrators."
   In Side-Walk Studies. London: Chatto & Windus, pp. 130–
   47.
   Discusses illustrations to the novels from 1779 to 1843,
   with special emphasis on Stothard's, Rowlandson's, Cruick-
   shank's, and Mulready's, and a brief sketch of German and
   French illustrated editions. [Text used: Oxford World's
   Classics edition (London: Oxford University Press, 1924),
   pp. 130–47.]

2 FERGUSON, ROBERT. "Goldsmith and the Notions Grille and
   Wandrer in Werthers Leiden." MLN 17 (November):411–18.
   Goethe's feelings toward Lotte Buff, who married Kestner
   in 1793, found an echo in his poem Der Wandrer, itself an
   echo of Goldsmith's Traveller, especially the passages
   dealing with Italy and Switzerland, and by Goldsmith's use
   of contrast in Traveller, Deserted Village, and the Vicar.
   "The tender pathos of his story is due not a little to the
   influence of the kind-hearted, though unfortunate and
   impecunious Irish poet, Oliver Goldsmith" (p. 418).

3 FISCHER, WILLI. "Goldsmith's Vicar of Wakefield." Anglia
   25:129–208.
   Considers the literary sources he believes Goldsmith
   used: Fielding's Parson Adams and Dr. Harrison,
   Richardson's Dr. Lewen and Dr. Bartlett, and Sterne's
   Yorick. Finds similarities between Oliva and Squire
   Thornhill and Pamela and Mr. B. George and Arabella Wilmot
   are patterned after Tom Jones and Sophia Western.
   "Burchell ist neimand anders als Sir Charles Grandison"
   (p. 150). After quoting Johnson's praise for Goldsmith as
   a compiler, he denies that Goldsmith was really a novelist
   but compiled the elements of the Vicar from previous
   English novels.

1903

A. Books

1 NEUENDORFF, BERNARD. Entstehungsgeschichte von Goldsmiths
   "Vicar of Wakefield." Berlin: Mayer & Müller, pp. 111.

Believes Goldsmith began the book toward the end of 1757
and finished it about 1764. Compares Mrs. Thrale's,
Hawkins's, Boswell's, Cooke's, and Cumberland's accounts
of the sale, preferring Boswell's. Finds similarities to
both Fielding and Richardson's novels, citing false
marriage in Pamela, prison scenes from Amelia and even from
Pilgrim's Progress. Stresses long tradition of the good
priest in English literature, going back to Chaucer, with
more recent examples from Fielding (Parson Adams, Dr.
Harrison) and Richardson (Mr. Williams, Dr. Lewen). Finds
eight specific points of similarity between Adams and
Primrose, though several of these are extremely general:
both make mistakes, both help the poor, both show concern
for their parishioners. Sees the use of contrasting sisters
as a motif from Restoration comedy and from the Tatler.
Disagrees with Fischer (1902.B3) that the sources for
Primrose's character are purely literary, since he finds an
element of Goldsmith's own character present and disagrees
with Fischer about literary sources of other characters.
Concludes that of the two schools of eighteenth-century
English fiction, that of Richardson and of DeFoe-Fielding,
Goldsmith belongs more to the Richardsonian school. Many
of the "sources" Neuendorff offers for characters in the
Vicar show only the more general similarities and often
merely one trait--Arabella Wilmot's greedy father is
patterned after Squire Western.

B. Shorter Writings

1   DOBSON, AUSTIN. "The Vicar of Wakefield and its illustrators."
    In Side-Walk Studies. London: Chatto & Windus.
        Second edition of 1902.B1. Reissued: 1923.B3;
    1924.B2.

2   WALZ, JOHN A. "Oliver Goldsmith and Goethe's Werther." MLN
    18 (January):31-33.
        Reply to 1902.B2. Ferguson should have consulted Goethe-
    Jahrbuch. Like Shakespeare, Goldsmith has always been dear
    to the Germans and "German scholars have always been ready
    to acknowledge his great influence upon Goethe and German
    literature" (p. 31). Walz cites Goethe's acknowledgment
    to Eckermann of his debt to Shakespeare, Sterne, and
    Goldsmith. Also cites S. Levy, 1885 Goethe-Jahrbuch,
    "Goethe und Oliver Goldsmith," which quotes passages
    Ferguson has used. Cites other German scholars who have
    noted similarities between Werther and The Vicar of
    Wakefield.

1904

1904

A. Books

1   SCHACHT, HEINRICH. Der Gute Pfarrer in der Englischen
     Literatur bis zu Goldsmiths "Vicar of Wakefield." Berlin:
     Mayer & Müller, 52 pp.
         Begins with the Good Priest in Wycliff and Chaucer and
     moves quickly through the Reformation, covering the drama
     to the Restoration. Chapters eight and nine deal with the
     Vicar: Primrose is a pathetic character with some
     humorous characteristics. Fielding's Harrison, not Adams,
     is the closer model for Primrose. Goldsmith makes Primrose
     the hero of the novel, putting him in situations like those
     Fielding uses for Adams, but makes him behave more like
     Harrison. Goldsmith raises his social level and makes him
     a Christian philosopher, but gives him humorous qualities
     and minor character flaws.

B. Shorter Writings

1   FISCHER, WILLI. "Zu Goldsmiths Vicar of Wakefield." Anglia
     27:516-54.
         Reply to Neuendorff (1903.A1). Does not find much new
     in the study, though there are minor errors of points of
     disagreement. Primarily quibbling about which particular
     literary sources for incidents in the Vicar are the
     "correct" sources. Does see Goldsmith using similar
     character types from work to work. Disagrees that Goldsmith
     is Richardsonian, since Richardson is almost without
     humor, and humor plays a large part in Goldsmith's novel.
     Fischer will grant some Richardsonian elements in the first
     half, but sees the second half as Fieldingesque, concludes
     it is among the liveliest of eighteenth-century novels, to
     be ranked with Tom Jones, Tristram Shandy, and Roderick
     Random.

1905

A. Books

1   KELLY, J. J. The Early Haunts of Oliver Goldsmith. Dublin:
     Sealy, Bryers & Walker & M. H. Gill, 91 pp.
         A reprint of 1879.B1, with a facsimile of Goldsmith's
     letter to Mrs. Jane Lawder, dated "Temple Exchange Coffee
     House near Temple Bar. London, 15 August 1758."

1907

B. Shorter Writings

1 COURTHOPE, W. J. History of English Poetry. 6 vols. London:
   Macmillan, 5:209-19.
      The major survey of English poetry of its time. Praises
   Dobson's Oliver Goldsmith (1885.A1) and discusses Deserted
   Village and Traveller with excerpts. Stresses Goldsmith's
   dislike of then-new forms: "He always seems glad to be
   able to deliver a side-stroke at the blank verse of
   Aikenside, the Pindarics of Gray, and the satiric manner of
   Churchill. . . . His own style may be described as the
   quintessence of the English classical manner" (5:216). "At
   the same time the style of Goldsmith is not directly
   imitated from the moral style of Pope; it differs from the
   latter to the same extent that the temperament of Goldsmith
   differs from the temperament of the greatest satirist of
   the eighteenth century" (5:217). Conclusion: "Generally
   speaking, Goldsmith's style is one of unadorned simplicity.
   He is perhaps the only English poet who has succeeded in
   introducing into the traditional treatment of the heroic
   couplet the note of individual pathos . . ." (5:218).
   Reprinted: 1962.B2.

1907

A. Books--None

B. Shorter Writings

1 OSGOOD, CHARLES G., Jr. "Notes on Goldsmith." MP 5 (October):
   241-52.
      Begins by noting the difficulty of defining the
   Goldsmithian quality, though his special tone is certainly
   perceptible. Discusses recent scholarship by Neuendorff
   (1903.A1), Schacht (1904.A1), and Fischer (1902.B3 and
   1904.B1). Schacht notes Goldsmith's interest in Methodism
   and the similarity of Primrose to Richardsonian characters,
   but more directly J. A. Swallow in Methodism and English
   Literature of the Last Century (Erlanger & Leipsig, 1895),
   cited allusions to Methodism by Goldsmith, all ridiculing
   it. Swallow sees no Methodism in the Vicar, but Osgood
   argues the sermon in Chapter 26 resembles passages in
   Wesley's Journal, believes Goldsmith may have adapted an
   open-air Methodist sermon he had heard, and finds the
   reforms the Vicar proposes for the prison like those
   Wesley argued for. Neuendorff believes Goldsmith's
   glorification of the humble life in the Vicar is

1908

Rousseauistic and derives it from the Johnson circle.
Discussion of problem of whether or not Goldsmith wrote
"The History of Miss Stanton," published in the British
Magazine, 1760. Prior, Forster, and Cunningham accept it,
but Dobson and Leslie Stephen reject it. All these studies
point to similarities to Fielding and other contemporary
novelists. Osgood recalls Goldsmith's published condemna-
tions of novels in his reviews.

1908

A. Books--None

B. Shorter Writings

1 CONANT, MARTHA P. The Oriental Tale in England in the
   Eighteenth Century. University Studies in English and
   Comparative Literature 17. New York: Columbia University
   Press, 338 pp., passim, but especially pp. 184-99.
       Discusses The Citizen of the World in relation to other
   oriental tales, praising it: "In general, the oriental
   decorations of the book are quite external. Yet the
   repeated references to what the author imagines or pretends
   to imagine, is the Chinese attitude of mind or turn of
   phrase, adds to The Citizen of the World a distinct and
   admirable element of humour. The book may justly be
   regarded as one of the best English oriental tales of the
   period" (pp. 198-99). Praises Goldsmith's use of Lien Chi
   Altangi's personality to unify the series of letters.
   Reprinted: 1966.B1.

2 GAUSSEN, ALICE C. C. Percy: Prelate and Poet. London:
   Smith, Elder, 336 pp., passim.
       Believes that Percy's first published work, a translation
   from a Portugese manuscript of the Chinese novel Hau Kiou
   Choaan, may have suggested to Goldsmith the idea for the
   Chinese Letters from his reading it before it was published.
   Of the Reliques: "To Oliver Goldsmith Percy owed more than
   to any other literary man of the day. His counsel was that
   of knowledge, for he had supported himself in early life by
   writing ballads which he sold for five shillings each to a
   small bookseller in Dublin, and had observed the popular
   taste by watching their reception in the streets" (p. 44).
   Also notes Goldsmith's interest in Irish folklore and the
   Irish bards, recorded in his essay "The History of Carolan,
   the last Irish Bard" (Works, 3:118-20). Dates Percy's and
   Goldsmith's first meeting as Wednesday, 21 February 1759,

as "guests of Dr. Grainger at the Temple Exchange Coffee House" (p. 140), followed by a succession of other meetings fairly soon. Believes Johnson and Goldsmith may have met through Percy about 31 May 1761. Provides a good summary of the delays in the collected edition of Goldsmith's works projected after his death to benefit his poor relatives, most of the problems arising from the bookseller Carnan's owning some of the copyrights--the edition being finally published only in 1801 (pp. 211ff).

3   HARRISON, FREDERIC. [Comment on Goldsmith's prose.] In Among My Books, Centenaries, Reviews, Memoirs. London: Macmillan, pp. 178-79.
    Considers Goldsmith the high-water mark of English prose: "To me dear 'Goldie' is the Mozart of English prose--the feckless, inspired, ne'er-do-well of eighteenth-century art" (p. 179). Reprinted: 1974.A6.

1910

A. Books

1   KING, RICHARD ASHE. Oliver Goldsmith. London: Methuen, 324 pp.
    The English frequently misunderstand Irish humor: "But, indeed, almost all other faults and virtues of Goldsmith which to his English contemporaries and biographers seem idiosyncracies, appear to his fellow countrymen natural and national characteristics. . . . But to Goldsmith's fellow countrymen much that seems silly in his talk and eccentric in his character appears natural and even rational" (p. xxviii). Argues that the real Goldsmith is better reflected in his works than in the accounts of his contemporaries or his biographers. His tendency to debt: "He lived as entirely in the present as a child, as he was a child also in guilelessness, anyone could impose on his simplicity, while no one could outweary his good-nature" (pp. 27-28). "The real trouble of his life--and it was life long--was a never-satisfied craving for sympathy and appreciation, of which he was almost as disappointed at the height of his fame in London as in these days of obscurity and scorn in Trinity College" (p. 29). Asserts, but gives no authority,that Goldsmith admitted more than once at Reynolds's dinner table that the "Wanderings of a Philosophic Vagabond" was "a transcript often down to the minutest details of his own adventures" (p. 56). Following in the tradition of Forster (1848.A2), King attacks the Newberys

1910

for not sharing with Goldsmith the supposed hundreds of
pounds they made from the <u>Vicar</u>, and sees Goldsmith's praise
of Newbery in the novel as misplaced. Few critical comments
on Goldsmith's work.

2   MOORE, FRANK FRANKFORT. <u>The Life of Oliver Goldsmith</u>. London:
Constable, 492 pp.
Points out that Goldsmith is one of the most loved of
authors, but that most readers form their opinion of his
personality from Boswell, whom Moore regards as extremely
jealous and prejudiced against Goldsmith. Relies heavily
on Goldsmith letters, usually quoted in full, and Mrs.
Hodson's narrative for detail. For Goldsmith's later life,
he draws heavily upon the large body of anecdotes available,
especially from Boswell, though often disagreeing with
Boswell's interpretation of Goldsmith's behavior. Much
quotation and paraphrase from Goldsmith's writings. Like
King (1910.A1), Moore believes most of his English
contemporaries did not understand his humor. Concludes:
"There was never a writer who put his own life into his
works to the same extent as did Oliver Goldsmith . . ."
(p. 467).

B. Shorter Writings

1   DOBSON, AUSTIN. "Percy and Goldsmith." In <u>Old Kensington
Palace</u>. London: Chatto & Windus, pp. 28-52 [41-52
discuss Goldsmith].
Chiefly a discussion of Gaussen (1908.B2). Rejects her
suggestion that Percy's translation of the Chinese novel
stimulated Goldsmith to <u>The Citizen of the World</u>, finding
Goldsmith's 1758 letter to Bob Bryanton, plus Walpole's
1757 <u>Letter from XoHo</u> more likely sources. Discusses
Goldsmith's meeting Percy, their rapid friendship. Reports
from Gaussen (p. 49) that after Chatterton's death,
Goldsmith called on Percy, asked him to be his biographer,
dictated the "Percy Memorandum," and gave him a bundle of
manuscripts. Regrets Johnson's and Percy's dilatoriness in
attending to writing Goldsmith's life, but at least their
delays led to biographies of Prior, Forster, and Irving, so
that we know more of Goldsmith than Percy or Johnson ever
did.

A. Books--None

B. Shorter Writings

1 LOWES, JOHN LIVINGSTON. "Wordsworth and Goldsmith." <u>Nation</u> (N.Y.), 23 March, pp. 289-90.
    Letter points out a parallel between "a famous passage" in Wordsworth's 1815 "Preface" and a paragraph in one of Goldsmith's essays. In discussing the difference between fancy and imagination, Wordsworth's illustration involves different meanings of <u>hang</u>. Goldsmith's essay is "Poetry distinguished from other Writing" (No. 5; Friedman excludes the series "On the Study of Belles Lettres" [<u>Works</u> 3:xiv], although Gibbs included them in his edition [1:323-86, No. 5 occupying 1:361-77]). Both Wordsworth and Goldsmith quote Virgil, <u>Eclogue</u> 1, and Shakespeare's <u>King Lear</u>: "half way down; <u>Hangs</u> one who gathers samphire." Both praise the passages, Wordsworth using the term "imaginative"; Goldsmith, "figurative."

1912

A. Books--None

B. Shorter Writings

1 FORSYTHE, R. S. "Shadwell's Contribution to <u>She Stoops to Conquer</u> and to <u>The Tender Husband</u>." <u>JEPG</u> 11 (January): 104-11 [only pp. 104-7 deal with Goldsmith].
    Rejects the claim that Goldsmith based Tony Lumpkin on Humphrey Gubbin in Steele's <u>Tender Husband</u>, arguing that the common model for both is Shadwell's Young Hartford in his <u>The Lancashire Witches</u>. Provides evidence that Goldsmith knew Shadwell's play, and argues that the main similarities of <u>She Stoops to Conquer</u> to <u>The Tender Husband</u> are those both plays share. Pp. 107-11 deal with only <u>The Lancashire Witches</u> and <u>The Tender Husband</u>.

1913

1913

A. Books--None

B. Shorter Writings

1   BARNOUW, A. J. "Goldsmith's Indebtedness to Justus Van Effen."
    <u>MLR</u> 8 (July):314-24.
        Goldsmith's name not on record in the <u>Album Studiosorum</u>
    of the University of Leiden and how well he knew Dutch is
    hard to tell, but No. 5 of the <u>Bee</u>'s first number, "Upon
    Political Frugality," praising the Dutch institution of
    "peace-makers" is probably based on a short pamphlet by
    Voltaire, which Goldsmith may have known from <u>Recuil de</u>
    <u>pièces fugitives en prose et en vers</u>, by M. de V**, 1740.
    Praise for the Dutch is not unusual for Goldsmith, his own
    letter from Leiden containing eighteenth-century common-
    places, as do <u>Traveller</u> and Letters 41 and 49 of <u>The</u>
    <u>Citizen of the World</u>. No. 1 of the <u>Bee</u> has the "Letter
    from a Traveller," dated Cracow, but is a translation, with
    Holland changed to England, and the source is the Dutch
    essayist Justus Van Effen, who travelled through Sweden in
    1719 as part of the entourage of a German princeling.
    Original was <u>Relation d'un voyage de Hollande en Suède</u>,
    <u>contenue en quelques lettres de l'auteur du Misantrope</u>,
    the <u>Misantrope</u> being Van Effen's imitation of the <u>Spectator</u>.
    Goldsmith's source is Van Effen's Letter 6. The sources
    for Goldsmith's "Some Particulars relative to Charles XII
    not Commonly Known" in No. 2 of <u>Bee</u> are Van Effen's Letters
    8 and 12.

2   DOBSON, AUSTIN. "Oliver Goldsmith." In <u>Cambridge History of</u>
    <u>English Literature</u>. Edited by A. W. Ward and A. R. Waller.
    Cambridge: University Press, 10:240-44.
        Follows 1888.A1 closely but emphasizes the interconnec-
    tion of Goldsmith's life and work even more emphatically:
    "'No man,' wrote that authoritative but autocratic
    biographer, John Forster, 'ever put so much of himself into
    his books as Goldsmith, from the beginning to the very end
    of his career.' To many authors, this saying is only
    partly applicable; but it is entirely applicable to the
    author of <u>The Vicar of Wakefield</u>." Dobson's discussion of
    <u>The Citizen of the World</u> and the <u>Vicar</u> illustrates his
    method: "But the strong point in each is Goldsmith
    himself--Goldsmith's own thoughts and Goldsmith's own
    experiences. . . . One may smile at the artless inconsis-
    tencies of the plot, the lapses of the fable, the presence
    in the narrative of such makeweights as poetry, tales,

political discourses and a sermon; but the author's genius
and individuality rise superior to everything, and the
little Wakefield family are now veritable citizens of the
world" (p. 234). Concludes: "His real vocation was
comedy; and on comedy, his ideas were formed, having been
in great measure, expressed in the Enquiry and in other of
his earlier writings" (pp. 235-36). Reprinted: 1933.B4.

1914

A. Books--None

B. Shorter Writings

1   [WELBY, LORD WARD, WILDRED; PROTHERO, G. W.; and KENYON,
    Sir F. G., eds.] Annals of the Club, 1764-1914. London:
    printed for the Club, 237 pp., passim. [A new edition of
    "The Club" by Sir M. E. Grant Duff.]
        Contains nothing not available elsewhere. During
    Goldsmith's membership, no formal records of meetings were
    kept.

2   CLARKE, ERNEST. "The Medical Education and Qualifications of
    Oliver Goldsmith." Proceedings of the Royal Society of
    Medicine 7:88-98.
        Rejects Macaulay's view that Goldsmith had no medical
    degree; of a degree from Padua, argues that no absolute
    evidence to disprove it nor any solid ground for believing
    he received a medical degree from any other foreign univer-
    sity, but gives Glover as authority for the Louvain degree
    which Prior rejected as improbable. Cites record found by
    Osler in Jackson's Oxford Journal for Saturday, 18 February
    1769, that Goldsmith was granted the Bachelor of Medicine
    degree by Oxford on the basis of his statement that he had
    received the Bachelor of Physic degree from the University
    of Dublin [Trinity College]. Speculates that Goldsmith
    may have applied for Bachelor of Physic degree from Dublin
    after his return to London in connection with his application
    for position with East India Company in 1758.

3   _____. "Oliver Goldsmith as a Medical Man." Nineteenth
    Century and After 75 (April):821-31.
        A general survey, using mostly evidence in print but
    also some newly discovered letters. Believes Goldsmith
    prepared seriously for a medical degree "so far as his
    roving and mercurial talent would permit" (p. 822). "The
    balance of opinion seems to be in favour of his having

1915

obtained from his <u>alma mater</u> of Dublin the degree of M.B.
in absentia some time between 1756 and 1763" (p. 829).
Covers Oxford degree and records his efforts about 1765
to establish a practice to secure more regular income.
"After this we hear no more of Goldsmith's medical
practice; and though no one need have any regrets at this,
it is a pity that Oliver did not utilise for his own
benefit the professional knowledge that he must have picked
up in his studies in the various capitals of Europe, for he
practically threw away his life by neglect of himself and
his ailments at the early age of forty-six on the 4th of
April 1774" (p. 831).

1915

A. Books--None

B. Shorter Writings

1   CRAWFURD, RAYMOND. "Oliver Goldsmith and Medicine."
     <u>Proceedings of the Royal Society of Medicine</u> 8:7-26.
        A reply to 1914.B1, summarizing Clarke's argument that
     Goldsmith's only medical degree was the Oxford one,
     conferred under the misapprehension Goldsmith had the
     Bachelor of Physic from Dublin before 1763. Goldsmith's
     1754 letter to his uncle Contarine from Edinburgh shows he
     left there without degree, with Paris his first aim, but
     wound up at Leyden, where the desire for travel seems to
     have overcome medical interests. The Percy Memorandum
     mentions no foreign degree, though belief in Louvain as the
     granting university was widely accepted by his friends and
     derives from Glover's account. Believes Goldsmith's
     statement to Oxford authorities that he had a Dublin
     Bachelor of Physic from Dublin before 1763. Goldsmith's
     1754 letter to his Uncle Contarine from Edinburgh shows he
     Padua in his <u>Life</u> as at least not improbable. Argues that
     from 1758-63 Goldsmith was working too hard at writing
     to be studying for the Dublin degree. Despite Osler's
     discovery of report on <u>Jackson's Oxford Journal</u>, no official
     Oxford records show degree granted, but a gap exists in
     Oxford Convocation records.

1919

A. Books--None

B. Shorter Writings

1   PATTON, JULIA. The English Village: A Literary Study. New
    York: Macmillan, 246 pp., passim.
         The Vicar shows an interest in well-marked, vigorous
    individual characters from lower social ranks since
    isolation in the country tends to preserve individual
    traits unchanged, as in some characters of higher rank
    like Squire Western or Sir Roger de Coverley. For all his
    warm feeling and ready sympathy, Goldsmith argues that it
    is natural that the distresses of lower classes affect us
    less than those of the higher, though Fielding gives an
    example of some breaking with this idea. "Finally, in the
    hands of a man of genius [Goldsmith], the village theme
    emerged from casual and desultory treatment into a
    distinctness and permanence it has never lost. And it was
    the old village of a happy community life to which Goldsmith,
    in indignation and distress at a devastation wrought by
    forces he only dimly understood, gave imperishable
    expression" (p. 84). The idyllic parts of the Vicar and
    Deserted Village tend to linger in the mind, yet Goldsmith's
    belief in the actuality of depopulation was based on his own
    observations and experience. Cites Dobson's, Macaulay's,
    and Black's disbelief in the eviction parts of Deserted
    Village, but Patton considers such events as commonplace in
    the 1760s because of the agricultural revolution.

1921

A. Books--None

B. Shorter Writings

1   CRANE, RONALD S., and SMITH, HAMILTON J[EWETT]. "A French
    influence on Goldsmith's Citizen of the World." MP 19
    (August):83-92.
         The Marquis D'Argens' Lettres Chinoises, most popular of
    D'Argens's works, listed as a possible model by Gibbs but
    not by L. J. Davidson (1921.B2), who lists his Chinese
    Letters as The Chinese Spy, 1751. The 1756 translation has
    162 letters and its scheme is summarized. Goldsmith knew
    the work when he began writing his letters for the Public
    Ledger in 1760, almost certainly in the original. Mentions

1921

D'Argens in <u>An Enquiry</u>, 1759, but gives no titles.
Goldsmith's previous interest in China demonstrated in his
1758 letter to Bob Bryanton, his reviews for the <u>Critical</u>
<u>Review</u>, and in seeing Percy's Chinese as-yet unpublished
novel. Shows clear use of D'Argens through parallel
passages of ten letters from D'Argens and Goldsmith.
Usually Goldsmith translates but sometimes freely adapts
French to English. Differences: Goldsmith avoids
metaphysical discussions, historical narratives, attacks on
religious fanaticism and superstition--all D'Argens's
propaganda as a <u>philosophe</u>; prefers humorous conventions,
with more concern for character and incident and less
preoccupation with manners and morals. These borrowings
help explain many details, some features of Goldsmith's
simplification of D'Argens's scheme, and throw some light
on Goldsmith's method of composition, but account for none
of the traits which constitute the originality of Goldsmith's work.

2 DAVIDSON, L. J. "Forerunners of Goldsmith's <u>Citizen of the</u>
<u>World</u>." <u>MLN</u> 36 (April):215-20.
   Lists and summarizes Marana's <u>Turkish Spy</u>, Montesquieu's
<u>Lettres Persanes</u>, Lyttelton's <u>Persian Letters</u>, and mentions
D'Argens's <u>Chinese Spy</u>, but does not realize the last is
the same as his <u>Chinese Letters</u>. For additional comment,
see 1921.B1.

<u>1922</u>

A. Books--None

B. Shorter Writings

1 OLIVER, JOHN W. "Johnson, Goldsmith and 'The History of the
Seven Years' War.'" <u>TLS</u> (18 May):324.
   Prior includes a "Preface and Introduction to the History
of the Seven Years' War" in his 1837 edition on the basis
that the manuscript was in Goldsmith's own hand, according
to Isaac Reed, who had owned it. Cunningham and Gibbs
printed it, with Gibbs recapitulating facts: Gibbs
located the piece in the <u>Literary Magazine</u>, December 1757;
January and February 1758, titled "History of Our Own
Times," with some omission and alteration from the text of
the "Preface and Introduction." The "Preface" is a
recasting of "Introduction to the Political History of
Great Britain," <u>Literary Magazine</u>, May 1756, with some
material from "Observations on the Present State of Affairs,"

Literary Magazine, August 1756. Both these 1756 articles
are included in collections of Johnson's works, largely on
the basis of internal stylistic evidence, which seems
convincing. Letter 17, Citizen of the World, also shows
some resemblances to "Observations on the Present State of
Affairs." Argues that this relationship might represent
some kind of Johnson-Goldsmith collaboration prior to their
meeting on 31 May 1761 through Percy. [Friedman rejected
these essays from the Literary Magazine and so does not
reprint them in Works 3:xiv.] see 1929.B8.

1923

A. Books--None

B. Shorter Writings

1   CRANE, RONALD S., and WARNER, JAMES H. "Goldsmith and
        Voltaire's Essai sur les Moeurs." MLN 38 (February):65-76.
        In August 1757, Goldsmith contributed a long favorable
    notice to the Monthly Review of the 1756 Geneva edition of
    Voltaire's Essai (Monthly Review 17 [August 1757]:154-64;
    Gibbs' edition, 4:277-82; Works 1:95-105). Repeats his
    praise in Memoirs of M. de Voltaire, 1759, has a letter
    of Voltaire to Theriot on impartiality, love of truth,
    zeal for human happiness--all themes in Essai. The
    results of this interest appear in his 1764 History of
    England in a Series of Letters. William Cooke's
    reminiscences in European Magazine, 1793.B1, describe
    Goldsmith's procedure of composition--Cooke lists Rapin
    and Hume as sources but not Voltaire. Goldsmith tones down
    the anticlericalism, sometimes combines phrases from
    Voltaire and Rapin, and sometimes translates freely from
    Voltaire, without acknowledging either source. It is
    harder to estimate Voltaire's influence on general
    interpretation and method, but both Rapin and Voltaire
    scorn medieval clergy, distrust republican institutions,
    sympathize with the middle class, oppose wars and conquests,
    realistically estimate nature of savage man, and distrust
    overseas colonies. Goldsmith said he was writing a history
    of men, not of kings--the same conception of history as
    Voltaire's, and similar to Hume's. The 1771 four-volume
    History of England for Davies uses much the same material
    but with revisions from Hume.

*2   DOBSON, AUSTIN. "Goldsmith's Poems and Plays." In A Paladin
        of Philanthropy and Other Papers. Oxford Standard Authors.

1923

London: Oxford University Press.
A reprint of 1898.B1.

3 _____ . "The Vicar of Wakefield and its Illustrators. In
Side-Walk Studies. Oxford Standard Authors. London:
Oxford University Press.
A reprint of 1902.B1.

1924

A. Books

1   LYTTON SELLS, ARTHUR. Les Sources Françaises de Goldsmith.
Bibliothèque de la Revue de Littérature Comparée, no. 12.
Paris: Librairie Ancienne Édouard Champion, pp. viii,
225.
Divided into four parts: Goldsmith's relations with
France, largely biographical; Goldsmith's critical
opinions of France and French literature; Goldsmith's
French sources; and the importance of French influences on
Goldsmith. 'In Part One, Lytton Sells cannot show how
Goldsmith acquired his good working knowledge of French
early in life, but believes he learned it from French-
trained Roman Catholic priests living in his home
neighborhood. Part Three is almost certainly the most
important, concentrating on Goldsmith's heavy debt to
Marivaux and to Voltaire especially, but also to lesser
writers like D'Argens, Montesquieu, Rapin, and Buffon.
He does speculate, pp. 89-90, that in The Citizen of the
World Goldsmith may have been writing a kind of parody of
orientalism for a select few and kind of "straight"
orientalism for the general reader.

2   PITMAN, JAMES H. Goldsmith's "Animated Nature": A Study of
Goldsmith. Yale Studies in English 66. New Haven: Yale
University Press, 159 pp.
Major divisions indicate the scope of this study: the
facts and circumstances of publications, Goldsmith's
method and manner in Animated Nature, his sources, and
Goldsmith's relation to his age. Emphasis is primarily on
his sources, especially Buffon. Reprinted: 1973.A3.

B. Shorter Writings

1   BOSWELL, JAMES. Letters of James Boswell. 2 vols. Collected
and Edited by Chauncey Brewster Tinker. Oxford: Clarendon
Press, 1:1-271, 2:272-550.

Includes some material not covered by Life, 1791.B1.
The Yale Edition of the Private Papers of James Boswell
(Research Edition): Correspondence, will ultimately
supersede this edition. Three volumes have appeared;
Volumes Two, 1969.B1, and Three, 1976.B3, contain Goldsmith
material.

2 DOBSON, AUSTIN. "The Vicar of Wakefield and its Illustrators."
   In Side-Walk Studies. World's Classic Edition. London:
   Oxford University Press, pp. 130-47.
      A reprint of 1902.B1 and 1923.B3.

3 TUPPER, CAROLINE F. "Essays Erroneously Attributed to
      Goldsmith." PMLA 37 (June):325-42.
      The series "On the Study of the Belles Lettres,"
   originally published in the British Magazine, July 1761
   to January 1763, was included in Percy's edition (1801.B2)
   and rejected only by Cunningham (1854.A1) among nineteenth-
   century editors, many including them under the title
   "Essays, originally published in the year 1765," implying
   Goldsmith had republished them himself. Gibbs reprints the
   series, 1:325-86, but notes Cunningham's objections (1:325
   n.) and discusses the whole problem of authenticity in his
   "Appendix," 1:406-8. Tupper reviews Gibbs's arguments and
   rejects them, primarily because the attack on Shakespeare
   and the praise of blank verse disagree with Goldsmith's
   opinions expressed in reviews and essays known to be his.
   Suggests the author may have been Smollett. Friedman does
   not reprint the series, accepting Tupper's arguments.

4 WILLIAMS, IOLO A. Seven XVIIIth Century Bibliographies.
      London: Dulau, pp. 117-77.
      Technical bibliographical descriptions of first
   editions of Goldsmith's works.

1925

A. Books--None

B. Shorter Writings

1 ANSON, ELIZABETH, and ANSON, FLORENCE, eds. Mary Hamilton,
      afterwards Mrs. John Dickenson, at Court and at Home, from
      Letters and Diaries 1756 to 1816. London: John Murray,
      pp. 180-82.
      For 14 May 1784, she records a conversation with
   Johnson: "I regret I cannot recollect everything Dr.

1925

Johnson said, for he was in good spirits & tho' just
recovered from a dangerous illness & in ye 75th year of
his age & very infirm, his faculties are as bright as
ever . . ." (pp. 180-81). Most of the opinions she records
are similar to Boswell's: "Dr. Johnson said of ye late
Dr. Goldsmith that he never saw a head so unfurnished; he
gave him credit for being a Clerical Scholar so far as he
had learnt at school, but that he knew very little of any
subject he ever wrote upon; that his abilities were equal
to any Man's he ever met with, but that he had no applica-
tion; upon the most common subjects he was very ignorant,
of which he gave many & daily proofs . . ." (p. 182).

2   CURTIS, HENRY. "The Ancestry of John Payne Collier (1789-
     1883), with a Reference to Oliver Goldsmith." N&Q 149
     (25 July):57-59.
        Photograph of a page of the Roll Book of the Medical
     Society of Edinburgh for admission 2 August 1755 shows
     Collier's signature and also Goldsmith's. The Medical
     Society was then a students' club, but is now the Royal
     Medical Society.

3   DOBSON, AUSTIN. "Goldsmith's Poems and Plays." In A Paladin
     of Philanthropy and Other Papers. World's Classic Edition.
     London: Oxford University Press, pp. 130-37.
        A reprint of 1898.B1, 1899.B1, 1923.B2.

                              1926

A.   Books

1   BALDERSTON, KATHARINE C. A Census of the Manuscripts of
     Oliver Goldsmith. New York: Edmond Byrne Hackett, Brick
     Row Book Shop, 81 pp.
        A very careful description of all the surviving pieces
     of Goldsmith's writings, including agreements, bills,
     receipts, as well as longer pieces, mainly letters,
     including ownership at the time of publication. Hardly
     any of the MSS. are "literary," the letters being the most
     nearly so.

2   _____. The History & Sources of Percy's Memoir of
     Goldsmith. Cambridge: University Press, 61 pp.
        A careful, critical account of 1801.B2, accounting for
     the twenty-five-year delay between Percy's undertaking
     Goldsmith's Life and its final publication in 1801. Her
     study of the sources Percy and his collaborators used to

                               70

put the Life together is extremely valuable. She prints
for the first time the complete text of the memorandum
Goldsmith dictated to Percy on 28 April 1773, pp. 12-17.
See also 1974.A6 and 1976.A1.

3   SMITH, HAMILTON JEWETT. Oliver Goldsmith's "Citizen of the
    World": A Study. Studies in English 71. New Haven: Yale
    University Press, 181 pp.
        Detailed study of the Citizen, especially of the French
    sources, stressing the influence of the contrast Voltaire
    draws in the Dictionnaire Philosophique between Chinese
    stability and European shallowness, though Smith does not
    point out that in the Citizen China turns out to be a
    tyranny, not a benevolent state, in its effect on Lien
    Chi's family life. Smith's description of D'Argens's
    general scheme of organization in the Lettres Chinoises
    does not show that D'Argens used several correspondents
    in several European cities, not one central correspondent
    as Goldsmith does, although the parallels he shows between
    particular letters are convincing. Smith also works from
    Brooke's translation of Du Halde, not the two-volume
    edition published by Cave, which Goldsmith clearly
    specified in his notes, and thus misses several instances
    of indebtedness to Du Halde.

B. Shorter Writings

1   BROWN, JOSEPH E. "Goldsmith's Indebtedness to Voltaire and
    Justus Van Effen." MP 23 (February):273-84.
        Lists various debts to Voltaire: In "Of Eloquence,"
    Bee, No. 7, about 400 words translated from Voltaire's
    "Éloquence" in Diderot's Encyclopedie, with other extensive
    borrowings from D'Alembert's "Elocution" in same source.
    Bee, No. 6, summarizes an oriental anecdote from Voltaire's
    Dictionnaire Philosophique. In Letter 2 of The Citizen of
    the World, the names of the two Chinese philosophers Lien
    Chi mentions are taken from Voltaire, where "he found a
    frequent vein of oriental local color, entertaining
    anecdote, and a frequent vein of satire" (p. 277), all
    important elements in the series. Letter 98, satirizing
    delays in law courts, has many similarities to Voltaire's
    Dialogue entre un Plaideur et un Avocat--its dialogue
    form, the length of the suit, the client's expectation
    that day and the absurdity of citing ancient precedents.
    Bee, No. 3, "Of Justice and Generosity," paralleled with
    Van Effen's Le Misantrope 22, 22 May 1712, showing strong
    similarity of more than half the essay. Sells believes
    Marivaux's Le Spectateur is source; Brown believes Marivaux

may also have drawn on Van Effen. Brown also believes
Goldsmith had met Voltaire, citing Gibbs's edition, 4:24-25.

2   DUMERIL, EDITH. "L'Élément Autobiographique dans The Travel-
    ler." Revue de L'Enseignement des Langues Vivantes 43
    (April):150-56.
        Divides Goldsmith's works into those which were
    commissioned and those based on what he had seen or
    experienced. Cites Thackeray and Bulwer-Lytton to support
    the idea that he reveals himself in George Primrose, in
    Mr. Burchell, in Young Marlow, and in Lien Chi Altangi.
    Argues a great part of The Traveller shows strong
    autobiographical elements, but even before we read the poem,
    his dedication to his brother Henry reveals him as the
    vagabond, the eternal wanderer. Notes origin of poem
    during his travels in Europe, summarizes his European
    wanderings as generally found in his biographies. Finds
    Goldsmith sympathizes politically with the poor and the
    monarchy, but not the rich, who dispossess the poor in
    Deserted Village and who do not encourage the talented like
    himself and Johnson. To Goldsmith, the common people show
    the distinctive traits of a nation, not its upper classes.
    Believes that the details in the poem do conform generally
    to those his best biographers cite, despite Macaulay's
    warnings about his lack of truthfulness.

3   MILNER-BARRY, ALDA. "A Note on the Early Literary Relations
    of Oliver Goldsmith and Thomas Percy." RES 2 (January):
    51-61.
        On the evidence of Percy's Diary for 31 May 1761, asserts
    Percy arranged Goldsmith's first meeting with Johnson:
    "This was the celebrated occasion when Johnson put on a new
    suit of clothes, as described in the so-called Percy Memoir
    of Goldsmith" (p. 51, n.). Describes their shared interest
    in China: Percy then in London seeking a publisher for his
    edition-translation of Kiou Choaan, eventually published by
    Dodsley in 1761 in four volumes. Sees Percy and Goldsmith
    using similar passages from Du Halde's A Description of the
    Empire of China.

4   POWELL, L. F. "Hau Kiou Choaan." RES 2 (October):446-55.
        A reply to 1926.B3. Disposes of Percy as a primary
    influence in Goldsmith's using Chinese materials for his
    framework in The Citizen of the World: "It has been
    suggested by various writers that Hau Kiou Choaan
    influenced Goldsmith's choice of medium for his Citizen of
    the World. Miss Milner-Barry has dealt with the question
    fully and sympathetically; the evidence adduced by her is,

however, not conclusive. We know Goldsmith copied
extensively from D'Argens's Lettres Chinoises and made use
of Du Halde. We know, too, that he took the name of his
Chinese philosopher 'Lien Chi Altangi' from Walpole.
Moreover, there is other evidence of Goldsmith's Chinese
reading prior to his introduction to Percy February 21,
1750. There is, I venture to think, little doubt that the
works mentioned suggested the medium of Goldsmith's
production, and that D'Argens's collection of pseudo-letters
served as a model" (pp. 454-55).

<u>1927</u>

A. Books

1 CRANE, RONALD S., ed. <u>New Essays by Oliver Goldsmith</u>.
    Chicago: University of Chicago Press, 188 pp.
       Ascribes eighteen essays to Goldsmith never before
    identified. Gives a resume of earlier editors' efforts to
    collect Goldsmith's periodical writing, justifies his own
    effort, defines his method--demonstrating Goldsmith's
    connection with the periodical involved and the identifying
    echoes of Goldsmithian ideas and phrasing. Argues most of
    these pieces are not among Goldsmith's first-rate work.
    Crane's appendix lists other essays for which he does not
    find enough evidence to make a definitive ascription.
    These essays all appeared in the <u>British Magazine</u>, the
    <u>Royal Magazine</u>, the <u>Public Ledger</u>, the <u>Lady's Magazine</u>, and
    <u>Lloyd's Evening Post</u>. Friedman prints (<u>Works</u> 3, passim)
    all but three: "A Letter Supposed to be Written by the
    Moorish Secretary in London, to his Correspondent in Fez,"
    <u>British Magazine</u>, January 1760; "A Letter from a Foreigner
    in London to his Friend in Rome," <u>Lady's Magazine</u>,
    September 1761; and "Thoughts on the Present Situation of
    Affairs," <u>Lady's Magazine</u>, October 1761, evidence for all
    of which Crane granted was among the weakest in his
    discussions.

B. Shorter Writings

1 BALDERSTON, KATHARINE C. "Goldsmith's Supposed Attack on
    Fielding." <u>MLN</u> 42 (March):165-68.
       Poses the question, is the attack on romances in letter
    83, <u>Citizen of the World</u>, an attack on Fielding? Believes
    Goldsmith did not intend it to attack Fielding or any other
    contemporary writer, since the entire letter is translated
    from Du Halde. Goldsmith gives a footnote with exact page

references and encloses borrowed passages in quotation
marks. Almost all modern editions do this, too, but some
editors seem a bit suspicious, even Gibbs thinking it may
refer to Richardson. Some of the problem may be caused by
there being another edition of Du Halde--J. Watts, 1736--
available besides Cave's, which Goldsmith used. Even if
Goldsmith was translating, he knew the general tenor, but
he is using the passage merely as an illustration of the
effect of reading on young people. Concludes the reference
is general, intended as an attack on no specific writer.

2 BROWN, JOSEPH E. "Goldsmith and Johnson on Biography." MLN
   42 (March):168-71.
        Goldsmith's remarks on the art of biography in the Life
   of Nash echo Johnson's Idler 84 and some resemblances may
   also be seen between Goldsmith's Life of Parnell and
   Johnson's Rambler 60. "Goldsmith accepted in advance of
   most of his contemporaries, in theory--and illustrated in
   practice, one may add--a conception of biography that was
   soon to be further perfected in The Lives of the Poets and
   Boswell's Life of Johnson, and was even to become the basis
   of present day methods" (p. 171). The emphases on truth,
   not panegyric; getting to the real man, not just the outer
   shell; and the use of details to show character all show
   Johnson's dominating influence on Goldsmith as well as on
   Boswell.

3 CRANE, RONALD S. "Goldsmith's Essays: Dates of Original
   Publication." N&Q 153 (27 August):153.
        In preparing New Essays (1927.A1), found original
   places of publication for four of the seven essays untraced.
   Essay 8, "A Specimen of a Magazine in Miniature,"
   originally published in Lloyd's Evening Post and British
   Chronicle, 8-10 February 1762, as No. 4 of a series called
   "The Indigent Philosopher"--the other three are printed in
   New Essays (1927.A1); Essay 16, "Asem, an Eastern Tale"
   appeared first in the Royal Magazine, or Gentleman's
   Monthly Companion, under the title "The Proceedings of
   Providence Vindicated" in December 1750; Essay 26, "On the
   Superabundance of Addresses to Royalty," added to the
   second edition of 1766, first appeared in the Public
   Ledger, 17 September 1761; and Essay 27, "To the Printer,"
   first printed in the Public Ledger, 24 September 1761. The
   original places of publication still unknown for Essay 25,
   "Supposed to be Written by the Ordinary of Newgate," and the
   two poems "The Double Transformation, a Tale" and "A New
   Simile in the Manner of Swift," Nos. 26 and 27 in the first
   edition of 1765, and Nos. 28 and 29 in the second edition
   of 1766.

4   _____. "The Deserted Village in Prose (1762)." TLS
     (8 September):607.
         Despite Strean's letter in Mangin's Essay on Light
     Reading (1808.B2) arguing that General Robert Napier's
     evictions near Lissoy provided the inspiration for the
     Deserted Village, believes it now fairly clear that
     Goldsmith's impulse to write came from England: the
     reference in the "Dedication" to Reynolds to "my incursions,
     for these four or five years past," being a typical sample.
     A short anonymous piece in Lloyd's Evening Post and British
     Chronicle, 14-16 June 1762 (p. 571), reprinted with cuts
     as "The Revolution in Low Life" in the Universal Museum, or
     Gentleman's and Ladies' Polite Magazine, June 1762 (1:323-
     24), concerns the depopulation of a village being enclosed
     by a rich London merchant to form his estate. Also
     discussion that foreign trade enriches only the few. Crane
     argues the essay is by Goldsmith on the basis of similarity
     of theme and expression. John Newbery was one of the
     owners of Lloyd's Evening Post, to which Goldsmith
     contributed a series of four essays, one of which he
     reprinted in Essays, 1765, and Goldsmith's primary
     publisher at this time.

5   HOLDER, ARTHUR S. Authorship in the Days of Johnson: Being
     a Study of the Relation Between Author, Patron, Publisher,
     and Public, 1726-1780. London: R. Holden, 278 pp.
         A general survey, tracing conditions in the book trade
     from the early part of the eighteenth century to the later.
     Emphasizes that both Goldsmith and Johnson rejected
     patronage ultimately, though both sought to work with the
     patronage system early in their careers. Both came to rely
     on booksellers and the public, though Johnson is somewhat
     more outspoken in favoring the booksellers and Goldsmith
     somewhat ambivalent, though he did not accept the Earl of
     Northumberland's thinly disguised offer and later he did
     accept the friendship of Lord Clare and enjoyed his
     hospitality both at his country estate and at Bath. Both
     Johnson and Goldsmith seem to have wanted to keep their
     independence, especially in politics.

*6   NICOLL, ALLARDYCE. A History of Late Eighteenth Century Drama,
     1750-1800. Cambridge: University Press.
         Goldsmith and Sheridan are very frequently mentioned as
     the finest playwrights of the period: "twin stars that
     shine in the darkness of this era" (p. 1). Much of his
     discussion concerns sentimental comedy, with Goldsmith and
     Sheridan in opposition to it, but finds elements of
     sentimentalism in Goldsmith, "as both The Vicar of

1927

Wakefield and The Deserted Village show" (p. 157),
especially in The Good Natur'd Man. Reports the play's
reasonable financial success, even though Kelly's False
Delicacy deliberately written at Garrick's instigation for
Drury Lane to rival Goldsmith's play at Covent Garden.
Finds She Stoops to Conquer a great improvement: "We may
cavil at the construction of the comedy; we may describe
certain of the incidents as farcical; we may criticise
some of the characterisation, but always Goldsmith's 'humor'
and his 'nature' prevail" (p. 159). [Annotation based on
Nicoll Allardyce, History of English Drama (Cambridge:
University Press, 1955), 3:157-60.] Revised ed.:
1955.B8.

7   SEITZ, R. W. "Goldsmith and 'A Concise History of England.'"
    N&Q 153 (2 July):3-4.
       Goldsmith's two definitely known histories of England
    are his History of England in a Series of Letters from a
    Nobleman to his Son, Newbery, 2 vols., 1764, and the
    History of England, Thomas Davies, 4 vols., 1771. In 1765,
    James Dodsley advertised a book, the second part of which
    Seitz attributes to Goldsmith: "The Geography & History
    of England/Done in the Manner of Gordon's and Salmon's
    Geographical and Historical Grammars./In Two Parts."
    Goldsmith had nothing to do with the first, geographical
    part, but the second part, "A/Concise History/of/England,"
    pp. 247-97, Seitz believes is Goldsmith's. The internal
    evidence suggests an abridgement of the epistolary history,
    and Seitz provides parallel passages supporting this point;
    external evidence includes a contract Goldsmith had signed
    with Dodsley in 1763 for a book of "British Lives," but
    had never delivered. Dodsley paid thirty guineas and by
    1763 had a contract right to publish other work by
    Goldsmith, which Seitz believes was this work.

1928

A. Books

1   BALDERSTON, KATHARINE C., ed. The Collected Letters of Oliver
    Goldsmith. Cambridge: University Press, 243 pp.
       A meticulous piece of work, of crucial importance to
    Goldsmith's biography. Prints nine new genuine letters,
    several forgeries--included to save future students from
    error--the complete text of Mrs. Hodson's narrative of her
    brother's early life, and some materials connected with
    Threnodia Augustalis and with the first production of She

Stoops to Conquer. Has provided new and sometimes fuller texts of thirty-one previously published letters, from collations with the originals, and in several cases has corrected dating by earlier authors. Introduction studies five important biographical problems--Goldsmith's relation to his family; the genuineness of the Fiddleback episode, including the authenticity of the letter he supposedly wrote his mother about--the letter rejected as not authentic; the conditions leading to his decision not to go to India; the composition of Threnodia Augustalis; and an account of the revision and production of She Stoops to Conquer.

2   ISAACS, J. [Temple Scott]. Oliver Goldsmith, Bibliographical-ly and Biographically Considered. Based on the Collection of Material in the Library of W. M. Elkins, Esq. Introduc-tion by A. Edward Newton. New York: Bowling Green Press; London: Maggs Brothers, 387 pp.
    Primarily a catalogue of the Elkins collection, with technical bibliographical descriptions, and uses passages from Goldsmith's life and works as explanation of Goldsmith's character and behavior. Sees Goldsmith as sometimes joking when Boswell did not perceive his attitude and recorded his words literally. Describes a good many of the Goldsmith-Newbery papers. Biographical material contains many quotations from manuscripts in the collection, and no footnotes to earlier biographies though Forster's and Prior's are both mentioned and obviously used, as are Boswell and Hawkins and others, so that the biographical parts of the book are derivative and undocumented, but the bibliographical descriptions are valuable.

B. Shorter Writings

1   BOSWELL, JAMES. Private Papers of James Boswell from Malahide Castle in the Collection of Lieut.-Colonel Ralph Heyward Isham. Vols. 1, 3, 4. Prepared for the Press by Geoffrey Scott and now First Printed. New York: William Edwin Rudge, passim.
    See also 1929.B2, 1930.B3, 1931.B1, 1931.B2, 1932.B1, 1933.B1, 1937.B2. This limited edition is being re-edited and reissued as The Yale Editions of the Private Papers of James Boswell, see 1950.B1, 1955.B1, 1956.B1, 1959.B1.

2   [CHAPMAN, R. W.] "Oliver Goldsmith, 1728(?)-1774." TLS (8 November):813-14.
    Front-page essay-review of Balderston's Collected Letters (1928.A1) and Crane's New Essays (1927.A1).

1928

"Goldsmith's character must remain enigmatical. It was an enigma to his contemporaries and it puzzled himself" (p. 813). Discussing the problem of Boswell's envy of Goldsmith, argues Boswell was fond of Goldsmith, and "it is unlikely he went far wrong" (p. 813). Believes Goldsmith's oddities stand out in his works, too, and finds little value in his early journalistic essays beyond their "easy manner. The style itself runs thin" (p. 813). "The paradox of Goldsmith--if we are to seek a paradox--is that his best things are so much better than his dead level that they come with a shock of surprise. . . . His great gift is for the particulars--a picture, an episode, a trait of oddity. . . . His genius is the genius of a poet, comic or tragi-comic" (p. 814). Reprinted: 1953.B1.

3   DIX, E. R. McC. "The Works of Oliver Goldsmith, a Hand-List of Dublin Editions before 1801." Transactions of the Bibliographical Society of Ireland 3:93-101.
         A bibliography.

4   DOUGHTY, OSWALD, ed. Introduction to The Vicar of Wakefield. London: Scholartis Press, 299 pp.
         Reprints the fifth edition, 1773, the last in which Goldsmith could conceivably have had a hand, though Friedman believes he made no more revisions after second [Works 4:11-12]. Lengthy introduction surveys and analyzes the different versions of the sale of the novel, quoting the accounts by Mrs. Piozzi, 1786; Sir John Hawkins, 1787; Boswell, 1791; Richard Cumberland, 1806; and briefer comments by William Cooke, 1793; and Joseph Craddock, 1826; and cites evidence from Welsh's 1885 biography of John Newbery, concluding that the Vicar was finished by 28 October 1762. Despite three editions of 1000 copies each, the novel did not show a profit until shortly before Goldsmith's death. Believes the setting is a compound of idealized memories of Lissoy, with some, perhaps, of Springfield, Essex. Finds Goldsmith's use of plot and structure not new, but a consolidation of themes and subject-matter from Richardson, Fielding, Smollett, and even some from Defoe, but does give "a new, imaginative field, that of simple, homely, domestic life" (p. xxiii). "Life as he presents it is ever the gentle idealisation of reality, an idealisation half-tender, half-cynical" (p. xxxvi).

5   TINKER, CHAUNCEY B[REWSTER]. "Figures in a Dream." Yale Review 17 (July):670-89.
         Considers the popularity of The Deserted Village and

its extensive influence. Formerly saw its descriptions and
characterizations as its real strength, but now does not.
Now finds its strength the archetypal sense of loss and of
the passage of time, finding parallels in the urbanization
of Connecticut. Also regrets the loss of the essay-
element in poetry, the disappearance of the rhetorical
element of persuasion through emotion.

1929

A. Books--None

B. Shorter Writings

1   BALDERSTON, KATHARINE C. "The Birth of Goldsmith." TLS
    (7 March):185-86.
        Since Percy's Life (1801.B]) 1728 has been accepted as
    the year of Goldsmith's birth. Argues for 1730, using
    three kinds of evidence: Goldsmith's own statements at
    various periods in his life; the record of his age in the
    Senior Lecturer's book at Trinity College, Dublin; and
    unsupported and conflicting statements by his sister
    Catherine Hodson and his brother Maurice.

2   BOSWELL, JAMES. Private Papers of James Boswell from Malahide
    Castle in the Collection of Lieut.-Colonel Ralph Heywood
    Isham. Vols. 2, 5, 6. Prepared for the Press by Geoffrey
    Scott and now First Printed. New York: William Edwin
    Rudge, passim.
        See general comment on 1928.B1.

3   CHAPMAN, R. W. "A Goldsmith Anecdote." TLS (13 June):474.
        Reports discovering a copy of D. Fenning's "The Young
    Man's Book of Knowledge," an elementary encyclopedia,
    inscribed as a gift to John Croft from Oliver Goldsmith and
    with a second inscription noting that Goldsmith cut out
    several pages and threw the book into the street where it
    was found. The cut pages are 5-92 and 93-110, which contain
    a history of England. Suggests Goldsmith may have either
    written the pages or wanted them, and Ronald S. Crane told
    him the printers were associated with Newbery and that the
    pages containing the chronological tables in Fenning are
    the immediate source of the chronological tables at the end
    of Goldsmith's History of England in a Series of Letters,
    1764, 2:255f.

1929

4   CHURCH, RICHARD. "Oliver Goldsmith." Criterion 8 (April):
    437-44.
        Considers various contemporary attitudes toward
    Goldsmith. Johnson supported him for original membership
    in the Club, praised his writing skill, criticized his
    lack of knowledge. Judge Day's account [in Prior's Life,
    1837.A1] stresses his boistrous good humour, solidity of
    information, frequent laughter. Another contemporary, a
    lady, saw him as plain but good-hearted. Church believes
    he spent nearly a year at Louvain and Padua and may have
    taken a medical degree at the latter, but he did perfect
    his French and Italian on his European trip. Despite hard
    experience in journalism, Goldsmith remained an innocent,
    squandering knowledge and money so that in his own work,
    he returns to his own childhood--Church accepts She Stoops
    to Conquer as based on an actual experience [from Mrs.
    Hodson]. Finds in him a carefree quality, the price he
    paid for never becoming fully mature.

5   COLUM, PADRAIC. "Young Goldsmith." Scribner's 86 (November):
    555-63.
        For the general reader. Covering the years 1749-52, a
    time Goldsmith spent gambling, singing, attempting to be a
    tutor, and trying to find a profession, Colum sets up a
    kind of interior monologue going in Goldsmith's mind
    covering these years when Goldsmith was refused ordination,
    gambled away the money that was to get him to London to
    study law and that which was to take him to America, and
    ends with him leaving for Edinburgh to study medicine.
    Most of Colum's imaginings are based on published sources.

6   ELTON, OLIVER. A Survey of English Literature, 1730-1789.
    2 vols. London: Macmillan, 1:98-123, passim.
        Finds Goldsmith's shift from Churchill's hard satire to
    the softer-toned Traveller is striking, and his rural
    pictures are free from the tired artifices of classical
    pastoral. Praises Retaliation and cites Goethe's praise of
    Vicar's morality and its pervasive irony. All its strength
    flows from his using the vicar as narrator-observer, but
    also sufferer, not just the self-centered narrator we see
    in Pamela and Roderick Random. "Goldsmith, in his writings,
    is happy without effort, and even when he is so poignant,
    he manages to leave us expectant of better times" (p. 113).
    Finds his comedies are his best work, though The Good
    Natur'd Man is stiff but Croaker saves it, and She Stoops
    to Conquer far better done. Believes Goldsmith learned
    "shaping, proportioning, omitting" and "some of his ease,
    transparency, and lightness of hand" (p. 122) from such

writers as Voltaire, Marivaux, and Buffon. Concludes by
praising him as a "master of that central, dateless, and,
in the true sense, classical style" (p. 123).

7   INGALLS, GERTRUDE VAN ARSDALE. "Some Sources of Goldsmith's
    She Stoops to Conquer." PMLA 44 (June):565-68.
        The nineteenth century considered both She Stoops to
    Conquer and the Vicar highly original, but she suggests
    some possible sources: Lady Bluemantle in Spectator 27, by
    Steele, as a parallel for Tony driving Mrs. Hardcastle
    about her own garden. Cites Spectator 289, by Addison, as
    an analogue to Harlow's [sic] mistaking Hardcastle's house
    for an inn. Grants similarity not so close here--though
    neither parallel is very apt. Cites Forster as authority
    for the idea the situation was autobiographical--source is
    Mrs. Hodson's narrative. Believes Goldsmith was unable to
    recognize the value of his own experience as literary
    material unless he had read something similar. Believes
    examples similar to his use of French materials will be
    found in English and cause a revision of judgments.

8   SEITZ, R. W. "Goldsmith and the Literary Magazine" RES 5
    (October):410-30.
        Seven articles or series of articles published in the
    Literary Magazine between December 1757 and July 1758
    have been ascribed to Goldsmith, four by Prior in 1837
    (1837.A2), the rest by Gibbs in 1885. The group consists
    of "The History of Our Own Times," "The Poetical Scale,"
    "The Sequel to the Poetical Balance, being Miscellaneous
    Thoughts on English Poets," "Phanor: or the Butterfly
    Pursuit, a Political Allegory," "The History of Our Own
    Language," "On the Character of English Officers," and
    "Of the Pride and Luxury of the Middling Class of People."
    Believes the case of the authenticity of these pieces was
    never conclusive and doubts have been increasing. Attacks
    all internal and external evidence advanced for attribu-
    tions, and "reduces Goldsmith's connection with the
    Literary Magazine to a reader who used a set of numbers
    from November, 1759, as an occasional source of the Bee,
    Lady's Magazine, Public Ledger, The Political View of the
    Result of the Present War with America, and History of
    England in a Series of Letters." Findings are mainly
    negative, but does make some positive points: John
    Campbell's Present State of Europe was a source for
    Goldsmith's Political View, and identifies some new
    borrowings in the Citizen of the World from Johnson's
    articles in the Literary Magazine for 1756. That Goldsmith
    did not write the central portion of "An Account of the

1929

Augustan Age of England" in Bee No. 8 may be seen by the
opinion of Tillotson there and its difference from that in
"Of Eloquence," Bee, No. 7.

9 _____. "Goldsmith's Lives of the Fathers." MP 26
(February):295-305.
Prior and others believed Goldsmith was responsible for
a Life of Christ and Lives of the Fathers (Prior, Life
I:479, 488; 22:57). Believes he has acquired a copy and
describes it bibliographically. The views expressed are
similar to those of Goldsmith on depopulation, miracles
(skeptical), persecution (merely makes new believers).
These were not serialized in the Christian's Magazine as
Prior thought, but both publications used a common source.

10 SMITH, HAMILTON J[EWETT]. "Mr. Tattler [sic] of Pekin: A
Venture in Journalism." University of California Publications in English 1:155-75.
Steele's Tatler was the original observer-critic of
journalism, the father of Mr. Spectator, grandfather of
Lien Chi Altangi of The Citizen of the World. Lien Chi was
pleasing as a familiar stranger after the somewhat heavy
tone of Johnson's Rambler and appealed to the Chinese fad
of the 1750s. Describes the major sources of the pseudo-
letter tradition. Believes it was necessary, at least in
the beginning, for the public to think the author was
Chinese. The purpose of the series, like all journalism,
was direct and practical, calling people's attention to
folly and indiscretion.

1930

A. Books--None

B. Shorter Writings

1 BALDERSTON, KATHARINE C. "A Manuscript Version of She Stoops
to Conquer." MLN 45 (February):84-85.
In the Larpent Collection belonging to the Huntington
Library is the Licenser's copy of the play, the text
substantially that of the printed first edition. This
manuscript version confirms Horace Walpole's story of Mrs.
Rachel Lloyd's taking offense, since the original reference
to Mrs. Rachel Buckskin appears, though was changed to
Miss Biddy Buckskin. Another significant change in Kate's
soliloquy in Act 4, from "I'll still preserve the character
in which I conquer'd," to "I'll still preserve the

character in which I stooped to conquer," suggests a
change after the title was finally chosen. The manuscript
is titled "The Novel," a fact that may offer problems,
but the title is not in Goldsmith's hand or that of the
copyist. "Whether or not the subtitle, 'The Mistakes of a
Night,' which was of course retained, was here first
suggested remains open to question" (p. 85).

2 BAUDIN, MAURICE. "Une Source de She Stoops to Conquer." PMLA
45 (June):614.
Argues that Marc Antoine Le Grande's Galant Coureur
(1722) has some similarities to Goldsmith's play--the
action takes place in a strange house, Kate's tactics are
somewhat like those of the Countess, and the revelation is
made gradually in both plays.

3 BOSWELL, JAMES. Private Papers of James Boswell from Malahide
Castle in the Collection of Lt-Colonel Ralph Heyward Isham.
Vols. 7, 8, 9. Prepared for the Press by Geoffrey Scott
and Frederick A. Pottle. New York: privately printed,
passim.
See note on 1928.B1.

4 CRANE, RONALD S. [Comment on K. C. Balderston, "The Birth of
Goldsmith." TLS (7 March 1929): 185-86] PQ 9 (April):190-
91.
Finds major objections to 1730 as the most probable
birth year are the unreliable Trinity College records and
Goldsmith's own statements in 1773 memorandum dictated
to Percy. Believes also that Mrs. Hodson's statement that
Maurice was seven years younger than Oliver may be based
on evidence from family Bible. Believes a clear decision
between 1729 and 1730 impossible and that of dates proposed,
1728 rests on the weakest contemporary evidence. Agrees
with Balderston that Goldsmith probably did not know or
much care exactly what year he was born.

5 _____. "The Text of Goldsmith's Memoirs of M. de Voltaire."
MP (November):212-19.
Originally intended by Goldsmith as a book, but the
only text we have was published in Lady's Magazine,
February to November 1761. Percy may have known it, but
Prior identified it, and Prior's text stood and was
reprinted by Cunningham, Masson, and Gibbs. Cunningham
thought a publisher's hack, J. Wright, rewrote heavily.
Goldsmith wrote carelessly both factually and grammatically,
and the 1837 Prior text is cleaned up and polished. What
the early nineteenth-century reader might see as

1930

indelicacies are removed, and some omissions occur, mostly
from the later parts.

6   ELIOT, T. S. [Comments on Goldsmith.] In London: A Poem and
     The Vanity of Human Wishes. . . . by Samuel Johnson.
     With an Introductory Note by T. S. Eliot. Haslewood
     Books Edition. London: F. Etchels & H. Macdonald, 44 pp.
       The first three comments associate Goldsmith and
     Johnson as poets who follow the tradition of Pope without
     becoming imitators only, whose originality is achieved with
     a minimum of change rather than a maximum, and whose verse
     exhibits the virtues of good prose, an idea familiar in
     Eliot's criticism; the last distinguishes Goldsmith from
     Johnson as being more in tune with his times in the use of
     the pastoral, but avoiding sentimentality by precise
     diction. Reprinted: 1935.B5; 1940.B1; 1942.B2; 1944.B4.

7   PASCHAL, The Rev. Father. "Goldsmith as a Social Philosopher."
     Irish Ecclesiastical Record, 5th ser. 55 (February):113-24.
       Finds "what is best in his social philosophy has a
     distinctly traditional or Catholic flavour" (p. 114). His
     Deserted Village shows a cold, commercial spirit disrupting
     traditional agricultural relationships, and "Goldsmith's
     views on trade and commerce have more affinities with those
     of the French School of Economists (known as the Physiocrats)
     than with the ideas of the prevailing English Mercantile
     School" (p. 118). Concludes that "Time and talent have
     often been devoted to such questions as Goldsmith's
     birthplace, the quality of his poetry, the defective
     technique of his novel, while the more enduring basis of
     his fame has been comparatively neglected" (p. 124).
     Finds Goldsmith presenting traditional values in virtually
     every respect, but does not identify Goldsmith with mid-
     eighteenth-century Tory writers like Johnson in any
     organized way.

8   SEITZ, R. W. "Goldsmith and the Present State of the British
     Empire." MLN 45 (November):434-38.
       Seitz argues for attribution to Goldsmith. About one
     hundred pages--devoted to the British empire in America
     transferred almost without change from Edmund and William
     Burke's Account of the European Settlements in America.
     The Monthly Review critic found the work confused, and
     Seitz believes Goldsmith made few changes from his source
     and the ten pounds he was paid was ample for what he did.
     "The text certainly shows no very clear trace of his hand.
     That this work, however, is the Present State, for which
     Goldsmith received ten pounds from Newbery in 1767, there

can be no reasonable doubt" (p. 437).

9   TUPPER, CAROLINE F.   "Goldsmith and the 'Gentleman Who Signs
    D.'" <u>MLN</u> 45 (February):71-77.
        In the <u>Monthly Review</u>, April 1757, Goldsmith reviewed a
    French version of the <u>Edda</u> by Mallet, a professor at Lyons.
    Many early Goldsmith reviews were neglected because of the
    tradition of Griffiths and his wife tampering, but this one
    was singled out by Prior and Forster as important for
    showing Goldsmith's interest in "Celtic" material, as Norse
    items were believed to be at the time. Finds that the
    entire article is an abridged translation of a review in
    the <u>Bibliothèque des Sciences et des Beaux-Arts</u> 6 (October-
    December 1746):285-303. Comparison of parallel passages.
    Finds the clue to authorship in the editorial note "The
    following paper was sent to us by the Gentleman who signs,
    D, and who, we hope will excuse our striking out a few
    paragraphs, for the sake of brevity" (p. 76). "D" had
    inaugurated the Foreign Books section in the <u>Monthly Review</u>
    in February 1758, and specifically cited the <u>Bibliothèque</u>.
    "D" signed four reviews from April 1755, six from September
    1756. Griffiths's marked copy in the Bodleian Library
    identifies "D" as Grainger for most of the reviews, but
    this one of Mallet's book is marked "Goldsmith."

<u>1931</u>

A. Books

1   WOOD, ALICE I. PERRY. Introduction to <u>The Grumbler, an</u>
    <u>Adaptation by Oliver Goldsmith</u>. Cambridge, Mass.: Harvard
    University Press, 43 pp.
        Goldsmith's adaptation of the translation by Sir Charles
    Sedley of Brueys's and Palaprat's <u>Le Grondeur</u> to a one-act
    farce for John Quick, the actor who had played Tony Lumpkin.
    Apparently acted only once, 8 May 1773. This edition is
    the only complete text, since Friedman did not reprint it.
    (<u>Works</u> 1:xi).

B. Shorter Writings

1   BOSWELL, JAMES. <u>Private Papers of James Boswell from Malahide</u>
    <u>Castle in the Collection of Lt-Colonel Ralph Heyward Isham</u>.
    Vols. 10, 11, 12. Prepared for the Press by Geoffrey Scott
    and Frederick A. Pottle. New York: privately printed,
    passim.
        See note on 1928.B1.

1931

2 POTTLE, FREDERICK A. and POTTLE, MARION S. The Private Papers
   of James Boswell from Malahide Castle in the Collection of
   Lt-Colonel Ralph Heyward Isham: a Catalogue. London and
   New York: Oxford University Press, [246 pp.].
       A description of the collection. See 1928.B1. A new
   catalogue of the full Boswell papers, compiled by Marion S.
   Pottle, is in press.

3 SEITZ, R. W. "Goldsmith and the 'English Lives.'" MP 28
   (February):329-36.
       The Concise History of England, which Dodsley published
   in March 1765, is practically an abridgement of the 1764
   History of England in a Series of Letters, published by
   Newbery. Includes an agreement of 1763 between Dodsley and
   Goldsmith for Goldsmith to write a "Chronological History
   of the Lives of Eminent Persons of Great Britain and
   Ireland" for about £210--almost his largest project so far,
   and the project was probably not abandoned until about the
   time the epistolary history appeared near the middle of
   1764. Dodsley appears to have shifted his interest to
   history since James Grainger was writing a series of English
   lives, since Goldsmith was unlikely to meet the commitment
   and since he realistically was trying to get what he could
   out of Goldsmith. Newbery was almost certainly involved,
   since he had published the epistolary history. Dodsley
   may well have returned what copy he had had from Goldsmith
   and taken the Concise History in exchange. "Certainly as
   far as our present knowledge goes, the biographical
   history is the only work of Goldsmith's which might be
   designated 'English Lives.' That Newbery published this
   work in a single volume I doubt. Whether he published any
   part of it in any of the numerous periodicals of the day
   remains to be discovered. Meanwhile our hypothesis may
   serve to throw some light on some of the obscure events in
   Goldsmith's career during 1763 and 1764" (p. 336).

1932

A. Books--None

B. Shorter Writings

1 BOSWELL, JAMES. Private Papers from Malahide Castle in the
   Collection of Lt-Colonel Ralph Heyward Isham. Vols. 13,
   14, 15, 16. Prepared for the Press by Geoffrey Scott and
   Frederick A. Pottle. New York: privately printed, passim.
       See general comment on 1928.B1.

2   PRICE, LAWRENCE M. The Reception of English Literature in
     Germany. Berkeley: University of California Press, pp.
     248-56.
          The great impact of Goldsmith's writing, especially the
     Vicar, on Herder and Goethe. Goethe's Wandrer influenced
     by The Traveller, but only on personal level, not by any of
     the political or economic ideas.

1933

A. Books

1   KENT, ELIZABETH E. Goldsmith and His Booksellers. Cornell
     Studies in English no. 20. Ithaca, N.Y.: Cornell
     University Press, xiv, 122 pp.
          Devotes one chapter to each of Goldsmith's principal
     publishers: Ralph Griffiths, Robert and James Dodsley,
     John Newbery, Thomas Davies, and William Griffin, with a
     biographical sketch and summary of Goldsmith's connection
     with each. Of Griffiths, the proprietor of the Monthly
     Review, who gave Goldsmith his start in writing, notes that
     he may have published Cleland's Fanny Hill, though believes
     it was only an expurgated edition. Forster (1854.A2)
     believed Griffiths had published the indecent original and
     censured what he believed was Griffiths's hypocrisy. After
     Goldsmith left the Monthly, his work received pretty
     consistently bad reviews beginning with the Enquiry, 1759,
     through She Stoops to Conquer, 1773, mainly written by
     Kenrick, but some upon Griffiths's direction, and adverse
     criticism continued after Goldsmith's death. Robert Dodsley
     had published Johnson's London in 1738 but retired from
     business in 1759, so that his brother James alone published
     the Enquiry in 1759; connection was desultory but
     continued, since he published the revised posthumous edition
     of the Enquiry in 1774. John Newbery was not only a
     publisher but a considerable entrepreneur, being the
     proprietor of Dr. James's Powders, among other things, and
     especially known for his books for children. He was not
     the actual publisher of the Vicar, but almost certainly had
     an interest in his nephew Francis's business. Davies began
     life as an actor, later kept a bookshop, where he introduced
     Boswell to Johnson, and commissioned the Roman history, the
     four-volume English history, and the lives of Parnell and
     Bolingbroke, primarily on the basis of the popularity of
     Goldsmith's History of England in a Series of Letters . . . ,
     published by Newbery. He generally defends Goldsmith in
     his Memoirs of Garrick, 1780.B2. William Griffin, an
     Irishman, published Essays, 1765; The Deserted Village, 1770;

and contracted with Goldsmith in 1769 for an eight-volume "Natural History," published as <u>Animated Nature</u>, 1774.

B. Shorter Writings

1   BOSWELL, JAMES. <u>Private Papers of James Boswell from Malahide Castle in the Collection of Lt-Colonel Ralph Heyward Isham</u>. Vols. 17, 18. Prepared for the Press by Geoffrey Scott and Frederick A. Pottle. New York: privately printed, passim. See general comment on 1928.B1.

2   CRANE, RONALD S. "'Oliver Goldsmith, M.B.'" <u>MLN</u> 48 (November): 462-65.
    Believes the crucial question is not the source of Goldsmith's medical degree or the validity of his claim to possession of such a degree, but the date at which the claim to have such a degree was made. The usual date given is 1763, based on the contract with Dodsley for the "English Lives," causing Forster and others to assume Goldsmith's decision to use the title coincided with this contract. Percy's diary for 1759 describes Goldsmith as "Mr. Goldsmith" with additional references using "Goldsmith" or "Mr. Goldsmith," but the style changes in the entry for 16 November 1764 to "Dr. Goldsmith." Usual interpretation has been that Goldsmith assumed the degree only toward the end of his anonymous authorship, perhaps to give prominence and importance to himself as he associated with more prominent people. But other evidence shows he was known by the title as early as 1759, a letter Shenstone wrote Percy 6 June 1759, again 15 February 1760 and 16 May 1762. Two early printed references refer to "Dr. Goldsmith": <u>Court Magazine</u>, December 1761, and William Rider's <u>Historical and Critical Account of the Lives and Writings of the Living Authors of Great Britain</u>, 1762.B3. Thus he was known as "Dr. Goldsmith" almost from the beginning of his literary career.

3   CRANE, RONALD S., and FRIEDMAN, ARTHUR. "Goldsmith and the Encyclopédie." <u>TLS</u> (11 May):331.
    Goldsmith drew heavily on the <u>Encyclopedie</u> and sixteen instances of previously unrecorded borrowings are presented, mostly in <u>Bee</u> papers but also various reviews, introductions, and one from the <u>Citizen</u>.

4   DOBSON, AUSTIN. "Oliver Goldsmith." In <u>Cambridge History of English Literature</u>. Edited by A. W. Ward and A. R. Waller. Cambridge: University Press; New York: Macmillan, 10: 220-44.

The "Cheap Edition" of 1913.B2, an exact reprint.

5   ELIOT, T. S. [Comments on Goldsmith.] In London: A Poem and
     The Vanity of Human Wishes. . . . by Samuel Johnson. With
     an Introductory Note by T. S. Eliot. In English Critical
     Essays: Twentieth Century. Selected with an Introduction
     by Phyllis M. Jones. London: Oxford University Press,
     World's Classics Edition, pp. 301-10.
          Reprinted: 1930.B6, 1940.B1, 1942.B2, 1947.B4.

6   FRIEDMAN, ARTHUR. "An Essay by Goldsmith in the Lady's
     Magazine." MP 30 (February):320-22.
          Crane's suggestion in New Essays (1927.A1) that "A Lady
     of Fashion in the Times of Anna Bullen" in Lady's Magazine,
     October 1760 (2:124-26) may be Goldsmith's is based on
     Crane's belief that Goldsmith was probably editing the
     magazine and the concluding paragraphs strongly parallel
     passages in the Bee and Deserted Village. Adds that the
     central part of the essay resembles a paragraph describing
     a lady of fashion of a somewhat earlier period in Gold-
     smith's "Reverie at the Boar's-Head Tavern in East Cheap,"
     published seven months earlier in the British Magazine,
     March 1760 (1:153). Possibly someone else was borrowing
     from Goldsmith, but since he was probably editing the
     Lady's Magazine, that possibility is unlikely, and the
     parallel shows Goldsmith borrowing from himself.

7   GALLOWAY, W. F. "Tne Sentimentalism of Goldsmith." PMLA 48
     (December):1167-81.
          Two opposed views of Goldsmith common, that he is a
     master of the sentimental, nostalgic vein--based largely
     on The Deserted Village and the Vicar, but partly on the
     nostalgia of The Traveller, too; and that he attacks
     sentimentality, mainly in his comedies--"a classicist out
     of touch with the tendencies of the future" (p. 1167), a
     wit and advocate of common sense. Finds the disagreement
     is not about the man but about the writer and seeks a
     clearer understanding of Goldsmith's sentimentalism and a
     better appreciation of his work, using a broad definition
     of sentimentalism: the belief in human nature as funda-
     mentally good, praising spontaneity and human sensitivity,
     and attacking form: "In his attitude toward man as an
     artist he is on the whole classicist, with slight
     indications of any tendency to indulge in sentimentalism"
     (p. 1167).
          Goldsmith recognizes the irrational attachments of the
     heart, but his admiration for goodness of heart in Primrose
     and Nash is balanced by recognition of their follies.

1933

Burchell praises greatness in virtue, not mere freedom from
fault. The Primrose family are not savages, and their
rusticity is that of the classical tradition of retirement,
not of Rousseau's primitive life, which Goldsmith attacks
in description of American colonies in Deserted Village.
Goldsmith sees folly, not virtue, as a fundamental human
attribute and is free of two sentimental obsessions, the
natural goodness of man and the superiority of primitive
life. "Though it must be granted that Goldsmith was
instinctively sensitive, and in the non-technical sense of
the word, sentimental, he was able to keep from being
entangled in the doctrinaire movement of Shaftesbury,
Richardson, and Rousseau" (p. 1180).

8   ROBERTS, W. "Goldsmith in France." TLS (30 November):855.
Discusses the vogue of his writings in France: among
the salons his books were never as popular as Richardson's
and Fielding's, though his own travels there and his
extensive knowledge of the literature gave him a good
understanding of the country. Early translations include
that of The Citizen of the World, Amsterdam, 1764; the
Vicar, 1767; The Deserted Village, 1770; and the Traveller,
1785. His popularity rose very rapidly in the middle of
the nineteenth century--from 1830 to 1870, there are thirty
editions of the Vicar, five of Fielding, none of Richardson,
twelve of Sterne. During the last quarter of the eighteenth
century, though, Goldsmith was introduced to French readers
through the widely circulated Mercure de France.

9   ROCHER, M. L. "Goldsmith l'Éternel Vagabond." Revue Anglo-
Américaine 2 (October):22-32.
Begins with biographical sketch, repeating familiar
ideas: In The Deserted Village he sketched his father as
the parson and Lissoy as Auburn. Finds few signs of family
feeling in his letters--no genuine letters to his mother
survive and he neglected his generous Uncle Contarine.
Sketches his travels from Edinburgh to Europe and to
England. Does not show that Goldsmith during his mature
life was largely a resident of London and his moves from
residence to residence there were the result of increased
income rather than a roving spirit.

10   SCHORER, MARK. "She Stoops to Conquer: A Parallel." MLN 48
(February):94.
Reminds reader that there is "no known record in which
Goldsmith himself asserted" that the play was based on his
boyhood experience, and argues that Mrs. Susanna Centlivre's
The Man Bewitch'd; or The Devil to Do About Her (1709) shows

a considerable parallel: mistaking private property for an
inn. Some similarity in phraseology. Grants there is no
evidence that Goldsmith knew the play.

11 _____. "Correspondence." <u>MLN</u> 48 (November):486.
Has discovered Walter and Clare Jerold, <u>Five Queer</u>
<u>Women</u> (London: Brentano's, 1929) had noted the parallel
in their chapter on Mrs. Centlivre.

12 SEITZ, R. W. "Goldsmith and the <u>Annual Register</u>." <u>MP</u> 31
(November):183-94.
For the section of his <u>History of England in a Series of</u>
<u>Letters</u> . . . , Newbery, 1764, dealing with the Seven Years'
War, Goldsmith seems to have had two sources. Prior refers
to a Newbery memorandum of books supplied to him at Canon-
bury House, Islington: four volumes of the <u>Annual Register</u>
[by Burke] and Smollett's "Continuation." The <u>Annual</u>
<u>Register</u> volumes are 1758, 1759, 1760, and 1761; the second
is Smollett's continuation of his <u>Complete History of</u>
<u>England</u>, 1759-60, eleven volumes, forming volumes twelve
through sixteen, published 1760-65. Sees Goldsmith as not
particularly interested in specific facts, but principles
"as an aristocratic English cosmopolite; . . . a philosophe.
. . . From his first appearance as a writer he approached
whatever subject he had in mind with a kind of fixed
emotional attitude--a pattern of prejudice, it might be
called--which made him sensitive to certain facts, phrases,
and ideas with which he came in contact, very often in his
reading and which he stored away for future use" (p. 187).

13 TILLOTSON, ARTHUR. "Dr. Johnson and the <u>Life of Goldsmith</u>."
<u>MLR</u> 28 (October):438-43.
Considers the problem of why Johnson did not write a
"Life of Goldsmith" for the booksellers' edition, but
believes Balderston's explanation (1926.A1) that Carnahan's
ownership of the copyright to <u>She Stoops to Conquer</u> and his
unwillingness to cooperate is wrong. Plays were not
commonly included in this collected edition--Dryden's were
not--and in the second edition of 1790, only Goldsmith's
poems were printed. "Johnson's forgetfulness and laziness
(he was getting old and the prefaces were not an easy task)
had doubtless much to do with the result . . ." (p. 443).

<u>1934</u>

A. Books--None

1934

B. Shorter Writings

1   TEMPLAR [pseud.] "Oliver Goldsmith." TLS (8 March):162
        Points out Croaker's close paraphrase in Act 1, Scene 1
    of The Good Natur'd Man of Sir William Temple's final
    sentence in "Of Poetry." [Gibbs notes the similarity in
    his edition, 2:155, note 1.]

2   de BLACAM, HIGH. "The Madan Family and Goldsmith." TLS (1
    February):76.
        Believes Goldsmith's genius may have come from Madden
    blood--one of his great-grandmothers was Jane Madden of
    Donore, County Dublin, believed connected with the Madans
    of Galway.

3   BAKER, ERNEST A. The History of the English Novel: The Novel
    of Sentiment and the Gothic Romance. London: H. F.
    Witherby & G. Witherby, 5:66-70, 77-85, passim.
        First section deals with orientalism and the Citizen.
    Notes that the tone varies considerably and finds this kind
    of satire analogous to Gulliverian satire, but believes
    Goldsmith was an unsystematic thinker, stringing desultory
    ideas together in the haste of journalistic writing.
    Several approximations to the novel--the narrative thread,
    especially in the son's adventures, and approaches the
    novel of manners best in characterizations of the Man in
    Black and the Tibbses.
        Accepts Vicar as finished in 1762, the year the Citizen
    published, and a natural progression from it. "Superficial-
    ly, The Vicar of Wakefield is an idyll, the benign comedy
    of simple domesticity and human charity, picturing a little
    household of blameless souls . . ." (p. 79). Considers the
    characterization of the Vicar a minor masterpiece in the
    tradition of Parson Adams and Uncle Toby. "There is good
    reason for misunderstanding, for, to put it briefly,
    Goldsmith started in one direction, lost his way before he
    had gone far, and presently found himself going in a direc-
    tion entirely opposite. The idyll was to have been a
    comic idyll, a bitter-sweet pastoral, the bitterness
    concealed in the irony. . . . It was to be a fable at the
    expense of sentimental optimism, complacent trust in the
    supremacy of good, confidence that honesty will have its
    rewards without a cautious sense of the wickedness of the
    world and the guile and unscrupulousness of others" (p. 81).
    His skill at characterization ranks him with the four great
    eighteenth-century novelists, and his use of first-person
    narrative point of view "makes the lesson of his [the
    Vicar's self-deception] all the more unmistakable. The
    lesson is that prudence is necessary, as a guard to virtue,
    without which it is not safe" (p. 85). Reprinted: 1964.B1.

92

4   CRANE, RONALD S. "Goldsmith and Justus Van Effen." <u>TLS</u>
    (1 March):144.
         <u>Essays and Criticisms</u>, 1798, attributed "A Dream,"
    from the <u>British Magazine</u>, May 1760, and was accepted by
    Percy and all later editors [including Friedman, <u>Works</u>
    3:115-18]. Crane identifies the essay as a somewhat
    abridged translation of the third and fifth "Discours" of
    Justus Van Effen's <u>Le Misantrope</u> (1712-13), and prints
    parallel passages.

5   _____. "A Neglected Mid-Eighteenth-Century Plea for
    Originality and Its Author." <u>PQ</u> 13 (January):21-29.
         <u>Critical Review</u> for January 1760, ridicules R. Kedling-
    ton's <u>Critical Dissertations upon the Iliad of Homer</u>, which
    Crane believes Goldsmith wrote and favored praising writers
    for the beauties "rather than fewness of their faults, in
    deprecating imitation of ancient models and in urging
    modern poets to strike out new paths to give their readers
    first-hand pictures of the distinctive manners of their
    own time" (p. 21). The fairly advanced opinions held by
    Johnson and the <u>Critical Review</u> circle make Goldsmith a
    likely candidate.

6   RITCHIE, G. S. "Oliver Goldsmith." <u>TLS</u> (15 March):194.
         A comment on 1934.B1: Goldsmith had used a paraphrase
    of Temple's words in the final paragraph of the <u>Enquiry</u>.
    [Gibbs also notes this paraphrase of Temple in his edition:
    3:527, note 1.]

7   ROBERTS, S. C. "Oliver Goldsmith." <u>TLS</u> (8 March):162.
         Argues that in estimating Boswell's attitude toward
    Goldsmith, Boswell's friendly letter of 29 March 1773
    (Tinker's edition, <u>Letters</u>, 1:193--1924.B1) should be
    considered, as should Goldsmith's very cordial reply printed
    in the Isham papers.

8   STEIN, HAROLD. "Goldsmith's Translation of the <u>Roman Comique</u>."
    <u>MLN</u> 40 (March):171-78.
         Issued by Griffin in 1775 after Goldsmith's death. Sells
    believes Goldsmith translated only the first nine chapters
    and perhaps the novel <u>The Rival Brothers</u>. Stein argues for
    only the first seven chapters: "It is now clear that
    Goldsmith worked without any reference to the French at
    all. He took Brown['s translation of 1700], condensed it
    in some places, amplified it in others, and devoted his
    energies toward making a smoother . . . version" (p. 174).

9   [WOOLF, VIRGINIA.] "Oliver Goldsmith." <u>TLS</u> (1 March):133-34.

1935

Front-page review-article. Discusses Goldsmith as an
author living in an age that saw the shift from patronage
to writing for booksellers, with a new public demanding
large compilations of information, a condition repugnant to
Goldsmith, although he eventually came to favor the change.
The writer could now be independent of aristocratic whims,
and Goldsmith was suited to take advantage of the changing
conditions.
Praises his "detached attitude and width of flavour"
(p. 133) as characteristic of his essays. Goldsmith's
narrators are always on the edge of the crowd as observers
of the common people, as seen in Citizen. The world of
Goldsmith's poetry is, of course, a flat and eyeless world;
swains sport with nymphs and the deep is finny" (p. 134).
Yet Goldsmith has a "peculiar reticence which forbids
us to dwell with him in complete intimacy . . .
he had only to write and he was among the angels, speaking
with a silver tongue in a world where all is ordered,
rational, and serene" (p. 134). Reprinted 1950.B3.

1935

A. Books

1   GWYNN, STEPHEN. Oliver Goldsmith. London: Butterworth;
      New York: Henry Holt, 332 pp.
         Strong on Goldsmith's early life in Ireland and on the
      special features of early eighteenth-century Ireland.
      Analysis of Goldsmith's character shows awareness of his
      Irish humor and tendency to tale-telling for effect.
      Otherwise, largely a rehash of Prior, Forster, and Dobson,
      though without Forster's sentimental view that Goldsmith
      was unmercifully exploited by the booksellers. Does not
      show knowledge of recent scholarship.

B. Shorter Writings

1   CHURCHILL, IRVING L. "Editions of Percy's Memoir of Gold-
      smith." MLN 50 (November):464-65.
         Corrects Balderston's misconception (1926.A) that the
      1801 edition is the only one. Reports at least six others:
      London: 1806, 1812, 1820, all published by the large
      group of booksellers who issued the 1801 edition, although
      the group's membership changed somewhat through the years.
      Other editions containing the Percy Life are the 1809
      Boston reprint by Hastings, Etheridge and Bliss, etc.;

the 1809 Baltimore edition published by Coale and Thomas, and the 1816 Baltimore edition issued by F. L. Lucas, Jr., and Joseph Cushing. Believes there were probably others. Two other editions contain a biographical preface clearly based on the Percy Life, but not identical to it: the 1816 Glasgow Miscellaneous Works, and the 1816 edition published at London, Liverpool, York, Edinburgh, and Glasgow, perhaps the edition used by Irving in preparing his 1825 prefatory Life (1825.B1).

2   FRIEDMAN, ARTHUR. "Goldsmith and the Weekly Magazine." MP 32 (February):281-99.
      December 1759 and the first half of 1760 were a fallow period for Goldsmith, but he appears to have been writing for the Weekly Magazine; or, Gentleman and Lady's Polite Companion, said to be "By a Society of Gentlemen" and published by I. Pottinger, who had published the Busy Body. Only one copy of the four numbers issued exists, in the Huntington Library; 29 December 1759 and 5, 12, and 19 January 1760. Goldsmith can be definitely connected with the magazine, since he published in it a poem and an essay later reprinted in Essays, 1765. Believes the following essays are by Goldsmith: "A Description of the Manners and Customs of the Native Irish," "Some Thoughts Preliminary to a General Peace," "Some Original Memoirs of the Late Famous Bishop of Cloyne," "The Life of the Hon. Robert Boyle," "Serious Reflections on the Life of the Late Mr. T----- C----- [Theophilus Cibber], by the Ordinary of Newgate," "A Sublime Passage in a French Sermon," "The Futility of Criticism," and "On the Present State of Our Theatres" [all reprinted by Friedman, Works 3:24-57; on 3:22, Friedman lists four other essays he believes Goldsmith may have written, but for which the corroborating evidence is not strong enough].

3   _____. "Goldsmith's Life of Bolingbroke and the Biographica Britannica." MLN 50 (January):25-29.
      Gibbs's introduction mentions the Biographica Britannica but does not indicate the depth of Goldsmith's use. Estimates about four-fifths borrowed from the source, with parallel passages for several instances. But Goldsmith added one of his characteristic metaphors--the idea that some liquors in fermentation become muddy, then clear, and some never clear.

1936

1936

A. Books--None

B. Shorter Writings

1   AUBIN, ROBERT C. Topographical Poetry in XVIII-Century
    England. Revolving Fund Series 6. New York: Modern
    Language Association, 428 pp., passim.
        Primarily concerned with minor poems, with little beyond
    incidental references, one of which concerning The Deserted
    Village is atypical: "It is this intrusion of the Industri-
    al Revolution and its patterns into the local poet's
    descriptions that particularly distinguishes Goldsmith's
    poem [The Deserted Village]" (p. 178).

2   FRASER HARRIS, D. F. "Goldsmith on his Teachers." DR 16:362-
    70.
        Of tangential interest at best, since discussion is
    mainly limited to Alexander Monro, his anatomy professor
    at Edinburgh, and Gaubius and Albinus, his chemistry and
    anatomy professors at Leyden, with a brief comment about
    Guillaume Francois Rouelle, a chemistry lecturer in Paris,
    briefly mentioned in chapter six of the Enquiry.

3   SEITZ, R. W. "Bibliographical Notes: Goldsmith to Sir William
    Chambers." TLS (26 September):772.
        Reports discovery of a letter and a note from Goldsmith
    to Sir William Chambers in volume two of Chambers's "Letter
    Books" (British Museum, Add. MS. 41, 134, f21b) of March
    1773. The first letter occasioned by a letter from Chambers,
    not surviving, concerning the production of She Stoops to
    Conquer. In return, Goldsmith is solicitous about Chambers's
    Dissertation on Oriental Gardening, the second edition of
    which had just been published, occasioning a satirical poem,
    which Goldsmith and Chambers thought was by Christopher
    Anstey, but actually written by William Mason, Walpole's
    friend. Elsewhere Chambers connects the poem with Mason.
    A letter from Chambers among the Goldsmith-Percy papers in
    the British Museum (Add. MS. 42, 515), accepts Goldsmith's
    offer to write a poem defending Chambers's book and then
    decides against it in a second version. Goldsmith's note
    reports Burke supports Chambers's views on his [Goldsmith's]
    and Reynolds's authority.

<u>1937</u>

A. Books--None

B. Shorter Writings

1 KENNY, R. W. "Ralph's <u>Case of Authors</u>: Its Influence on
   Goldsmith and D'Israeli." <u>PMLA</u> 52 (March):104-13.
       James Ralph's <u>Case of Authors by Profession</u>, a 1758
   pamphlet defending authors against booksellers, theatre
   managers, and politicians, was favorably reviewed by both
   the <u>Monthly Review</u> and the <u>Critical Review</u>. It may have
   suggested some ideas for Goldsmith's <u>Enquiry</u>, and Isaac
   D'Israeli quoted it extensively without acknowledgment in
   his <u>Calamities of Authors</u>. Ralph sees the bookseller and
   writer caught in a vicious circle, aiming at popular taste
   and thus both corrupt. Theatre managers put on revivals,
   not new plays, or write for political factions. Both
   Ralph and Goldsmith were on the staff of the <u>Monthly Review</u>
   in 1756-57 and may have discussed these problems. Goldsmith
   echoes Ralph's three points in the <u>Enquiry</u>, and seems to
   have lost the Secretaryship of the Society for the Arts
   because of Garrick's angry reaction to his unflattering
   remarks on theatre managers in the <u>Enquiry</u>.

2 POTTLE, FREDERICK A., et al., comps. <u>Index to the Private</u>
   <u>Papers of James Boswell from Malahide Castle in the</u>
   <u>Collections of Lt-Colonel Ralph Heyward Isham</u>. London:
   Oxford University Press, 379 pp.

3 SCHULZE, IRVING L. "An Inconsistency in the Thought of Goldsmith." <u>MLN</u> 52 (March):206-7.
       The inconsistency is the sympathy shown for the bold
   peasantry in <u>The Deserted Village</u> and the idea expressed
   in the "Essay on the Theatre" that "the great excite our
   pity by their fall; but not equally so of comedy, since
   the actors employed in it are originally so mean that they
   sink little by their fall" [<u>Works</u> 3:211].

4 SEITZ, R. W. "The Irish Background of Goldsmith's Social and
   Political Thought." <u>PMLA</u> 52 (June):405-41.
       Notes Goldsmith's habit of repeating favorite phrases and
   a few favorite ideas: admiration for the middle rank of
   society came from his Irish experiences, having become
   aware once in England that Ireland had virtually no middle
   group. Goldsmith argues that severe laws could be relaxed
   without endangering the constitution. His distrust of the
   magnates was that of an Irishman who had not moved outside

his own limited circle. Sir William Thornhill represents
the ideal Irish landlord, his nephew the villainous
squireen. Believes this aloofness with lords arose from
his countryman's prejudice. Usually the great are Goldsmith's villains.

When he arrived in England, his Irishness marked him.
Often adopted the pose of an Englishman in some early
essays, but frequently the Irishman breaks through. His
desire to stifle the Irishman in him sprang from an awareness of his own shortcomings as compared with the "moral
assets of the English middle class" (p. 407). He proceeded
to build his social and political philosophy largely from
elements absorbed in Ireland. Seitz sees a conflict
between his "English" and his "Irish" selves. The wealthy
merchant becomes a symbol of Goldsmith's bogeyman, luxury.
"The significant element in Goldsmith's social and political
thought depends on his having remained an Irishman" (p. 408).
Thus, he opposed the rise of commerce and imperialism.

1938

A. Books--None

B. Shorter Writings

1   EMERY, JOHN P. "An Unpublished Letter from Arthur Murphy to
    Goldsmith Concerning She Stoops to Conquer." PQ 17
    (January):88-90.
        Warns Goldsmith about Garrick and regrets that the press
    of his own law business prevents him from doing an epilogue
    for the play.

2   FRIEDMAN, ARTHUR. "Goldsmith and the Marquis d'Argens." MLN
    53 (March):173-76.
        The British Magazine, May 1760, contains the anonymous
    essay "A Dream," first ascribed to Goldsmith by Thomas
    Wright in Essays and Criticisms by Goldsmith, 1798, and
    ever since has appeared in most collected editions. It
    is closely imitated from "Dix-neuvième Songe," Songes
    Philosophiques by the Marquis d'Argens, as evidence from
    parallel passages shows.

3   _____. "The Immediate Occasion of Goldsmith's Citizen of
    the World, Letter XXXVIII." PQ 17 (January):82-84.
        The trial of Earl Ferrers for murdering his steward, a
    notorious crime in early 1760, was widely reported, but
    Goldsmith did not mention it until 19 May 1760, two weeks

after the earl's execution, praising the impartiality of
justice. Letters pro and con were frequent in the news-
papers about the time of the trial. It seems highly
probable that the immediate occasion was a defense in the
Public Ledger on 8 May of impartiality, attacked by "Anglo
Britannicus" in a letter to Read's Weekly Journal; or,
British Gazeteer for 17 May, especially citation of the
Prince of Charolais's being pardoned by the King of France
three times for murder.

4   HOWARTH, R. G. "Proverbs in The Good Natur'd Man." N&Q 174
    (2 April):245.
        Quotes Croaker's own paraphrase of Temple's conclusion
    to his "On Poetry." Honeywood's reply is one of George
    Herbert's "Outlandish Proverbs," 1640 [translated proverbs]
    which existed in a versified form by the Rev. Rowland
    Watkins. Goldsmith may have known the phrase as a proverb
    without knowing its origin. Both Croaker and Honeywood
    are speaking with second-hand sententiousness. Previous
    dialogue may contain quotations other than from Citizen,
    letter 40. See 1934.B1 and 1934.B6.

5   REYNOLDS, W. VAUGHAN. "Goldsmith's Critical Outlook." RES 14
    (April):155-72.
        Goldsmith's criticism was "based upon sound and reason-
    able principles. He shared the general opinions of the
    Augustan critics, but his judgment was guided by commonsense,
    honesty, and courage" (p. 155). In Goldsmith's criticism,
    the "rules" do not replace feeling, and he follows the
    principles of Pope's Essay on Criticism, emphasizing
    instruction and hoping pleasure is possible.

6   SEITZ, R. W. "Some of Goldsmith's Second Thoughts on English
    History." MP 35 (February):279-88.
        A comparison of his political views expressed in his
    1764 History of England in a Series of Letters . . . and
    his 1771 History of England shows some changes in emphases
    between his earlier and later attitudes toward monarchy,
    aristocracy, and the people, the conventional classifica-
    tions used at the time. Believes the changes are to be
    accounted for more by changes in Goldsmith's personal
    situation, although some may be accounted for by changes in
    politics. In 1771, Goldsmith shows less tendency to stress
    a strong monarchy, and is even farther from finding an ideal
    king among those since Henry VII. Seitz infers Goldsmith's
    growing desire for a pension was a strong factor in many of
    these changes. His sense of his own dignity led him to
    reject Parson Scott's indirect offer of a pension about

1939

1767-70. Goldsmith was probably not aware of all his
motives in his position, but he desired to maintain his
reputation for independence while still hoping for reward,
and was caught in something of a labyrinth.

1939

A. Books--None

B. Shorter Writings

1   IGNOTO [pseud.]. "Goldsmith Repeating Himself at Length."
N&Q 176 (17 June):424.
    The "City Night Piece" in Bee, No. 4, is reprinted in
Citizen, Letter 117. [Noted by Gibbs in his edition, 3:422,
note 3].

2   CHEN SHOU-YI. "Oliver Goldsmith and his Chinese Letters."
T'ien Hsia Monthly 8 (January):34-52.
    Believes Goldsmith's letter series marks the culmination
of English interest in Chinese culture, which was important
but did not become the dominant force it did in France. In
1758 and 1759, he had reviewed books concerning China, and
Bee, No. 6, uses a Chinese story. Took Fum Hoam's name
from Gueullette's Contes Chinoises and the first half of
Lien Chi's from Walpole's Letter from XoHo, 1757. Mainly
used Le Comte's Nouveau Memoires and Du Halde's Description,
and acknowledged both. He reflects both the "contemporary
English taste for things Chinese, but also reveals the
author's own interest in Chinese people" (p. 43), but does
not aspire to be a critic or interpreter of Chinese culture,
and generally criticizes or satirizes England without
exalting China. China is sometimes ridiculed. Most "quotations" by Confucius are fabricated by Goldsmith.

3   WALCUTT, CHARLES C. "Goldsmith and Franklin on Sheep's Tails."
N&Q 177 (6 December):438-39.
    In 1765, in London representing Pennsylvania Franklin
wrote "To the Editor of a Newspaper" (quoted from Smyth's
edition of Franklin's Works; whether or not ever published
is not known) of American sheep with tails so woolly they
have a little car or wagon to support the tail. He took
the reference almost certainly from Goldsmith's reference
to fat-tailed Indian or Asiatic sheep in "On Dress," just
then republished in Essays, 1765, from Bee, 1759, when
Franklin was also in London. Borrowing from the more
recently published book seems more likely.

1940

A. Books

1 PADEN, WILLIAM D., and HYDER, CLYDE KENNETH. A Concordance to
   the Poems of Oliver Goldsmith. Lawrence: University of
   Kansas Press, 192 pp.
       A useful tool.

B. Shorter Writings

1 ELIOT, T. S. [Comments on Goldsmith.] In London: A Poem and
   the Vanity of Human Wishes. . . . by Samuel Johnson. With
   an Introductory Note by T. S. Eliot. In English Critical
   Essays: Twentieth Century. Selected with an Introduction
   by Phyllis M. Jones. World's Classics Edition, London:
   Oxford University Press, pp. 301-10.
       A reprint of 1930.B6.

2 FRIEDMAN, ARTHUR. "Goldsmith and Jean Rousset de Missy." PQ
   19 (October):409-11.
       The Lady's Magazine for September 1760, contains the
   anonymous essay "Of the Assemblies of Russia," which
   Goldsmith later reprinted in Essays, 1765. He did not use
   a Russian source for Peter the Great's "Rules for Governing
   Assemblies," but translated it from de Missy's Memoires du
   Regne de Catherine Imperatrice & Souveraine de Toute de
   Russie, La Haye, 1728. Prints parallel passages. Rules
   eight and nine do not appear in de Missy, and Friedman
   suggests he may have invented them, although they may have
   been suggested by other passages in de Missy.

3 _____. "Goldsmith and Steele's Englishman." MLN 55
   (April):294-96.
       Letter 78, Citizen of the World, has for its source a
   letter describing the French signed "Ralph English" in
   Steele's Englishman, No. 40 (5 January 1713/14). Paragraph
   two has some paraphrase, paragraph six has a longer one, and
   the close of paragraph eight is another paraphrase.
   Paragraph nine is slightly expanded from Steele's original.

4 HAYDON, FRANCIS M. "Goldsmith as a Biographer." SAQ 39
   (January):50-57.
       Goldsmith holds a place of double importance in the
   history of biography as a literary form, as a disciple of
   Samuel Johnson and as a forerunner of Boswell. He
   illustrated advanced theories of biography which were an
   advance beyond most of his contemporaries in the theory

1940

and practice of biography. Primarily for the general reader.

5   HEILMAN, ROBERT B. "The Sentimentalism of Goldsmith's <u>Good-Natur'd Man</u>." In <u>Studies for William A. Read: A Miscellany Presented by Some of his Friends</u>. Edited by Nathaniel M. Caffee and Thomas A. Kirby. University: Louisiana State University Press, pp. 237-53.
    Argues that Goldsmith sought to attack sentimentalism by presenting his attack as a burlesque--Honeywood is a burlesque of the sentimental hero who believes he is animated by benevolence. The play's plotting owes something to the <u>Vicar</u> in that Honeywood's uncle, Sir William Honeywood, untangles the problems very much as does Sir William Thornhill in the novel. Part of the problem with the play is that Honeywood is so similar to heroes of sentimental comedies that the burlesque nature of the play is not entirely clear, chiefly because Goldsmith had not discovered ways to signal his audience he was satirizing sentimental comedy.

<u>1941</u>

A. Books--None

B. Shorter Writings

1   C[RANE], R[ONALD] S. "Goldsmith." In <u>The Cambridge Bibliography of English Literature</u>. Edited by F. W. Bateson. New York: Macmillan; Cambridge: University Press, 2:636-50.
    The definitive bibliography of Goldsmith's own writings and of writings about him at the time of its publication; some ascriptions have been added and deleted by Friedman in the <u>NCBEL</u> (1971.B1).

2   De C., J. P. "Dr. James's Powders." <u>N&Q</u> 180 (18 January): 48.
    Quotes a letter from Mrs. Nora Monckton from the London <u>Times</u> of early January 1930, stating that the powders were not always effective as shown by a letter from Comte de Cely written during Wellington's Peninsular Campaign, describing how Lady Lainage Osborn gave a "bootler" [butler] eight grains of James's powders for indigestion and he survived because of a strong constitution.

3   HAGGIS, A. W. "Dr. James's Powders." <u>N&Q</u> 180 (25 January): 68-69.

Gives a brief history of James's powders from A. C. Wotton's Chronicles of Pharmacy, London, 1910: patented in 1747 with antimony oxide the active ingredient. Has not heard of any other famous person's death ascribed to the powders besides Goldsmith's. The debate after Goldsmith's death was never settled, and the exact causes of his death are still being debated.

4   HEAL, AMBROSE. "Dr. James's Powders." N&Q 180 (18 January): 48.
        The question of the role of the powders in Goldsmith's death has already been amply debated; reports the only authenticated fatality was an ox killed by Lady Lainage Osborn about 1809.

5   LYTTON SELLS, ARTHUR. "Oliver Goldsmith's Influence on the French Stage." Durham University Journal, 33 (March):88-101.
        The high prestige of French drama in Georgian England led to much adaptation from French drama from Molière, Destouches, etc. "Goldsmith with a lighter touch . . . appeared to follow his [Arthur Murphy's] example. In both The Good Natur'd Man and She Stoops to Conquer, the central scenes were inspired by Marivaux" (p. 89). Goldsmith was steeped in French drama, and the sale catalogue of his library shows eighteen titles, most of them multi-volume sets of French drama. Many scenes derive from J. C. Dancourt's Le Glorieux, unknown to most Goldsmith students, and also D'Ancourt's La Maison de Campagne. Among the French imitations of She Stoops to Conquer are the anonymous La Fausse Auberge, then in 1821 La Voyage à Dieppe uses the false night-journey motif, and in 1876 Henri Crisafulli's L'Hôtel Godelot also imitates the play. The Good Natur'd Man was not widely known in France, but besides these imitations, there were frequent editions of She Stoops to Conquer.

6   POWELL, L. F. "Dr. James's Powders." N&Q 180 (18 January):48.
        The effect of the powders on Goldsmith is discussed in Birkbeck Hill's Boswell 3:501 [Hill-Powell, ed., 3:501].

1942

1942

A. Books--None

B. Shorter Writings

  1   BELL, HOWARD, Jr. "Goldsmith and the Pickle-Shop." <u>MLN</u> 57
       (February):121-22.
            The reference is to <u>Boswell</u>, ed. Hill, 2:217-19 [Hill-
       Powell, ed., 2:218-19], whether or not pickle-shops are
       necessary. "Goldsmith's argument here should not, then, be
       construed as an attack on all luxury or as a contradiction
       of the opinion expressed in Letter 11 of the <u>Citizen</u> that
       the innocent indulgence of human desires for pleasure is
       socially beneficial" (p. 122).

  2   ELIOT, T. S. [Comments on Goldsmith.] In <u>London: A Poem and</u>
       <u>the Vanity of Human Wishes</u>. . . . by Samuel Johnson. With
       an Introductory Note by T. S. Eliot. In <u>English Critical</u>
       <u>Essays: Twentieth Century</u>. Selected with an Introduction
       by Phyllis M. Jones. World's Classics Edition, London:
       Oxford University Press, pp. 301-10.
            Reprint of 1930.B6.

  3   LYNSKEY, WINIFRED. "Pluche and Derham: New Sources of
       Goldsmith." <u>PMLA</u> 57 (June):435-45.
            The sources are Abbe Pluche, <u>La Spectacle de la Nature</u>,
       Paris, 1732-51, eight volumes, and William Derham, <u>Physico-</u>
       <u>Theology</u>, London, 1713, both of which use the argument from
       design. Lytton Sells had previously asserted there was no
       proof of debt to Pluche, and Pitman similarly for Derham.
       Lynskey shows how he drew on both for his prefaces to
       <u>Brookes' Natural History</u> and to <u>Animated Nature</u>, but some-
       what surprisingly Goldsmith avoids using the argument from
       design in <u>Animated Nature</u> or certainly uses it far less
       than any other contemporary popularizers.

  4   PIOZZI, HESTER LYNCH THRALE. <u>Thraliana: The Diary of Mrs.</u>
       <u>Hester Lynch Thrale (later Mrs. Piozzi), 1776-1809</u>.
       2 vols. Edited by Katharine C. Balderston. Oxford:
       Clarendon Press, passim.
            The raw material out of which Mrs. Thrale mined her
       <u>Anecdotes of Samuel Johnson</u> (1785.B2) and from which later
       editors mined her <u>Diary</u> (1861.B1).

1943

A. Books--None

B. Shorter Writings

1   LYNSKEY, WINIFRED. "The Scientific Sources of Goldsmith's
     <u>Animated Nature</u>." <u>SP</u> 40 (January):33-57.
          Pitman divided the sources for <u>Animated Nature</u> into
     three groups--those like Linnaeus, Gesner, or Boyle, which
     are purely scientific, or like Buffon, which aims to
     popularize genuine science; second, travels and voyages,
     which contain much description of animals and natural
     events even though their primary purpose is not scientific;
     and the ancient writers who serve to provide details and
     anecdotes rather than scientific information. Pitman saw
     Goldsmith's principal sources as Gesner, Swammerdam,
     Willoughby, Ray, Brisson, Linnaeus, and Reamur; but Lynskey
     argues his principal sources are Willoughby, Pluche,
     Pennant, and R. Brookes.

2   MOORE, JOHN ROBERT. "Goldsmith's Degenerate Song-Birds: An
     Eighteenth-Century Fallacy in Ornithology." <u>Isis</u> 34
     (Spring):324-27.
          In <u>Deserted Village</u>, lines 346-49, draws upon Buffon's
     idea that all animal species had degenerated in America, so
     that the birds did not sing in Georgia.

3   SMITH, JOHN H. "Tony Lumpkin and the English Booby Type in
     Antecedent English Comedy." <u>PMLA</u> 58 (December):1038-49.
          Notes that Forster (1848.A2) had remarked the similarity
     between Humphry Gubbin in Steele's <u>Tender Husband</u>, a
     similarity supported by Forsythe (1912.B1). Sees similarity
     in Tony's spelling out a letter to Dryden's <u>Wild Gallant</u>,
     to Wycherley's <u>Plain Dealer</u>, to Cibber's <u>Woman's Wit; or
     the Lady in Fashion</u>. Goldsmith was indebted to five old
     plays: "It is my impression that this principle holds, in
     the main, for both his comedies, which seem to result not
     from first-hand observation and copying after nature, but
     from reworkings of conventional materials by his highly
     creative sense of the comic. In Tony's case Goldsmith's
     genius is revealed as the sort that works with literary
     materials" (p. 1049). Most of these similarities are
     equally explainable as coincidences. Smith speculates
     (p. 1047) that "Surely he would have owned and been
     familiar with sets of Dryden, Steele, Cibber, and Shadwell,"
     but the sale catalogue of Goldsmith's library (1774.A6,
     1837.Al, and 1973.B9) shows he owned only Cibber from this
     group.

1944

1944

A. Books--None

B. Shorter Writings

    1   BELL, HOWARD, Jr. "The Deserted Village and Goldsmith's
         Social Doctrines." PMLA 59 (September):747-72.
              The poem was written as a warning of what might happen
         to every other village in England, and this side of the
         poem has been neglected by modern critics: argues
         Goldsmith wrote the poem to discuss current social issues.
         Concerned to show what ideas Goldsmith was trying to
         present, what made him consider the problem not merely
         unfortunate but virtually fatal to national health. His
         attack is on commerce and the commercial revolution
         conquering the agrarian interest. Finds the poem congruent
         with his ideas on luxury, an aristocracy of wealth and
         commerce expressed in other writings, especially the Vicar
         and Citizen.

    2   KNIGHT, DOUGLAS. "Two Issues of Goldsmith's Bee." N&Q 187
         (16 December):276.
              Describes an unbound set of the Bee in the Yale Library
         in which No. 1 differs typographically from most other
         copies and argues this one may be an earlier version.

    3   KRAUSE, GERD. "Oliver Goldsmiths Stellung zum Bauerntum in
         Zuzammenhang seines Dichterischen Werkes." Anglia 67-68:
         341-52.
              Emphasizes the large number of rural elements in Gold-
         smith's work--the setting, characters, idealization of the
         village, even though Goldsmith himself seems to have
         identified with urban culture. But he was concerned with
         peaceful, homely family circle and idealizing a simpler
         life. Especially in his verse, the importance of a free
         and independent peasantry is repeatedly stressed in both
         The Traveller and The Deserted Village.

    4   LYNSKEY, WINIFRED. "Goldsmith and the Warfare in Nature."
         PQ 23 (October):333-42.
              Argues Goldsmith is not nearly as optimistic as his
         sources and other popularizers about the beneficence of
         the universal order--most are quite complacent about the
         struggle in nature. In discussing the problem of predator
         and prey, Goldsmith sometimes alters his sources to favor
         the prey among carnivorous creatures. "So to put the
         matter bluntly, in the struggle for existence, as it

prevails in <u>Animated Nature</u>, Goldsmith neither permitted,
praised, nor justified the warfare in nature on grounds of
rational and necessary evil. Goldsmith escaped from the
strictures of that eighteenth-century philosophy which,
as Voltaire had remarked, cried out in a lamentable voice
that everything was good" (p. 342).

5   PRICE, LAWRENCE M. "The Works of Oliver Goldsmith on the
     German Stage, 1776-1795." <u>MLQ</u> (December):481-86.
         <u>She Stoops to Conquer</u> was translated and produced in
     1773, printed in 1777. Adapted with German characters and
     settings and became a permanent repertory piece of the
     German stage either in the 1773 translation with aristo-
     cratic characters or the slightly later middle class
     adaptation. <u>The Good Natur'd Man</u> was also translated, but
     never so popular. The <u>Vicar</u> was dramatized as were other
     eighteenth-century English novels. Generally, the plays
     were treated like those of other eighteenth-century authors
     --simplified, nationalized, and moralized, so that poetic
     justice prevailed.

6   STARKEY, JAMES [Seumas O'Sullivan]. "Goldsmith and the <u>Bee</u>"
     and "Goldsmith's Birthplace." In <u>Essays and Recollections</u>.
     Dublin: Talbot Press, pp. 24-37.
         "Goldsmith and the <u>Bee</u>" offers nothing new and attacks
     those who have pointed out how much of <u>The Bee</u> is borrowed
     from other writers. "Goldsmith's Birthplace" discusses the
     evidence set forth in Mangin's <u>Essay on Light Reading</u>
     (1808.B2) for Smith-Hill as Goldsmith's birthplace without
     realizing that Mrs. Hodson's narrative, the Goldsmith
     family Bible, and Goldsmith's 1773 memorandum to Percy all
     identify Pallas as his birthplace, not just Johnson's
     epitaph. Ignores recent scholarship.

<u>1945</u>

A. Books--None

B. Shorter Writings

1   BARNETT, GEORGE L. "Two Unacknowledged Adaptations from
     Goldsmith." <u>MLQ</u> 6 (March):29-30.
         Letter 69, <u>Citizen</u>, "The Fear of Mad Dogs" republished
     much altered in the <u>Gentleman's Magazine</u> 30 (August 1760).
     The "Life of Parnell," prefaced to Davies's selection of
     Parnell's poems, published 13 July 1770, appears prefaced
     to Bell's small, two-volume edition of Parnell in the

1945

"Poets of Great Britain" series, with considerable
rearrangement, alteration, and condensation sometimes for
the sake of compression; however, "Other changes seem to
have been made for the sole purpose of concealing the
source" (p. 30).

2   HAMMER, CARL, Jr. "Goethe's Estimate of Goldsmith." JEPG 44,
no. 2:131-38.
Goethe's comments in Dichtung und Wahrheit of 1811-12
record experiences related to Werther and slightly later
periods much after the fact. What Goethe speaks of as
coming from Goldsmith may well have happened to him in his
subjective experience and was a "cultural experience" of
great personal intensity. He makes continual references in
his late writings to the influence of Shakespeare, Sterne,
and Goldsmith as deeply influential on him: "Again and
again he turned to the writings of that 'productive poet,'
whose genial insight into humanity called forth his
admiration. . . . Goldsmith . . . in Goethe's own words,
represented for him one of the most far-reaching formative
influences of his youth" (p. 138).

3   LYNSKEY, WINIFRED. "Goldsmith and the Chain of Being." JHI
6 (June):363-74.
Argues that Goldsmith used the chain-of-being idea as a
principle of organization in Animated Nature: "I know of
no other writer of natural history in the eighteenth
century--even including Buffon, the chief source of Goldsmith's natural history--in whom the chain is presented
both philosophically and literally." Argues that for
Goldsmith the chain offered a simple means of classification
for the popular reader, but points out Goldsmith abandons
the argument from design, urging a philosophical basis for
his system, not a theological one. See 1946.B3.

4   SEEBER, EDWARD D. "Goldsmith's American Tigers." MLQ 6
(December):417-19.
The reference to tigers in Deserted Village, line 355,
has been used as an instance of Goldsmith's ignorance, but
Buffon referred to American tigers, meaning cougars or
pumas, both of which are common in Alabama, not jaguars,
which do not range north of Texas. Cites support from the
Dictionary of American English.

1946

A. Books--None

B. Shorter Writings

1   FRIEDMAN, ARTHUR. "Goldsmith's Contributions to the Critical
    Review." MP 44 (August):23-52.
        Reconsiders the ascriptions to Goldsmith and drops
    eight reviews from the canon and considers six others
    doubtful. These changes are reflected in Works 1:145-238.

2   JONES, CLAUDE E. Goldsmith's 'Natural History'--A Plan."
    N&Q 191 (21 September):116-18.
        Four months after the publication of Animated Nature,
    the Critical Review published a four-part review in
    August, September, October, and November 1774. The November
    issue prints "A Plan" different from the scheme for the
    work described in the preface. Jones reprints this "Plan"
    in full and speculates that it may have been drawn up for
    the publisher William Griffin five years earlier when the
    work was contracted for.

3   LOVEJOY, ARTHUR O. "Goldsmith and the Chain of Being." JHI
    7 (January):91-98.
        A reply to 1945.B3. Finds Lynskey's argument greatly
    exaggerated and argues that she tries to make Goldsmith
    more consistent than he is. Finds he fails to classify
    because his classes are not logical and his criteria for
    ranking various species are inconsistent. "But he did not
    exhibit, nor make any very sedulous and consistent attempt
    to exhibit, the entire animal kingdom as constituting such
    a chain" (p. 98).

4   NEVEU, RAYMOND. "Oliver Goldsmith, Poète et Médecin."
    Mémoires de la Société Française d'Histoire de le Médecin
    2:3-9.
        A general account, emphasizing Goldsmith's versatility
    in writing.

5   SEEBER, EDWARD D., and REMAK, HENRY H. "The First French
    Translation of The Deserted Village." MLR 41 (January):
    62-67.
        Usually Chevalier J.-J. Rutledge's Le Retour de
    Philosophe (Bruxelles, 1772) is considered the first French
    translation, though an "imitation libre." Charles-Michel
    Campion, a prominent tax collector, poet, and engraver of
    Orleans and Marseilles, left a manuscript translation

1946

which Seeber and Remak believe antedates Rutledge's.
Campion's translation is remarkably faithful compared with
other eighteenth-century French translations of English
authors but does expand the original 430 lines to 560 and
uses names with a classical flavor instead of the English
ones Goldsmith had used.

6 TRACY, C. R. "Browning and Goldsmith." <u>PMLA</u> 61 (March):600-1.
Letter 117, <u>Citizen of the World</u>, may have suggested
elements to Browning for "Love among the Ruins"--musing on
London solitude at two a.m. that the city will pass away
and make solitude permanent. The descriptions of ruined
cities are similar, and neither author particularizes any
certain city. Lien Chi argues decay is inevitable;
Browning's faith lies in the perpetual renewal of the race
through romantic love. Browning's father liked Goldsmith
and had a copy of <u>The Citizen of the World</u> in his library,
so that Browning could have read the letter in question.

<u>1947</u>

A. Books--None

B. Shorter Writings

1 ATKINSON, A. D. "Goldsmith Borrows." <u>TLS</u> (25 January): 5.
Letter 6 of Defoe's <u>Tour through England and Wales</u>
contains a description of Bath and the bathing there to
which Goldsmith's description of a lady bathing in the <u>Life
of Nash</u> has close verbal similarities.

2 [CAMPBELL, THOMAS.] <u>Dr. Campbell's Diary of a Visit to England
in 1775</u>. Newly edited from the manuscript by James L.
Clifford, with an Introduction by S. C. Roberts. Cambridge:
University Press, 162 pp.
A new edition of 1854.B1.

3 COWLEY, PATRICK. "The Eighteenth-Century Divine." <u>Theology</u>
50, no. 3 (July):258-63.
Argues that because both his father and his maternal
grandfather were clergymen, Goldsmith deserves a hearing
on what the typical eighteenth-century clergyman was like,
offering his early training for the clergy as an additional,
supporting reason. Notes the Vicar's high standard of not
using a curate, and his more personal Whistonian view
favoring clerical monogamy. In the <u>Deserted Village</u>,
Goldsmith stresses the parson's willingness to stay in his

living, without ambitions for a better one, attending
strictly to his pastoral duties. Finds his best comments
on pristly life and work in a not very widely known essay
["Of Eloquence," Bee, No. 7; Works 1:476-483]. "The
picture of the eighteenth century divine which emerges from
Goldsmith's pages is a high ideal, even though it is lack-
ing in any view of sacramental belief and practice" (p. 263).

4 ELIOT, T. S. [Comments on Goldsmith.] In London: A Poem and
   The Vanity of Human Wishes. . . . by Samuel Johnson. With
   an Introductory Note by T. S. Eliot. In English Critical
   Essays: Twentieth Century. Selected with an Introduction
   by Phyllis M. Jones. World's Classics Editions, London:
   Oxford University Press, pp. 301-10.
      A reprint of 1930.B6.

5 JACKSON, R. WYSE. "Goldsmith in Camouflage." Dublin Magazine,
   n.s. 22, no. 3 (July-September):47-53.
      Considers the problems associated with Goldsmith's life,
   finding much still needs explanation. Argues that what
   his contemporaries said about him is mostly wrong, what he
   said about himself is certainly false, and what he did not
   say is most likely to be true. Believes Boswell misunderstood him, that Marlow is a self-portrait. Argues the need
   for fuller psychological study, drawn from his writings,
   remembering he is always the complete Irishman. Commends
   King's biography (1910.A1).

                              1948

A. Books--None

B. Shorter Writings

1 BROWN, WALLACE C. "Goldsmith: The Didactic Lyric." In The
   Triumph of Form: A Study of Later Masters of the Heroic
   Couplet. Chapel Hill: University of North Carolina Press,
   pp. 142-61.
      Considers The Deserted Village undoubtedly his best,
   but surveys Goldsmith's lesser works in heroic couplet,
   especially his epilogues. The Traveller is simpler, more
   panoramic, with its structure of introduction, survey of
   four countries, and conclusion. Notes no triplets or
   alexandrines, citing Pope's influence, and the repetition
   of identical syntactical structures. Finds Goldsmith's
   contribution chiefly in his use of word repetition for
   such effects as emphasis, progression of thought, and
   increased unity, with repetition and alliteration both
   insinuating a lyric quality. Finds his peculiar quality

1948

seen most clearly in The Deserted Village, with only Gray's
"Elegy" comparable in this respect. Uses not panoramic
method but contrasting themes for a more complex structure
than The Traveller. Argues that Deserted Village's
structure is "like sonata form" (p. 154).

2   McKILLOP, ALAN D. English Literature from Dryden to Burns.
New York and London: Appleton-Century-Crofts, pp. 338-41.
A manual for college students, but reliable, if brief
discussion, stressing lack of reliable biographical infor-
mation except for his fifteen-year London literary career.
Traces writing chronologically, with a critical sentence or
two about the major works, the fullest discussion being of
The Deserted Village, reflecting a somewhat outdated taste.

3   SHERBURN, GEORGE. "The Restoration and Eighteenth Century
(1660-1789)." In A Literary History of England. Edited by
Albert C. Baugh. New York and London: Appleton-Century-
Crofts, pp. 1042-44, 1056-62.
A major critical estimate in a major literary history.
Emphasizes Goldsmith's opposition to sentimental comedy in
theory and practice, especially praising She Stoops to
Conquer. Traces Goldsmith's development from essayist to
novelist, an essayist who "excels in human details . . .
[and] creates his persons not merely as mouthpieces or
as gorgeous eccentrics: strange as they are, he really
likes them" (p. 1058), with high praise for the Citizen as
"perhaps Goldsmith's best sustained work" (p. 1059). Points
out that unlike his French philosophe models, Goldsmith did
not need to attack political tyranny and religious bigotry
and so could be more relaxed, literary, and "less of the
revolutionary" (p. 1059). Goldsmith portrays simplicity in
the Vicar: "The tone of the novel is emotional and benevo-
list, but it must be noted that the good vicar is
habitually caustic as to the absurdities of his socially
ambitious females" (p. 1061). Finds verse "interesting
but unimportant" (p. 1062). "Aesthetically he was a
traditionalist; mentally he was of the Enlightenment; he
was too hard-headed to be a sentimentalist, and too
sympathetic to be an outright satirist" (p. 1062). Second
edition: 1967.B7.

4   THORPE, JAMES. "Issues of the First Edition of The Vicar of
Wakefield." Papers of the Bibliographical Society of
America 42:312-15.
Iolo Williams's opinion that four issues of the first
edition of the Vicar exist, distinguishable by variant
misprints, has caused much higher prices for the one

Williams hesitantly identified as the first issue. Thorpe
concludes, on the basis of extensive collation, that the
variants are insignificant: "There is every reason to be
certain that there was only one issue of the first edition
and that the existence of the three variable points (and
of others postulated) was occasioned by corrections made
in the press while sheets were being run off" (p. 314).
Quotes Williams's similar conclusion about variants in the
first edition of The Good Natur'd Man to support his
argument.

1949

A. Books--None

B. Shorter Writings

1   ANGUS-BUTTERWORTH, L[IONEL] M. "Goldsmith as Historian."
    SAQ 48 (April):251-57.
        Written for the general reader, but praises the reada-
    bility of the histories and notes their popularity as
    textbooks. Reprinted: 1961.B2.

2   McADAM, EDWARD L. "Goldsmith, the Good-Natured Man." In The
    Age of Johnson: Essays Presented to Chauncey Brewster
    Tinker. [Edited by Frederick W. Hilles.] Introduction by
    Wilmarth S. Lewis. New Haven: Yale University Press,
    pp. 41-47.
        Primarily a character sketch rather than a discussion of
    his writing. Sees his dilemma as being generous but in-
    secure. Notes he knew a good bit about London low-life,
    citing Lien Chi's experience with the prostitute,
    references in Nash, and Marlow's easy behavior with such
    women, and similarly with gambling, citing Citizen, Letter
    6. Finds the Vicar "primarily a humorous idealization of
    Goldsmith's early life" (p. 46), and idealization of the
    past in The Traveller and The Deserted Village, the latter
    the final expression of Goldsmith's insecurity in London"
    (p. 47). Conclusion: "But he exists for us still as the
    good-natured man, whom he portrayed so often, always
    seeking a security which he did not find and pleasure
    which could not wholly satisfy him, justifying and then
    condemning the luxury which he loved--a weak man who never
    gave up, a great artist who, even displaying his own
    weaknesses, contributed far more than did Garrick to the
    gaiety of nations" (p. 47).

1950

1950

A. Books--None

B. Shorter Writings

  1   BOSWELL, JAMES. Boswell's London Journal, 1762-1763. Now
      first Published from the Original Manuscript, with an
      Introduction and Notes by Frederick A. Pottle, with a
      Preface by Christopher Morley. [Yale Editions of the
      Private Papers of James Boswell.] New York: McGraw-Hill,
      xxix, 320 pp., passim.
         Describes Boswell's first meeting with Goldsmith and
      growing knowledge of him and other members of the Johnson
      circle. The basis for Boswell's account of these years in
      1791.B1.

  2   JEFFERSON, D. W. "Observations on The Vicar of Wakefield."
      Cambridge Journal 3 (July):621-28.
         Analysis of Goldsmith's treatment of the Vicar's mis-
      fortunes shows Goldsmith deliberately reduces their
      emotional effect by "echoing literary convention half way
      to parody" by general reduction of scale: all disasters
      occur on a small scale and open with "almost comic
      abruptness" (p. 622). The Vicar's telling the story is of
      great importance: we cannot be sure if he is emotionally
      limited or urbane and controlled in the face of disasters,
      even those without a comic element like the burning of his
      house: "The way the vicar's misfortunes are precipitated
      makes him seem the victim of a series of practical jokes
      on the part of an unkind fate. . . . Reduction of scale by
      the manipulation of traditional and conventional features
      is the technical formula on which the novel is based.
      Everywhere we meet the familiar and the archetypal, neatly
      scaled down" (p. 624). This effect presents a seriously
      admirable life, while its neat smallness and his genial
      complacency amuse us. Mixing various conventions--
      comedy of manners, the picaresque, the digressive tale-
      within-a-tale, the didactic digression of the sermon, all
      clearly identifiable in reduced form--emphasizes artifice
      and establishes aesthetic distance.

  3   WOOLF, VIRGINIA. "Oliver Goldsmith." In The Captain's Death
      Bed and Other Essays. New York: Harcourt, Brace, pp. 3-
      14.
         Reprint of 1934.B9.

1951

A. Books

1   JACKSON, R. WYSE. <u>Oliver Goldsmith: Essays Toward an
     Interpretation</u>. Dublin: Association for Promoting
     Christian Knowledge, 47 pp.
         Ten very rambling, digressive essays arranged in rough
     chronological order. Stresses the importance of
     Goldsmith's Irish background, praising King's (1910.A1)
     and Gwynn's (1935.A1) biographies. Uses Boswell but
     discounts his version of Goldsmith. Main topics are
     his Irish background, his education at school and at
     Trinity, his plays, the discovery of new essays by Crane
     and Friedman, and his humility in religion.

B. Shorter Writings

1   BARBIER, C. P. "Goldsmith en France au XVIIIe Siècle: <u>Les
     Essays</u> et <u>le Vicar de Wakefield</u>." <u>Revue de la Littérature
     Comparée</u> 25, no. 3 (December):385-402.
         The impact of Goldsmith's essays including the <u>Citizen</u>
     and <u>Vicar</u> was small until after 1780. The <u>Citizen</u> was
     translated by Pierre Poivre immediately following its
     English publication, but since it shows its derivation from
     both Montesquieu and d'Argens it had few readers. <u>Essays</u>,
     1765, made little impression, as did the <u>Bee</u>, and only the
     appearance of Mme. de Montession's translation of the <u>Vicar</u>
     in 1767 really introduced Goldsmith to the French. Early
     critics are hard on the translation but note pleasure in
     reading book for its nature and truth, finding it somewhat
     unoriginal and lacking verve of Fielding.
         <u>Essays</u> were considered indifferent work until Prince
     Boris de Golitzin praised them in 1787 in <u>L'Année Litteraire</u>,
     as did De Larival elsewhere. Goldsmith was beginning to be
     ranked immediately after Richardson and Fielding, and the
     public showed an interest in <u>Essays</u> because they were
     written by the author of the <u>Vicar</u>, and <u>Essays</u> became a
     book recommended to young people for its morality. "Asem"
     especially popular. Attributes Goldsmith's rise in
     popularity after 1780 to a new interest in England, almost
     Anglomania, in which all English authors' popularity
     increased greatly.

*2   CHURCH, RICHARD. <u>The Growth of the English Novel</u>. London:
     Methuen, Home Study Books, 179 pp.
         Sees Goldsmith as typically English: "and in his one
     novel <u>The Vicar of Wakefield</u> he had added to English fiction

one of its more central and representative examples" (p. 90). Summarizes plot. "The reader not only condones the obvious stage craft of the happy ending, but welcomes it as part of the atmosphere of good-fellowship and religious faith, based on happiness in little things, which Goldsmith imported into the English novel . . . (p. 91). [Text used: 1961.B3: University Paperbacks, pp. 89-93, passim.] Reprinted: 1957.B2; 1961.B3.

3   FRIEDMAN, ARTHUR. "Goldsmith and Hanway." MLN 66 (December): 553-54.
     Letter 94, Citizen of the World, contains a description by Hingpo of the "Wolga Pirates," which seems on grounds of verbal similarity and like ideas to derive from Jonas Hanway's An Historical Account of the British Trade over the Caspian Sea, London, 1753, but may have come from an extract published in the London Magazine 22 (1753):232-33, or from a translation of the passage in Journal Étranger (Juin 1754):60-64.

4   _____. "The Year of Goldsmith's Birth." N&Q 196 (1 September):188-89.
     A letter Goldsmith wrote his brother Henry in January 1759, states Henry was seven or eight years older than he. Draws two conclusions: the probability of the early years 1727, 1728, and 1729 is lessened; the chief alternative to 1730 would appear to be 1731, a conclusion which agrees with the memorandum Goldsmith dictated to Percy in 1733 when he said he was born in 1731 or 1730.

5   HILLES, FREDERICK W. Introduction to The Vicar of Wakefield, by Goldsmith. New York: E. P. Dutton; London: J. M. Dent, Everyman's Library, New American Edition, pp. vii-xv.
     Argues that internal evidence shows Goldsmith planned the book very carefully: "The first three chapters serve as a kind of prologue. The story proper begins in the new home described in Chapter IV. And balancing the prologue are the final three chapters in which the various threads are held together. The central part of the book falls into two roughly equal parts" (p. xi). Interpolations in the story like the ballad of Edwin and Angelina and the tale of Mathilda both foreshadow the reversal in plot and the happy ending, as well as complementing the tone for the part of the book in which they appear.

6   PACEY, DESMOND. "The Goldsmiths and their Villages." UTQ 21 (October):27-38.

A comparison between <u>The Deserted Village</u> and "The Rising Village," a poem by a Canadian nephew of Goldsmith's.

7   SANDS, MOLLIE. "Oliver Goldsmith and Music." <u>Music and Letters</u> 32 (April):147-53.
A love for music was deeply ingrained in Goldsmith and his numerous references to music range from ballads to Italian opera. In childhood he may have heard some Gaelic songs. Heard his cousin Jane play the harpsichord at the Contarines and of course himself played the German flute. Wrote and sold ballads at Trinity. Wrote the words for two oratorios of at least middling quality and the essays "On the Different Schools of Music" and "Letter on the Different Schools of Music" for the <u>British Magazine</u>. Most notable for his love of country songs and ballads.

<u>1952</u>

A. Books

1   FREEMAN, WILLIAM. <u>Oliver Goldsmith</u>. London: Herbert Jenkins; New York: Philosophical Library, 286 pp.
Argues he is using new manuscript material in the British Museum, but except for some manuscript sheets of <u>Animated Nature</u>, these materials were published by Balderston in her <u>History and Sources of Percy's Memoir of Goldsmith</u> (1926.A2) and her edition of the <u>Collected Letters</u> (1928.A1). Sees Goldsmith as overwhelmed as a writer and as a person by the influence of Johnson and his circle, but especially Johnson: the "poor Goldy" of the Irving-Forster tradition.

2   JOHNSTONE, CORAGREENE.   "The Literary Views of Oliver Goldsmith." Ph.D. dissertation, University of Michigan.
Aims at systematizing Goldsmith's literary opinions, since he was not a systematic critic, under three headings: his concept of the characteristics of an author; his concept of the purpose and technique of literature; and his opinion of the effect a literary work should have on an audience. Sees the artist as a seer and teacher, retains the neoclassic belief in the primacy of judgment, with taste deciding between reason and imagination. Believes in Aristotelian mimesis, but artist should copy nature, not models, even ancient models. Literary works should represent an idealized nature, mingling the useful and the delightful. Disliked modern epics, elegies, pastorals, and pindaric odes, preferring narrative, descriptive, and didactic poetry. Disliked blank verse, preferring the

1952

pentameter couplet. Generally disliked romances of his
day, as well as sentimental comedies, which he saw as
mixing genres. Both defends and attacks features of the
neoclassical tradition, preferring to concentrate on
beauties, not faults, and displayed aesthetic relativism.
More a general than a specific critic.

B. Shorter Writings

1   CONGLETON, JAMES E. Theories of Pastoral Poetry in England,
    1648-1798. Gainesville: University of Florida Press,
    pp. 146, 159, 168, 187.
        In the Critical Review, Goldsmith shows a conservative
    attitude by arguing for strict observance of the law of
    genres and a rigid use of the law of decorum. Some of his
    brief comments suggest he favored some contemporary changes
    and shifts in pastoral theory. Letter 106, Citizen,
    ridicules conventional elegies. In 1762, revised Newbery's
    Art of Poetry Made Easy and published it under the title
    The Art of Poetry on a New Plan, emphasizing the pictorial
    element. In his anthology The Beauties of English Poesy,
    1767, he praises Gay's Shepherd's Week for capturing the
    real spirit of the pastoral. Goldsmith argued against the
    theory that pastoral is the oldest poetic genre, pressing
    the claims of religious poetry of praise.

2   FRIEDMAN, ARTHUR. "The First Edition of Essays by Mr. Gold-
    smith." SB 5 (1952 for 1953):190-93.
        Presents evidence that the edition with an engraved title
    page is the first edition and that the one with a title page
    printed from type is a piracy.

3   GRAHAM, W. H. "Oliver Goldsmith." Contemporary Review 181
    (May):304-8.
        For the general reader. Considers Mrs. Thrale's view of
    him an anomaly, with Reynolds's and Johnson's friendship
    ample testimony to his worth. Summarizes biography and
    argues that he drew upon biographical details in later
    writings. Cites Johnson's dislike of the Vicar, but argues
    the critical consensus (Forster, Scott, and Cambridge History
    of English Literature, but does not cite Dobson by name) is
    against him. Argues Vicar is "no more or less than a fairy
    tale of the good old type" (p. 306), with characters in
    eighteenth-century clothing, with Dr. Primrose as its
    lovable hero. Argues the value of re-reading classics like
    this one.

4   REYNOLDS, JOSHUA. Portraits by Sir Joshua Reynolds.
     Character Sketches of Oliver Goldsmith, Samuel Johnson,
     and David Garrick, together with Other Manuscripts of
     Reynolds Discovered among the Boswell Papers and now First
     Published. Prepared for the Press with an Introduction
     and Notes by Frederick W. Hilles, Yale Editions of the
     Private Papers of James Boswell, New York: McGraw-Hill,
     pp. 27-59, passim.
          A major document. Hilles comments: "what we have here
     is a group of preliminary notes, a rough draft of the
     central part of the essay, and a revised and expanded
     version which lacks a beginning and an ending. The revised
     version consists of twelve pages, the first of which is
     numbered '2' by Reynolds. In other words, the first page
     of the revised version has not survived. The last two and
     a half pages of the revised version are given over to
     comments on Goldsmith's writing" (p. 42). "Accordingly the
     text given here is a composite, including, with trifling
     exceptions noted below, everything which Sir Joshua wrote
     on the subject. The structure of the sketch is that which
     is revealed in the revised version. Into this version have
     been woven the random notes and the sentences and para-
     graphs of the rough draft" (p. 43).
          Emphasizes Goldsmith's essential honesty and simplicity,
     but also that: "A great part of Dr. Goldsmith's folly and
     absurdity proceeded from principle, and partly from a want
     of early acquaintance with that life to which his reputation
     afterward introduced him" (p. 46). Stresses his sociability,
     desire to be liked, and awkwardness in conversation, but
     great discernment in writing.

                         1953

A. Books--None

B. Shorter Writings

   1   CHAPMAN, R. W. "Oliver Goldsmith, 1728(?)-1774, "Percy and
       Goldsmith," In Johnsonian and Other Essays and Reviews.
       Oxford: Clarendon Press, pp. 104-14; 170-73.
          "Oliver Goldsmith, 1728 (?)-1774" is a reprint of
       1928.B2.

   2   HARTH, PHILLIP. "Goldsmith and the Marquis D'Argens." N&Q
       198 (December):529-30.
          Points out the popularity of D'Argens's Lettres Chinoises
       in French and in English translations titled The Chinese

1953

Letters and The Chinese Spy both before and after Goldsmith's series. The problem of which edition Goldsmith
used puzzles, since he refers to D'Argens only once, in
Letter 43. However, in Letter 23, Goldsmith quotes a
fairly long passage from p. 174 of Abbe de Choisy's Journal
ou Suite d'un Voyage de Siam, a book D'Argens refers to
several times. Crane and Smith (1921.B1) believed Goldsmith had seen the book itself, but the passage appears in
its original French in the 1755 edition of Lettres Chinoises.
Since D'Argens wrote a new preface for each edition, this
was the first appearance of the Choisy quotation, which
does not appear in any of the English translations. Thus,
the 1755 edition is "with reasonable certainty" (p. 530)
the one Goldsmith used.

3   TODD, WILLIAM B. "The 'Private Issues' of The Deserted
     Village." SB 6 (1953 for 1954):25-44.
          All the twenty-six "private" or "trial" issues of the
     poem are piracies and were "apparently printed within the
     copyright period (ranging in this instance from 1770 to
     1784), or immediately upon its expiration . . . " (p. 28).
     "All of the separate editions represent a series of degraded
     texts cheaply produced at various times and places with the
     obvious intention of cutting in on the profits due the
     author and his publisher" (p. 30).

                              1954

A. Books

1   EICHENBERGER, KARL. Oliver Goldsmith: Das Komische in den
     Werken seiner Reifeperiode. Schweizer Anglistische
     Arbeiten, Band 35. Bern: G. Franke, 126 pp.
          Mainly considers the Vicar and the two plays as
     belonging to Goldsmith's mature period, with some glances
     at The Citizen of the World. Uses the term "comic" in the
     broadest possible sense, with the Vicar as a kind of way
     station on the road to dramatic comedy. Major divisions
     are the humorist attitude, discussing literary genre,
     sentimentalism, the humorous level, and the apparent
     harmony of the ironic style; the comic situation, discussing
     the staging of the comic, the themes of comic situations,
     the techniques of arousing tension, and the change of
     character and situation; the comic character, discussing
     the presentation of character, the ridiculous type, the
     tragic precipice, and the main forms of the comic; and the
     ordering instant, discussing the irresolutions of society,

the strength of instinctive nature, the ideal of pure
naturalness, and the conception of the natural human
being--most fully embodied in Kate Hardcastle.

2   TODD, WILLIAM B., ed. A Prospect of Society, by Goldsmith.
    King's College, Cambridge: privately printed at the
    Water Lane Press, 22 pp.
        Todd presents the unique half-quarto sheets discovered
    in 1902 by Bertram Dobell, discusses their possible origin,
    and reconstructs the text of the poem that later became
    The Traveller.

B. Shorter Writings

1   DAVIE, DONALD. "The Deserted Village: Poem as Virtual
    History." Twentieth Century 156 (August):161-74.
        Expounds Suzanne Langer's thesis from Feeling and Form
    that all art is abstracted form become a symbol "expressive"
    of human feeling. "'Poesis' creates the semblance of
    virtual experience or virtual events, which differ from
    actual experience or actual events in that every item of
    the experience presented is an emotional factor, having
    emotional value" (p. 164). Differs with Langer's analysis
    of Deserted Village, lines 7-24, which she argues present
    the dance on the green to contrast later with the overgrown
    green, the choked brook, unvisited church, and abandoned
    farms, seeing Goldsmith as moralizing and thus weakening
    his poem rather than letting contrast do the main work.
    Davie quotes six more lines to show the dancing on the
    green is merely one of several activities occurring there.
    "As a virtual history of village life Goldsmith's poem
    differs from Blake's ["The Echoing Green"] only in
    presenting a different semblance and so a different
    feeling. . . . 'The Deserted Village' expresses it as frail
    and thoroughly vulnerable" (p. 171).

2   TODD, WILLIAM B. "The 'Private Issues' of The Deserted
    Village." SB 7 (1954 for 1955):239.
        Bibliographical examination of the 1775 Belfast edition
    of Goldsmith's Poems shows it is the text used for the one
    of the "private" pirated issues of The Deserted Village
    falsely dated 1770, reset, and printed on paper with a
    Belfast watermark. See 1953.B3.

3   _____ . "Quadruple Imposition: An Account of Goldsmith's
    Traveller." SB 7 (1954 for 1955):103-11.
        Of the four quarter half-sheets discovered by Dobell in
    1902, three (B, C, and D) are headed "A PROSPECT OF SOCIETY."

1955

> Sheet E contains only the text, signature, and catchwords.
> Sheets B,C, and D appear to be in their final state.
> Friedman, Works 4:239, summarizes Todd's view: "the
> galleys were stored in reverse order, and when the
> compositor made the type up into pages he started with
> galley 11 and worked through to galley 1. Half-sheets B-E
> in P[rospect] were thus printed from type in galleys 11-4
> and the first part of galley 3; the rest of galley 3 and
> galleys 2 and 1 supplied the type for the pages of lost
> half-sheet F." Todd concludes: "From every indication,
> A Prospect of Society should thus be described, not as a
> random essay, nor as an uncorrected proof, but as an
> abortive edition, well conceived, badly bungled, and
> finally suppressed" (p. 110).

<u>1955</u>

A. Books--None

B. Shorter Writings

1   BOSWELL, JAMES. Boswell on the Grand Tour: Italy, Corsica,
    and France, 1765-1766. Edited by Frank Brady and Frederick
    A. Pottle. Yale Editions of the Private Papers of James
    Boswell. New York: McGraw-Hill, pp. 295-97.
        Describes a London street encounter with Goldsmith.

2   FRIEDMAN, ARTHUR. "Goldsmith and the Jest Books." <u>MP</u> 53
    (August):47-48.
        Several incidents in various works parallel situations
    in jest books: Mrs. Hardcastle's discovery of the lost
    jewels parallels one in Archie Armstrong's seventeenth-
    century <u>Banquet of Jests</u>; in <u>Bee</u>, No. 4, Bidderman the Wise
    has an analogue in <u>Pasquil's Jests with the Merriment of
    Mrs. Bunch</u>, 1650?; <u>Bee</u>, No. 2, "Happiness in a Great
    Measure Dependant [sic] upon Constitution" is borrowed
    with little change from a story in <u>Oxford Jests Refined
    and Enlarged</u>, 1684; and <u>Citizen of the World</u>, Letter 102,
    drawn from some changes in detail from "Arliquiniana" in
    the <u>Miscellaneous Remains of Cardinal Perron, President
    Thuanus, Mon^{sr} St. Evremond</u>, &c., London, 1707.

3   GOLDEN, MORRIS. "Goldsmith and 'The Distresses of an Hired
    Writer.'" <u>N&Q</u> 200 (April):165-65.
        Argues on the basis of differences in style and thought
    that the essay, which appeared in the <u>British Magazine</u>
    April 1761, was not written by Goldsmith. Friedman does

not reprint the essay in <u>Works</u> 3.

4   _____. "Goldsmith and 'National Concord.'" <u>N&Q</u> 200 (October):436-38.
      Internal evidence indicates this essay, published in the <u>British Magazine</u>, December 1760, is not by Goldsmith. Friedman does not reprint the essay in <u>Works</u> 3.

5   _____. "Goldsmith and 'The Present State of Russia and France.'" <u>N&Q</u> 200 (September):393-94.
      Crane suggested this essay in the <u>Royal Magazine</u>, February 1761, might be by Goldsmith. The subject is linked with <u>The Political View of the Result of the Present War with America</u>, which Goldsmith was then compiling. The style is smooth, rather fuller of images than Goldsmith's usually is, and includes none of his characteristic phrasing, as well as contradicting his political opinions. With the external evidence discredited, the internal evidence negative, Crane's even tentative ascription can be rejected.

6   HENNIG, JOHN. "The Auerbachs Keller Scene and <u>She Stoops to Conquer</u>." <u>Comparative Literature</u> 7 (Summer):193-202.
      Using circumstantial evidence only, argues that some features of the Auerbachs Keller scene in Goethe's <u>Faust</u> are based on the alehouse scene in <u>She Stoops to Conquer</u>.

7   HILLES, FREDERICK W., ed. Introduction to <u>The Vicar of Wakefield and Other Writings</u>, by Goldsmith. New York: Modern Library, pp. xiii-xxii.
      High praise for Goldsmith's major literary works: "Goldsmith as an essayist is best seen in the individual letters making up <u>The Citizen of the World</u>" (p. xx), arguing that the essay series was a way station on his road to becoming a novelist. Praises the <u>Vicar</u> and <u>The Deserted Village</u> for "the same idyllic atmosphere, the same felicity of expression, the same gentle humor mixed with sentiment" (p. xxi), and notes, "<u>The Traveller</u> comes very near being perfect of its kind" (p. xxi). Praises comedies for making audiences laugh. This collection is also interesting textually, since Hilles uses "the earliest version of each selection . . ." (p. xxiii).

8   NICOLL, ALLARDYCE. <u>History of English Drama</u>. Cambridge: University Press, 3:157-60, passim.
      A revision of 1927.B6.

1955

9   SHERBO, ARTHUR. "A Manufactured Anecdote in Goldsmith's <u>Life</u>
    <u>of Richard Nash</u>." <u>MLN</u> 70 (January):20-22.
        <u>Bee</u>, No. 3, "On Justice and Generosity" is taken mainly
    from Justus Van Effen, but two sentences about Lysippus
    are not: he refuses a friend a loan, but then borrows
    money to help an indigent, which winds up with the friend
    who first asked for the loan. An anecdote with the same
    general idea occurs in the <u>Life of Nash</u> (Gibbs ed. 4:59-60;
    <u>Works</u> 3:296-97). Sherbo believes the story about Nash was
    manufactured from the story in the <u>Bee</u> and that other Nash
    anecdotes may be equally suspect.

1956

A. Books

1   TODD, WILLIAM B., ed. <u>A Prospect of Society</u>, by Goldsmith.
    Reconstructed from the Earliest Version of <u>The Traveller</u>.
    Charlottesville: University of Virginia Press for the
    Bibliographical Society of the University of Virginia,
    32 pp.
        Reproduces the text of 1954.A2 and reprints 1954.B3.

2   WOODS, SAMUEL H., Jr. "The Literary Mode of Goldsmith's
    Essays and of <u>The Vicar of Wakefield</u>." Ph.D. dissertation,
    Yale University.
        Argues that Goldsmith's special literary mode combines
    three features, the use of a <u>persona</u>, the use of irony, and
    the "serious burlesque" of form. The <u>persona</u> is usually
    the dramatic speaker or narrator, but coupled with a
    "spokesman," who more nearly represents Goldsmith's own
    views. The views of these two figures are usually not
    diametrically opposed and the <u>persona</u> usually represents
    a partial truth, the spokesman a fuller truth. "Serious
    burlesque" of form means that Goldsmith does not take the
    literary genre he has chosen very seriously, even though he
    uses that same form as his basic literary structure. The
    study is limited to the miscellaneous essays, <u>The Citizen</u>
    <u>of the World</u>, and <u>The Vicar of Wakefield</u>, even though this
    mode may well apply to Goldsmith's major poems and plays,
    too.

B. Shorter Writings

1   BOSWELL, JAMES. <u>Boswell in Search of a Wife, 1766-1769</u>.
    Edited by Frank Brady and Frederick A. Pottle. Yale
    Editions of the Private Papers of James Boswell. New York:

McGraw-Hill, pp. 308, 317-18, 320.
Details describing Boswell and Goldsmith's relationship.

2 FRIEDMAN, ARTHUR. "Goldsmith and Wood." <u>TLS</u> (2 November):
   649.
   Evidence that Goldsmith borrowed parts of <u>The Life of</u>
   <u>Nash</u> from John Wood's <u>Essay towards a Description of Bath</u>.

3 _____. "Goldsmith's 'Essay on Friendship': Its First
   Publication and the Problem of Authorship." <u>PQ</u> 35 (July):
   346-49.
   Essay appeared about a month after Goldsmith's death in
   the <u>Universal Magazine</u>, April 1774, headed "For the
   UNIVERSAL MAGAZINE, ESSAY <u>ON FRIENDSHIP, written by the</u>
   <u>late Dr. Goldsmith</u>. (Never before published in his <u>works</u>),"
   and continued to be accepted in the Goldsmith canon.
   Apparently someone knew the essay was by Goldsmith: had
   appeared in 1767 as No. 81 in the collected edition of Hugh
   Kelly's <u>Babler</u> [sic] (2:78-81), probably reprinted from the
   original series in <u>Owen's Weekly Chronicle</u>. General tenor
   of essay is Goldsmithian: it attacks romance writers and
   argues the need for friendship to be free of obligation and
   dependence, though there are no close verbal parallels to
   other Goldsmith pieces. Kelly probably sent it to the
   <u>Universal Magazine</u>, even though he and Goldsmith had
   quarrelled in 1768 over rivalry between their plays <u>False</u>
   <u>Delicacy</u> and <u>The Good Natur'd Man</u> and had not reconciled,
   but Kelly was among the small group attending Goldsmith's
   funeral.

4 GOLDEN, MORRIS. "Goldsmith Attributions in the <u>Literary</u>
   <u>Magazine</u>." <u>N&Q</u> 201 (October):432-35; (November):489-93.
   Rejects Seitz's arguments (1929.B8) against attributing
   any material in the <u>Literary Magazine</u> and argues one series
   of four articles on "The History of Our Language" is
   Goldsmith's, two others probably his, and two more possibly
   his, all published in 1758.

5 _____. "Goldsmith Attributions in the 'Weekly Magazine.'"
   <u>N&Q</u> 201 (August):350-51.
   Refers to Friedman's earlier discussion (1935.B2),
   finding further evidence to support Friedman's ascription
   of "Introduction," 29 December 1759, in similar satire of
   the hypocrisy of such introductions in <u>Bee</u> and some similar
   phrasing. Finds more internal evidence supporting
   Friedman's attribution of "On the Present State of Our
   Theatres." Rejects "A Description of the Manners and
   Customs of the Native Irish, In a Letter from an English

1956

Gentleman," arguing Goldsmith wrote only the introduction
and conclusion, although grants he may have edited the
copy, and believes "Some Original Memoirs of the Late
Famous Bishop of Cloyne" is too clumsily written to have
been done by Goldsmith, although he grants the author may
have received the Contarine anecdote from Goldsmith.
Friedman rejected Golden's arguments, and prints all the
essays in <u>Works</u> 3.

6   WATSON, MELVIN R. <u>Magazine Serials and the Essay Tradition</u>,
     <u>1746-1820</u>. Louisiana State University Studies, Humanities
     Series, 6. Baton Rouge: Louisiana State University Press,
     170 pp., passim.
          No direct discussion of Goldsmith since <u>Citizen</u> appeared
     in a newspaper, not a magazine. Some discussion of his
     influence, especially on George Brewer's <u>Essays after the</u>
     <u>manner of Goldsmith</u>, which Watson finds more like Addison
     than Goldsmith.

1957

A. Books

1   WARDLE, RALPH. <u>Oliver Goldsmith</u>. Lawrence: University of
     Kansas Press, x, 330 pp.
          Comprehensive biography based on available manuscript
     materials, including the Goldsmith-Percy manuscripts in
     the British Museum and the Boswell papers at Yale,
     resulting in a factual account of very high quality,
     revealing study of specialized scholarship. Critical
     judgments are somewhat old-fashioned: "If he had had full
     confidence in his convictions and had had the leisure to
     develop them, he might well have been a leader in the
     Romantic Revival in English literature" (p. 296).

B. Shorter Writings

1   BARNETT, GEORGE L. "<u>Rasselas</u> and <u>The Vicar of Wakefield</u>."
     <u>N&Q</u> 202 (July):303-5.
          In <u>Joseph Andrews</u>, book four, chapter eight, Adams
     lectures Joseph on submitting to Providence, and shows his
     inconsistency in his extreme grief at the reported death
     of his son. G. B. Hill had pointed out that the philosopher
     in chapter eighteen of <u>Rasselas</u> shows a similar incon-
     sistency in mourning the death of his daughter. Barnett
     argues that <u>Vicar</u>, chapter seventeen, shows Primrose
     behaving in a similar manner after Olivia's loss and

likewise in the later chapter when Sophia is reported lost.
Argues that the Vicar is not used as a figure of laughter
like Adams or subordinated to morality like Johnson's
philosopher, but that these episodes enrich his character.

2   CHURCH, RICHARD. The Growth of the English Novel. London:
Methuen, Home Study Books.
A reprint of 1951.B2.

3   GOLDEN, MORRIS. "Another Manufactured Anecdote in The Life of
Richard Nash?" N&Q 202 (March):20-21.
Believes an even more striking example than Sherbo's
(1955.B8) occurs in Nash in the story of the impoverished
Col. M., who loves the heiress Miss L., becomes an actor and
is recognized by her. She faints, he catches her in his
arms, and they are reconciled. In Vicar, chapter nineteen,
George, appearing in the Fair Penitent, becomes speechless
on seeing Arabella Wilmot in the audience, and the two are
reunited and eventually marry.

4   _____. "Goldsmith and 'The Universal Museum and Complete
Magazine.'" N&Q 202 (August):339-48.
The preface to the 1765 volume of the magazine; of the
series "The Hermit in Town," finds No. 2 and No. 3 similar
to Goldsmith; "The Diary of a Country Gentleman in the Days
of Queen Elizabeth" like "A Reverie at the Boar's-Head
Tavern"; "The Life of the Celebrated Dr. Edward Young";
and a letter to the theatre column by "A Penitent Prodigal."
Friedman, Works 3:xi, note 1, remarks that Golden "may be
right in some of these ascriptions, but the evidence does
not seem to me sufficiently strong to justify reprinting
any of the essays."

1958

A. Books

1   STORM, LEO [F.]. "Melange of Literary Type and Idea in
Goldsmith's Deserted Village." Ph.D. dissertation,
University of Washington, 205 pp.
Argues that the poem is a fusion of four literary genres:
the topographical poem, the georgic, the Theophrastian
character, and Juvenalian satire. The topographical and
georgic are the basic formal elements, with the Theophrastian
character and Juvenalian satire subordinated to them.
Goldsmith observes the major conventions of topics and
themes for each genre.

1958

B.   Shorter Writings

1   DAHL, CURTIS. "Patterns of Disguise in The Vicar of Wake-
    field." ELH 25 (June):90-04.
        Despite critical objections to the supposed incoherence
    of the novel's plot, Dahl argues that the frequent use of
    disguise, literally and figuratively, helps unify the
    novel thematically. Sir William Thornhill's disguise as
    Mr. Burchell and Ephraim Jenkinson's as an honest man
    illustrate literal disguise, as do Lady Blarney and Miss
    Caroline Wilhelmina Skeggs. Much disguise is figurative,
    like Squire Thornhill's disguised "proposal" to Olivia and
    his attempt to conceal his evil conduct from his uncle when
    the Primroses are in prison. Thus distinguishing reality
    from appearance becomes a central theme in the novel. Both
    the ballad of Edwin and Angelina and the story of Mathilda
    hinge on this distinction, as do George's adventures. "Out
    of the painful stripping from reality of its various layers
    of disguise comes deeper wisdom and broader truth" (p. 103).

2   DAVIE, DONALD, ed. Introduction to The Late Augustans: Longer
    Poems of the Later Eighteenth Century. London: Macmillan,
    pp. vii-xxxiii.
        Discusses other elements besides the verse, especially
    finding his character "extremely elusive and contradictory"
    (p. xxiv). Describes the mood of The Deserted Village as
    "white melancholy" (p. xxv). Davie prints The Traveller,
    The Deserted Village, and Retaliation.

3   DEMSBOLTON, JOHN. "Definition of 'Berserk.'" N&Q 203 (March):
    127.
        Among other early uses, cites Citizen's description of
    Siberian tribes [earliest OED definition is dated 1822].

4   FRIEDMAN, ARTHUR. "The First Edition of Goldsmith's Bee,
    No. 1." SB 11:255-59.
        Friedman expands his earlier bibliographical argu-
    ments that the variant text Knight discovered is a
    reprint, not the original edition: based on his experience
    in collating many Goldsmith texts, he believes that "in
    reprints the punctuation becomes heavier and more regular"
    (p. 256, Friedman's italics), and argues that Knight's
    variant edition is probably later because more regularly
    punctuated. Further, Goldsmith used the commonly accepted
    texts, not the variant Knight described, when he reprinted
    Bee material in Essays, 1765. See 1944.B2.

5   GOLDEN, MORRIS. "The Family-Wanderer Theme in Goldsmith."
    ELH 25 (September):181-93.
         Goldsmith's "most pervasive and characteristic theme"
    (p. 181) is the contrast between the family circle and
    the wandering son, present in his work from early to late,
    it "unconsciously fills his mind" (p. 181). Lien Chi is
    "a lonely, wandering alien" (p. 182), and the Man in
    Black has to fend for himself at his father's death. In
    the Vicar, George is the main wanderer, and even here the
    family is static and endearing. The Traveller is his
    clearest example of the self as exiled wanderer, and by the
    time of The Deserted Village, the static dream-home has
    been destroyed, he having finally discovered that home does
    not exist any more.

6   _____. "A Goldsmith Essay in the 'Complete Magazine.'"
    N&Q 203 (November):465-66.
         Argues that because the Annual Register, 1764, reprinted
    "On the Use of Language" from the Bee under the title "On
    Friendship and Pity" and credited the essay to "Traveller
    V" in the Universal Museum and Complete Magazine, these
    events offer "further proof of Goldsmith's connection with
    the 'Universal Museum and Complete Magazine'" (p. 466).
    See 1957.B4.

7   _____. "Notes on Three Goldsmith Attributions." N&Q 203
    (January):24-26.
         Accepts "On the Different Schools of Music," British
    Magazine, February 1765; rejects "A Parallel between Mrs.
    Vincent and Miss Brent," British Magazine, May and June
    1760; and rejects the review of Francklin's "The Tragedies
    of Sophocles," Critical Review, June 1759. Crane (1941.B1)
    had accepted the first and marked the second and third as
    doubtful. Friedman prints only the first, Works 1:91-93.

8   HOPKINS, ROBERT H. "The Vicar of Wakefield, A Puzzler to the
    Critics." N&Q 203 (March):113-14.
         Forster quotes Southey as using the phrase about the
    novel; Hopkins points out that the phrase occurs in
    Southey's Common-Place Book, Third Series, London, 1850,
    p. 718, describing not the novel but the original review
    in the Monthly Review, 1766.

9   LUCAS, F. L. The Search for Good Sense; Four Eighteenth-
    Century Characters: Johnson, Chesterfield, Boswell,
    Goldsmith. London: Cassell, pp. 283-338, passim.
         Primarily a character sketch, reconstructing "a few
    living scenes that may quicken that dull catalogue of

1958

dates" (p. 287) usually found in a biography. Even when
writing the novel, Goldsmith had a playwright's "sense
both of character and dialogue" (p. 297). Goldsmith shows
his skill in Primrose's characterization and his artistry
in making him narrator. Lengthy discussion of poems, with
The Deserted Village preferred as revealing more of
Goldsmith. Finds plays hard to admire, especially The Good
Natur'd Man. "With a spirited cast, She Stoops to Conquer
still passes pleasantly enough; though not with very high
honours . . . (p. 337).

10   TODD, WILLIAM B. "The First Editions of The Good Natur'd Man
and She Stoops to Conquer." SB 11:133-42.
A bibliographical study pointing out the many misprints
and careless errors in William Griffin's printings of both
plays.

1959

A. Books

1   JEFFARES, A. NORMAN. Oliver Goldsmith. Writers and Their
Work, no. 107. London: Longmans for the British Council
and the National Book League, 44 pp.
Brief biographical and critical survey, reflecting the
most recent scholarship.

B. Shorter Writings

1   BOSWELL, JAMES. Boswell for the Defense, 1769-1774. Edited
by William K. Wimsatt, Jr., and Frederick A. Pottle. Yale
Editions of the Private Papers of James Boswell. New York:
McGraw-Hill, 428 pp., passim.
Mainly references to Goldsmith's death and reactions
connected with it.

2   FIELDING, K. J. "The Deserted Village and Sir Robert Walpole."
English 12 (Spring):130-32.
Argues that the poem refers to the enclosure acts used
to evict farmers to build Houghton Hall.

3   GOLDEN, MORRIS. "The Broken Dream of The Deserted Village."
L&P 9 (Summer-Fall):41-44.
Argues that the poem is "authentic poetry, unified and
made meaningful through a connected symbolic pattern that
not only catches the author's peculiar orientation to life
at this stage of his career but also catches a psychological

state occasionally shared by most of his readers" (p. 41).
The poem is clearly an idealized image of childhood and the
two fullest portraits are both father-figures. Other
contrasts exist besides the past-present one: the idyllic
country and the horrible city, the idealized village and
barbarous America, and childhood ideals and world where
adults must act.

4   _____. "Image Frequency and the Split in The Vicar of
     Wakefield." BNYPL 63 (September):473-77.
          Argues that frequency of images in the prose is a clear
     index to the amount of work Goldsmith expended. Thus, the
     number of images in the first twenty-seven chapters show
     considerable care, while the last five chapters seem to
     have been written hastily. Golden's examples of hasty
     writing do not include any of the longer compilations, so
     that his sampling is not entirely representative.

5   _____. "Two Essays Erroneously Attributed to Goldsmith."
     MLN 74 (January):13-16.
          Two essays, "On National Prejudices" and "On the Proper
     Enjoyment of Life" (reprinted with the title "Riches
     without Happiness"), both first published in the British
     Magazine, 1760, are not by Goldsmith. Finds no character-
     istic phrases of images in "On the Proper Enjoyment of
     Life." The anglophobia of "On National Prejudices" suggests
     Smollett may have been the author.

6   MINER, EARL. "The Making of The Deserted Village." HLQ 22
     (February):125-41.
          Finds the poem liked but little admired and suggests as
     reasons Goldsmith's reputation as a literary hack and easy
     stylist, "a buffoon who graces all he touches" (p. 126),
     and changed poetic standards as well as indifference.
     Finds much recent Goldsmith criticism unsatisfactory in
     representing Goldsmith as a muddled thinker, citing Seitz
     (1937.B4) and McAdam (1949.B2), but praises Crane's New
     Essays (1927.A1) and Bell (1944.B1). Politically, the
     poem reflects his Toryism; literarily, it redefines the
     pastoral elegy. Through careful analysis of the poem,
     presents Goldsmith as a thoughtful Tory of considerably
     skilled artistry and seriousness. Through analysis of the
     way luxury functions in the poem, Miner shows Goldsmith
     a moralist like other Tories.

7   RAWSON, C. J. "Some Unpublished Letters of Pope and Gay and
     some Manuscript Sources of Goldsmith's Life of Parnell."
     RES, n.s. 10, no. 40 (November):371-87.

1960

The manuscript materials Goldsmith used for his Life of
Parnell, besides their intrinsic interest, shed some light
on editions of Pope's letters.

1960

A. Books

1 MANLOVE, GEORGE KENDALL. "The Intellectual Background of
   Goldsmith's Deserted Village." Ph.D. dissertation, Duke
   University, 303 pp.
       Ideas set forth in the poem have their roots in the
   conflict between mercantilism and agrarianism, ideas
   reflected from Hume, Wallace, Cantillon, William Bell,
   Harte, Nathaniel Forster, Price, Young, Adam Smith,
   Montesquieu, and Mirabeau the elder. Writers interested in
   agriculture were involved in disputes over the nature of
   wealth, the effects of luxury, increasing and decreasing
   population, the value of colonies, conditions of life among
   the poor, the disappearance of small landowners. Goldsmith
   stands with those who oppose luxury and depopulation.
   Cites three other important influences: Goldsmith's
   interest in history, shaped by Montesquieu, generally
   pessimistic; his interest in natural history and travel
   literature led him to contrast civilized and primitive
   peoples; and specific evidence from his personal observation, especially the example of Springfield, Essex, rather
   than Lissoy.

B. Shorter Writings

1 DAICHES, DAVID. A Critical History of English Literature.
   2 vols. New York: Ronald Press, 1160 pp.
       Discussion of Goldsmith is by genre, so that no
   coherent estimate emerges. Poetry is "more centrally
   [than Macpherson's or Chatterton's] in the tradition of
   mid-eighteenth-century verse, moralizing and descriptive
   and often sententious" (p. 681). Goldsmith opposed other
   verse forms than the heroic couplet. "Goldsmith lacks wit,
   and his use of abstractions and generalizations often seems
   to be the result of no compelling poetic need but to be
   merely a mechanically skillful use of convention" (p. 682).
   "This argues a general sloppiness in the handling of
   language. Yet the Poem [The Deserted Village] has a
   kind of charm" (p. 683). Some verse portraits do charm,
   but the serious ones do not hold the reader. "This is
   Augustan verse weakened by sententious rhetoric" (p. 683).

The vicar is a sentimental character in a "deliberately
simple-minded novel, done with quiet grace of style, about
innocence and worldliness" (p. 737). Finds many of the
same problems in the essays and the Citizen, "but their
geniality, ease of movement, and what might be called their
purity of tone give them a charm that is not often found in
the essays of the mid-eighteenth century" (p. 797). "It is
perhaps an indication of the poverty of eighteenth-century
drama that this simple-minded comedy [She Stoops to Conquer]
should enjoy the reputation it does, but it does possess
genuine comic life" (p. 1097).

2   FRIEDMAN, ARTHUR. "The Problem of Indifferent Readings in
    the Eighteenth Century, with a Solution from The Deserted
    Village." SB 13:143-47.
        Evidence Goldsmith was responsible for deleting a couplet
    from the fourth edition, printed from standing type.

3   _____. "Two Notes on Goldsmith." SB 13:232-35.
        Bibliographical discussion of the first edition of The
    Life of Bolingbroke and the 1772 edition of The Traveller.

4   GASSMAN, BYRON. "French Sources of Goldsmith's The Good
    Natur'd Man." PQ 39 (January):56-65.
        The review in the London Magazine, February 1768,
    disparages this play and asserts he used six French sources:
    Marc Antoine Le Grand, Le Philantrope, acted in Paris 1724,
    printed 1724; Molière's L'Avare, 1668, 1675; Nericault
    Destouches, Le Dissipateur (no performance date given) 1736;
    David de Brueys and Jean Palaprat, Le Grondeur, 1691, 1711;
    David de Brueys, L'Important, 1693, 1694; and Racine, Les
    Plaideurs, 1668, 1668. No clear evidence Goldsmith knew
    any of them, since most are not listed in the sale catalogue
    of his library (1774.B6 and 1837.A1): de Brueys and
    Destouches are listed in his library but when he acquired
    them or how he used them is unknown. The reviewer was
    probably trying to buttress his disapproval of the play.

5   MONTAGUE, JOHN. "Tragic Picaresque: Oliver Goldsmith, the
    Biographical Aspect." Studies: An Irish Quarterly Review
    49 (Spring):45-53.
        Finds usual biography of Goldsmith a travesty, partly
    because of Johnson idolaters, the delay in publishing
    Percy's Life, so that Mrs. Thrale, Hawkins, and Boswell all
    used Goldsmith as a foil to Johnson and often a fool, too.
    Only Reynolds's recently discovered portrait sketch creates
    a consistently fair picture. Excepts Wardle's book as a
    fine work. The "melancholy process of distortion" (p. 45)

had begun in Goldsmith's lifetime. From 1759 to 1774, Goldsmith was producing the best literary work in England in
three major literary forms: poetry, the drama, and the
essay. Finds Goldsmith a comic writer presenting serious
ideas about life, his doctrines of Augustan classicism com-
plicated by his admiration for French literature, especially
Voltaire and Montesquieu, so that his manner is often that
of a philosophe. With Wardle's biography and Crane's projected edition, "critical revaluation becomes increasingly
possible" (p. 53).

6 STEVENSON, LIONEL. The English Novel, a Panorama. Boston:
    Houghton Mifflin, pp. 128, 133, 140-42, 217, 263, 502, 520.
        Discussing the Vicar, Stevenson notes Goldsmith's
    versatility and naturalness. Suggests Francis Newbery had
    logical reasons for withholding the novel from publication:
    it was short, "deficient in melodramatic action, the humor
    was gentle and tolerant, devoid of either satire or
    obscenity. It could not be put into the category of
    propaganda fiction, for the author recommended nothing
    more remarkable than family affection and Christian good
    will. But when it got into print, these negative qualities
    proved to be its positive virtues" (p. 141). The main
    technical stroke is the use of first person point of view,
    so that the vicar seems convincing and lovable instead of
    being the object of comedy like Fielding's Adams.

                              1961

A. Books

1   HOPKINS, ROBERT H. "The Creative Genius of Oliver Goldsmith."
    Ph.D. dissertation, University of Pennsylvania, 265 pp.
        Goldsmith's easy prose causes most readers to miss his
    subtle satire dependent on verbal irony and use of rhetoric.
    Analyzes the first edition text of Traveller rhetorically,
    not biographically. Finds Citizen partly burlesquing of
    the fad for orientalism and partly attacking on the pride
    of rationalism, British jingoism, and the idea of universal
    benevolence. Goldsmith's theory of humor mocks corruption
    of taste by the decadent aristocracy who have separated
    manners and morals. Life of Nash continues satire of merely
    genteel manners, but with somewhat less subtlety. Vicar
    satirizes clerical complacency, the fallibility of human
    nature, and the belief that men's manners depend on their
    fortunes. It burlesques sentimental fiction and sentimen-
    tal comedy. Analyzes the verbal irony in the second half

of the <u>Vicar</u> to show that the satire is sustained. Central
thesis is that Goldsmith's true forte is comic or amiable
satire, as opposed to Swift's savage indignation.

2   SHERMAN, OSCAR. <u>Goldy</u>. New York: Twayne, 367 pp.
       This book contains no notes, even though sources are
    paraphrased and quoted extensively. A popularization of
    the best known events of Goldsmith's life and times.
    Sherman's title shows something of his literary tactless-
    ness--Goldsmith disliked the nickname "Goldy," even from
    Johnson.

B. Shorter Works

1   ADELSTEIN, MICHAEL E. "Duality of Theme in <u>The Vicar of Wake-
    field</u>." <u>CE</u> 22 (February):315-21.
       Argues that "Goldsmith did have the general outlines of
    his plot in mind but that he switched from the theme of
    prudence to that of fortitude" (p. 315). Sees Vicar
    changing from a naive fool to a courageous, resolute hero.
    In first half, the Primroses are characterized as "'generous,
    credulous, simple, and inoffensive'" (p. 316) and all their
    misfortunes except for their house burning result from the
    Vicar's imprudence. Sees the Vicar undergoing several
    spiritual crises caused by the loss of Olivia, the reported
    abduction of Sophia, and the appearance of George in chains
    at the prison. All these show Primrose resolving his inner
    conflict. His sermon best expresses his resolution and
    acceptance of the lesson of submitting to Providence, but
    "the contrivance of the happy ending has usually obscured
    the character transformation" (p. 319). The book's
    popularity may be related to the "fault" of a shift in
    theme since it allows for a mixture of comedy and tragedy
    and melodramatic trappings: "a representation of life
    which views the real and the ideal, recognizes the good and
    does not deny the evil, and laughs at humanity but yet
    sympathizes with it" (p. 321).

2   ANGUS-BUTTERWORTH, LIONEL M. <u>Ten Master Historians</u>. Aberdeen:
    Aberdeen University Press, pp. 39-55.
       Reprint of 1949.B1.

3   CHURCH, RICHARD. <u>The Growth of the English Novel</u>. London:
    Methuen, University Paperbacks, pp. 89-93, passim.
       Reprint of 1957.B2.

4   GOLDEN, MORRIS. "The Time of Writing of <u>The Vicar of Wake-
    field</u>." <u>BNYPL</u> 65 (September):442-50.

1961

> After studying Goldsmith's borrowings from himself, Golden believes that the book was the object of steady work from about 1759 to the fall of 1762, with some touching up done in 1763.

5   HAWKINS, Sir JOHN. Anecdotes of Goldsmith in <u>The Life of Samuel Johnson, LL.D.</u> Edited, Abridged, and with an Introduction by Bertram H. Davis. New York: Macmillan, 371 pp., passim.
    Abridgement of 1787.B1.

6   MORGAN, LEE. "Boswell's Portrait of Goldsmith." In <u>Studies in Honor of John C. Hodges and Alwin Thaler</u>. Edited by Richard Beale Davis and John Leon Livesay. Knoxville: University of Tennessee Press, pp. 67-76.
    Argues Boswell's portrait of Goldsmith is substantially the same as that of other contemporaries, and thus it is unlikely that Boswell denigrated Goldsmith. Goldsmith's conversation was generally regarded as lacking in wit, especially in repartee. His vanity was noted by most contemporaries, but seen as compensation for his ugliness by Black, Dobson, Irving, and others. His impulsiveness, untruthfulness, gambling, affairs with women, all get fuller treatment from other biographers than from Boswell, who generally praises Goldsmith's works.

1962

A. Books--None

B. Shorter Writings

1   ARTHOS, JOHN. "The Prose of Goldsmith." <u>Michigan Quarterly Review</u> 1, no. 1 (Winter):51-55.
    His prose is much like Dryden's though Goldsmith's mind lacks the strength of Dryden's. He follows his own advice about writing given in the <u>Enquiry</u>: prefers the natural to the regular, the familiar over the periodic and writes "a plain, open, loose style where the same thought is often exhibited in several points of view" (p. 51). He generally avoids "a system of balances, the rounding out of contrasts and parallels, the matching of cadences and capricios--this comes to bore him, to seem as 'dronish' as the very iambic rhythm he tells us almost forces itself upon English prose" (p. 52). However, he will use this kind of balanced style for "something elaborate and artificial" (p. 52) like "Asem." Sees Goldsmith writing the familiar style as practiced by Dryden, Addison and

Steele, and Swift, carrying further than Dryden the
"delight in the diaphanous, in the laying before the reader
of the thing" (p. 53). Finds Goldsmith's prose shows the
"style of wit, unencumbered, unembarrassable, virginal"
(p. 55), and sees Goldsmith as generally avoiding irony.

2 COURTHOPE, W. J. History of English Poetry. 6 vols. New
    York: Russell & Russell, 5:209-19.
        A photographic reprint of 1905.B1.

3 MAYO, ROBERT D. The English Novel in the Magazines, 1740-1815,
    with a Catalogue of 1375 Magazine Novels and Novelettes.
    Evanston, Ill.: Northwestern University Press, pp. 705,
    passim.
        "Goldsmith brought to the magazines the greatest talent
    for fiction of his generation, Smollett and Fielding
    excepted; yet, like Fielding, he gave little impetus to
    the development of the magazine novel. . . . Of all
    familiar works of eighteenth-century fiction, The Vicar of
    Wakefield shows the most profound influence of the single-
    essay periodical" (pp. 117-18). Finds this influence
    primarily in the chapter length, in that each is about as
    long as an individual essay in an essay serial. Finds the
    Citizen conspicuously in the tradition of the Tatler and
    Spectator despite its pseudo-letter form.

4 MONTAGUE, JOHN. "The Sentimental Prophecy: A Study of The
    Deserted Village." Dolmen Miscellany 1, no. 1:72-79.
        The poem concentrates on nabobs dispossessing peasants,
    and continues Goldsmith's vision of decay first set forth
    in the Enquiry, and a sequel to the Traveller, providing a
    description of Goldsmith's ideal society, a local culture
    based upon retreat and frugal content, also seen in Vicar,
    chapter four. Destruction of Auburn is not only destruction
    of childhood memory but also of the "dream of ideal retreat
    and escape" (p. 60). The didactic portion, 11. 250-300,
    is strongly rhetorical, and the strong emotion of 11. 309-
    384, the flight from the land, follows the poem's rhetori-
    cal pattern. "Imperceptibly, therefore, the destruction of
    Auburn has come to signify the destruction of many things:
    the narrator's childhood and his dreams of escape and
    peaceful retirement . . . , 'rural virtues,' and all the
    connexions of kindred in the family unit, 'the spontaneous
    joys' as opposed to unnatural artifice, virginal innocence,
    and, finally, poetry itself, even perhaps religion. . . .
    Auburn, in fact, is identified with the good of society and
    of England and The Deserted Village is one of the first
    statements of a great modern theme, the erosion of

traditional values and natural rhythms in a commercial
society: the fall of Auburn is the fall of a whole social
order" (p. 75).

5   SCHWEGEL, DOUGLAS M. "The American Couplets in The Deserted
Village." Georgia Review 16 (Spring):148-53.
       The eighteen-line description of the Georgian locale
where the immigrants from Auburn are going contrasts
sharply with the rest of the poem, presenting Georgia as
forbidding and inhospitable. Goldsmith presents Georgia
as virtually tropical, with songless birds, scorpions, and
tigers (panthers or cougars), and menacing Indians--not
noble savages. The poem's attack on luxury naturally
opposes colonialism, since it increased trade and hence
luxury. The future colonists are made to seem as forlorn
as possible. "Goldsmith paints so forbidding a picture of
America that he almost seems to be trying to frighten
prospective immigrants away from going there. His inten-
tion, however, is the sentimental one of arousing emotions
of pity and sympathy, and through such sentiment to protest
against the rapacity of the newly rich" (p. 153).

6   WEBB, JAMES W. "Irving and His 'Favorite Author.'" University of Mississippi Studies in English 3:61-74.
       Describes Irving's long-standing interest in Goldsmith,
with detailed accounts of his writing the 1825, 1840, and
1849 biographies and the critical reception of each,
emphasizing the favor the 1849 version long enjoyed.
"Quite obviously the degree of Goldsmith's influence on
Irving cannot be settled. Nevertheless, his influence is
obvious" (p. 73).

1963

A. Books

1   EMSLIE, MACDONALD. Goldsmith: "The Vicar of Wakefield."
Studies in English Literature 9. London: Edward Arnold,
74 pp.
       The principal figures fall into three groups: the
Primroses, the innocents; the worldly squire and his
agents, not trusting human nature; and Burchell/Sir William
Thornhill, representing prudence, but ultimately above the
action. The Vicar usually treats his womenfolk ironically,
even Sophia. His wife and daughters are often more openly
materialistic than he and appear more credulous than he
chiefly because he is narrator, as Jenkinson's defrauding

him at the fair shows. In the second half, most of his
criticism of his wife and daughters is sharper and less
gently ironic. Under Nature and Society, the contrast
between deeds and words soon broadens into the larger
contrast of reality and appearance. The Vicar appears to
be on the side of reality, recognizing their loss of
fortune and Squire Thornhill's bad reputation, though
Olivia accepts his attractive appearance. The Primroses
belong to the rural community, not the beau monde, by their
nature as well as their changed fortune.

Language: The semi-Johnsonian rhetoric underlines
Primrose's sententiousness, with greater formality occurring at more formal occasions like the Vicar's denunciation
of Squire Thornhill and his sermon. The Action: Not
realistic since chance and accident dominate the second
half too heavily. The ending is much like the final
tableau of a stage comedy with all the principals on stage.
Finds mixture of absurd and pathetic probably deliberate,
but finds lapses in the humor, too, so that Emslie questions
consistent subtlety and considers it "not a novel of the
first rank" (p. 78).

2   JEFFARES, A. NORMAN, ed. A Goldsmith Collection. London:
     Macmillan, 200 pp.
         The collection is brief though fairly representative,
     even with only nine letters from the Citizen. Nothing
     from the Vicar or the plays, though these are intelligently
     discussed in the introduction, which concludes: "He is
     eighteenth-century man at his best: well-read, well-
     traveled, and well-disposed to his readers." (p. xxiv).

B. Shorter Writings

1   FRIEDMAN, ARTHUR. "The Time of Composition of Goldsmith's
     Edwin and Angelina." In Restoration and Eighteenth-
     Century Literature: Essays in Honor of Alan Dugald
     McKillop. Edited by Caroll Camden. Chicago: University
     of Chicago Press for William Marsh Rice University, pp.
     155-59.
         The poem was first printed privately in an undated
     pamphlet "'for the amusement of the Countess of Northumber-
     land'" (p. 155), of which two copies now exist. The
     probable date of publication of the pamphlet is 1765.
     Friedman argues convincingly that the poem goes back at
     least as far as 1764 and may well have been composed when
     chapter eight of the Vicar was written, perhaps in 1762.

2   GARROD, H[EATHCOTE] W[ILLIAM]. "Goldsmith." In The Study of
     Good Letters. Edited by John Jones. Oxford: Clarendon

1963

Press, pp. 73-79.
A general essay. Goldsmith survives the prigs like
Boswell, Macaulay, and the sentimentalists like Thackeray.
His proper character is that of the good natured man and
his strength is his humor. Finds more to praise in his
prose than his poetry.

3 PLUMB, J[OHN] H[AROLD]. "Oliver Goldsmith and The Vicar of
Wakefield." In Men and Places. Boston: Houghton Mifflin,
pp. 288-94.
A very general biographical account and survey of
Goldsmith's literary career by a distinguished political
and social historian. Literary criticism very rudimentary.

1964

A. Books--None

B. Shorter Writings

1 BAKER, ERNEST A. The History of the English Novel: The Novel
of Sentiment and Gothic Romance. New York: Barnes & Noble,
5:66-70, 77-85, passim.
A photographic reprint of 1934.B3.

2 BALDERSTON, KATHARINE C. "New Goldsmith Letters." Yale
University Gazette 39 (October):67-72.
Two letters, both written in 1766, to John Bindley.

3 JEFFERSON, D. W. "Speculations on Three Eighteenth-Century
Prose Writers." In Of Books and Human Kind: Essays and
Poems Presented to Bonamy Dobrée. Edited by John Butt,
assisted by J. M. Cameron, D. W. Jefferson, and Robin
Skelton. London: Routledge & Kegan Paul, pp. 81-91.
Writers and works chosen are Smollett's Ferdinand Count
Fathom, Goldsmith's Vicar, and Johnson's Rasselas.
Discussion of Goldsmith, pp. 83-85. Shows that as early
as Enquiry (1759), Goldsmith's style shows wit and elegance
in antitheses. "Goldsmith had an idiosyncratic liking for
neatness and small-scale effects" (p. 84). Concentrates on
Primrose's sermon to the prisoners in chapter twenty-nine:
"The sermon as a whole is a perfectly serious discourse
on faith in adversity. . . . It seems probable that Goldsmith, though he intends the Vicar to be comic and light-
weight in some respects, expresses unconsciously a good
deal of his own temperament through him, and that these
turns of phrase reflect the almost too easy poise of his
Augustanism" (pp. 84-85).

1965

4   QUINTANA, RICARDO. "Logical and Rhetorical Elements in The
     Deserted Village." CE 26 (December):204-14.
         The poem has a design, a shape and involves two
     organizing principles, logical and rhetorical. Logical
     thesis: "There must be an end to the folly and injustice
     of these enclosures, which are wiping out of existence
     old, established villages, casting their folk adrift, and
     in consequence weakening the nation" (p. 205), though
     never set forth so baldly. The logical and poetic elements
     are fused to reveal a new dimension in the poem through
     contrasting scenes of the village flourishing and the
     village desolated, followed by the nostalgic descriptions,
     then a crucial set of contrasts--nature and art, thrift
     and luxury, country and city. The final section presents
     the horrors of immigration in the dreary colonies, ending
     with the hope and prophecy that Poetry can recall erring
     man to virtue. The poem does carry a very strong emotional
     charge, but this fact does not mean it expresses direct,
     personal emotion. In all these elements Goldsmith follows
     the Augustan tradition: "Though the idiom and tone of
     The Deserted Village are something far different from what
     we have in the great satires of Swift and Pope, Goldsmith's
     moral indignation was on this occasion no less than theirs"
     (p. 214).

                            1965

A. Books

1   COULTER, JOHN KNOX. "Oliver Goldsmith's Literary Reputation,
     1757-1801" Ph.D. dissertation, Indiana University, 179
     pp.
         The Enquiry is not just an overly ambitious effort by a
     young man but sets the pattern for all later works. Point
     of view is that of the objective observer, subject is
     creativity, and chief fear it expresses is not of license
     but of lack of innovation; discovery is of the variety of
     patterns in Europe, each suitable to its own society. The
     Citizen repeats many of these characteristics: as a
     pseudo-letter series, it emphasizes the detached observer,
     finds variety in several societies, and offers considerable
     social criticism. The Traveller and The Deserted Village
     follow, the first underscoring exile as its theme with
     a strong element of nostalgia. The second emphasizes
     nostalgia but also criticizes rapid industrialization and
     depopulation. Both poems are often wrongly seen as
     sentimental by those who prefer emotion to argument. The
     Vicar is also labeled sentimental, but is more nostalgic.

                            141

1965

Its real significance lies in its realistic appraisal of
the sentimental Vicar because of his inability to control
emotion. In recent criticism, the criticism of individual
works has shown considerable realization of the antisentimental strain in Goldsmith, but so far these individual
criticisms have not settled into a wholly consistent view
of his works or of his personality.

2   GRIFFIN, ROBERT J. "Goldsmith's Augustanism: A Study of His
Literary Works." Ph.D. dissertation, University of
California, Berkeley, 270 pp.
Goldsmith's ideas, attitudes, and techniques are those
of a late Augustan. His prose reveals a reliance on
"polite" literature as a practical, useful element in a
civilized society; a respect for neoclassical wit; rational
simplicity; and an insistence on the values of the English
Augustan writers: moderation, symmetry, belief in comedy
and satire as correctives, and Goldsmith's own persistent
antisentimentalism. His two major poems are primarily
didactic: The Traveller deals with the mind and happiness
of man, The Deserted Village with the social and moral
problem of England degenerating through luxury. The poetic
structure of both is Augustan. The Vicar as essentially
mock-sentimental clarifies Goldsmith's position as a
consistent late Augustan, though it does not necessarily
make him an antisentimental literary genius.

3   HAWKINS, MARION E. "Oliver Goldsmith the Essayist: A Study
of Themes and Styles." Ph.D. dissertation, University of
Wisconsin, 265 pp.
Reveals his receptivity and sensitivity to the main
currents of his own time and communicates these ideas and
attitudes in a natural style. Includes a description of
his personal career, a summary of research on his life and
writings, a survey of his relationship to the periodical
essay, the mirror of eighteenth-century society--and the
genesis of his various series of essays with analysis of
selected themes and stylistic qualities. His urbane, easy
style reinforces his most important themes: the decline in
learning, the role of taste, the position of writers, the
pursuit of happiness, and the need for laughing comedy.

B. Shorter Writings

1   ANON. "Goldy's Ballad." TLS (11 February):116.
Traces history of the privately printed "Edwin and
Angelina" from the 1770s, when owned by Isaac Reed, to
Prior, to Sir John Murray, who loaned it for English Poetry

exhibition at National Book League in 1947. This copy was sold at Sotheby's 11 June 1963, when bought by the Free Library of Philadelphia.

2   FERGUSON, OLIVER W. "The Materials of History: Goldsmith's Life of Nash." PMLA 80 (September):372-86.
       Goldsmith's biography uses anecdotes in Goldsmith's easy style with an attitude "perfectly balanced between irony and compassion" (p. 372). Offers more specific information about Goldsmith's sources plus some new information about Nash's last years, most of it found through trying to identify George Scott, who played a vital part in the Life. Ferguson discovered a large collection of Scott's letters in the British Museum, covering the years 1746 to 1799, in the Egerton MSS. 3725-58. Finds no direct evidence linking Goldsmith and Scott. "The biography's greatest appeal lies in Goldsmith's view of his hero and in the tact and humanity with which that view is presented" (p. 385).

3   FUSSELL, PAUL. The Rhetorical World of Augustan Humanism: Ethics and Imagery from Swift to Burke. Oxford: Clarendon Press, pp. 22, 59, 188-89, 238, 240-41, 262-63.
       Argues that the "ethical convictions and the related rhetorical techniques" of Swift, Pope, Johnson, Reynolds, Gibbon, and Burke resemble "a sort of central nervous system running through the whole eighteenth century . . . and . . . largely redeem the period from its occasional but highly publicized faults of grandiosity, sentimentality, self-satisfaction, and archness" (p. vii). Cannot decide whether Goldsmith belongs with this group of Augustan humanists or opposes it: includes him by name among writers "against the humanist tradition bounded at one end by Defoe and on the other by Burns and Blake" (p. 22), but later associates him with the humanist admirers of the ancients: "The traditions in collision here in the quarrel between [George] Adams [author of Essays on the Microscope, 1787, a defender of studying insects] and Goldsmith are essentially those of the Ancients and Moderns" (p. 241). Reprinted 1969.B3.

4   PRIVATEER, PAUL. "Goldsmith's Vicar of Wakefield: The Reunion of the Alienated Artist." Enlightenment Essays 6, no. 1: 27-36 [MLA Bibliography 1976, item 4666, p. 89, dates this volume in 1965; it should probably read 1975].
       In Deserted Village inhabitants dispossessed as is speaker-poet, and Poetry leaves the land. In Vicar dispossession is revealed in the action, especially Primrose's bankruptcy and eviction from Wakefield. Gold-smith's awareness of artist's alienation from society

leads to creation of Sir William, who reunites these
alienated elements, restores value of art and creates
narrative and social harmony. Fielding's Allworthy and
his narrator-historian correspond to Thornhill-Burchell
combination of Vicar, not as similar types but in function-
ing to set up moral norms, control vision, and point of
view--both Allworthy and Thornhill are agents of civil and
moral authority. Burchell repeatedly described as giving
instruction and pleasure, the Horatian formulation of
art's purposes, and his views coincide with those expressed
in Goldsmith's criticism. Argues Goldsmith's awareness of
a need to reunite artistic and moral authority in age when
decline of traditional models of such authority and threat
of social disruption among classes was so strong.

5   QUINTANA, RICARDO. "Goldsmith's Achievement as a Dramatist."
     UTQ 34 (January):159-77.
         Goldsmith stressed the natural and the simple: "For him
     they meant . . . the avoidance of anything like falsifica-
     tion and affected sophistication in art, in literary style;
     in tragedy they meant genuine feeling instead of bombast
     or trite rhetoric, in comedy a realistic portrayal of
     everyday life, particularly in its most laughable aspects
     (p. 163). Superficially The Good Natur'd Man seems a
     typical Georgian drama, but its central theme certainly
     warns against the folly of extreme benevolence. She Stoops
     to Conquer is a dramatic triumph, using Georgian conven-
     tions, succeeding by its naturalism of dialogue, tone, and
     setting. It too uses deceptions and false identities,
     especially in Tony's misrepresentation of the Hardcastle
     house as an inn and in Kate's misrepresentation of herself
     as a barmaid and a poor relation and in Marlow's confusion
     about his own identity. Goldsmith's irony is subtle but
     never bitter. His geniality shows in seeing faults as
     deviations from nature rather than as "moral evils arising
     from culpable irrationality" (p. 174).
         A condensed version appears in 1967.A5.

6   _____. "Oliver Goldsmith as a Critic of the Drama." SEL
     5 (Summer):435-54.
         Goldsmith believed drama is vital to a civilized
     society, a view set forth early in the Enquiry (1759);
     he reflected his own time in his appreciation of good-
     natured humor and in understanding hard-hitting satire,
     admiring Swift's in particular. His "Essay on the Theatre"
     makes three main points: comedy and tragedy are separate
     genres, comedy makes us laugh by presenting human folly
     naturally, and weeping comedy illegitimately mixes comedy
     and tragedy, views consistent with the English critical

Tradition Expressed By Dennis, Johnson, and Bishop Hurd, as well as with Voltaire's attack on French comédie larmoyante. Goldsmith's idea of naturalism is basic to his dramatic theory: a depiction of normal events, but not mere reproduction.
Main ideas appear in 1967.A5.

7 STEEVES, HARRISON R. Before Jane Austen: The Shaping of the Novel in the Eighteenth Century. New York: Holt, Rinehart, & Winston, pp. 193-97.
The Vicar was long popular for its shortness, simplicity, good humor, moral weight without solemnity, and leaving "no aftertaste of pessimism or cynicism" (p. 193). The plot is modelled on that of a play, even though Goldsmith's own plays came later. The theme is "the designs of a wealthy man of fashion upon the simplicity of a charming but too trusting virgin" (p. 194). Is the real plot the Vicar's character? "The Vicar himself is, in an obvious sense, the story. For the action is haphazard and arbitrary, except in so far as it illumines the character of a man whose problems repeatedly involve conflicts between old precept and personal judgment" (p. 197). Believes "In our own century its melodrama, its providential interventions, its sentimentality, and its pietism have been kicked about mercilessly by another order of critics," though he does not specify particular critics. Finds Goldsmith a sentimentalist in the sense that honest sentiment is well assimilated into a highly sympathetic nature.

8 SUTHERLAND, W. O. S., Jr. "Satiric Ambiguity: The Vicar of Wakefield and the Kindly Satirist." In The Art of the Satirist: Essays on Satire of Augustan England. Austin: Humanities Research Center, University of Texas, pp. 84-91.
If the satirist's desire to reform the world declines, he may change from the harsh moralist to the patient, humorous, kindly satirist. Goldsmith uses the devices of the harsher Augustan satirists like Swift, but his attitude is more complex. He presents the Vicar ambiguously, since virtue and foolishness blend, and his naivete is a key trait. Notes the idyllic quality of the first half of the novel and elements of sorrow and anxiety in the second half, where the Vicar shows less naivete. "The Vicar may cause difficulty to his friends and family, but he is not a threat to his society. Since the Vicar's moral virtues extenuate his error, the reader's disapproval is weakened. Rather than moral denunciation, he tends to show condescension, pity, or even compassion. In addition, the reader's own sophistication makes him constantly aware that his

1966

acceptance of the Vicar's world is ironic. Goldsmith makes
the reader, and the reader alone, omniscient, and to know
all is to forgive the Vicar" (pp. 90-91).

<u>1966</u>

A. Books

   1   FRIEDMAN, ARTHUR, ed. <u>Collected Works of Oliver Goldsmith</u>.
       5 vols. Oxford: Clarendon Press, 1:518 pp., 2:495 pp.,
       3:487 pp., 4:448 pp., 5:504 pp.
          Now the definitive edition of Goldsmith's works,
       consisting of those works generally classified as "literary":
       the reviews, essays, biographies, novel, poems, plays,
       prefaces and introductions, and some miscellaneous pieces.
       Friedman's introductions provide information, if available,
       about "composition, publication, and early reception . . . ,
       a consideration, when necessary of the question of author-
       ship, and . . . a discussion of the text. The introductions
       make no effort to set the works in the context of literary
       history and offer no critical evaluations or analyses"
       (1:xx). Now standard authority for the canon of Goldsmith's
       works.

B. Shorter Writings

   1   CONANT, MARTHA P. <u>The Oriental Tale in England in the
       Eighteenth Century</u>. New York: Octagon Books, 348 pp.
          A photographic reprint of 1908.B1.

   2   EVERSOLE, RICHARD. "The Oratorical Design of <u>The Deserted
       Village</u>." <u>ELN</u> 4 (December):99-104.
          Two possible organizational schemes available to Gold-
       smith were ironic satire or vulgar propaganda. The mode
       adopted is well fitted to the argumentative requirement of
       the material. Cites Quintana's analysis of logical and
       rhetorical elements (1964.B4) and argues that the structure
       is that of the classical oration and that the seven parts
       appear in their usual order, but not apparently based on
       "any single rhetorical scheme" (p. 100), but cites
       Goldsmith's review of John Ward's <u>A System of Oratory</u> for
       various observations. "For Goldsmith's mode of persuasion
       is frequently pathos, either the compassionate appeal for
       human distress in the <u>reprehensio</u> or the sympathetic
       aesthetic response to an inanimate description in the
       <u>narratio</u>" (p. 104).

3   McDONALD, DANIEL. "The Vicar of Wakefield: A Paradox."
     College Language Association Journal 10, no. 1:23-33.
         Argues that the various theories of unity that have
     been proposed to explain the novel simply distort it.

4   POTTLE, FREDERICK A. James Boswell: The Earlier Years, 1740-
     1769. New York: McGraw-Hill; London: Heineman, pp. 59,
     381-83, 432, passim.
         Most comments are simply mentions of Goldsmith's name.
     No discussion of the degree of friendship between the two
     men nor of Boswell's opinion of his personality in this
     first volume.

5   RODWAY, ALLAN. "Goldsmith and Sheridan: Satirists of Senti-
     ment." In Renaissance and Modern Essays Presented to
     Vivian de Sola Pinto in Celebration of his Seventieth
     Birthday. Edited by G. R. Hibbard, with the assistance of
     George A. Panichas and Allan Rodway. London: Routledge &
     Kegan Paul, pp. 65-72.
         Goldsmith and Sheridan were affected by the Genteel or
     Sentimental mode they profess to attack. Goldsmith admired
     Farquhar, who is stylistically late Restoration "but is
     surely early Sentimental in terms of plot" (p. 65). We
     find an index of Hanoverian taste in Goldsmith's having to
     cut the Bailiff scene in The Good Natur'd Man. Goldsmith
     censures Honeywood from beginning to end through his uncle,
     Sir William. The mixture of virtue and folly in Honeywood
     makes satire of him difficult--he is improbable rather than
     complex. Goldsmith's plays basically are dramas of
     situation and hence the characters are often "humour"
     characters, funny but not absurd. His "plots do not depend
     on characters; that is, they need it so desperately" (p.
     70). "Goldsmith's characters--in She Stoops to Conquer,
     anyway--know they are only for fun and often play up to,
     rather than play their allotted parts. They display, as
     it were, a private feeling that after all there is more in
     them than first met the author's eyes" (p. 70).

6   SPECTOR, ROBERT D. English Literary Periodicals and the
     Climate of Opinion During the Seven Years' War. Mouton
     Studies in English, 34. The Hague: Mouton, 408 pp.,
     passim.
         Brief discussion of Goldsmith's opinion expressed in the
     Monthly Review, the Busy Body, and the Bee on literature,
     aesthetics, and chinoiserie, most of which have little or
     no connection with the war or politics.

1967

1967

A. Books

1   ABBOTT, Sister M. JOHN VIANNY. "Irony in Oliver Goldsmith's
        The Citizen of the World." Ph.D. dissertation, St. Louis
        University, 147 pp.
            Primary irony shows itself in the oriental visitor who
        is both spokesman for the author and the object of satire.
        Studies frame-tale, through which Goldsmith ironically
        presents primitivism, cosmopolitanism, and philosophical
        optimism. Considers the primary irony as it appears in
        letters criticizing English life. Here the oriental
        visitor is sometimes the unwitting spokesman for the
        author and sometimes the conscious satirist. In his three
        roles as observer, actor, and instructor, Lien Chi creates
        secondary ironies. Finds more unity in the work than
        usually ascribed to it, with irony an important contribu-
        ting factor. Emphasizes Goldsmith's reasonable and
        realistic response to trends of thought in his time as
        they apply to problems of universal significance.

2   GANNON, SUSAN R. "The Rhetorical Strategy of Oliver Gold-
        smith." Ph.D. dissertation, Fordham University, 301 pp.
            Such causes as the decline of patronage, the rise of
        the novel, the emergence of a mass reading public changed
        the intellectual climate in the mid-eighteenth century,
        producing a new writer-audience relationship and called
        forth changes in rhetorical strategies. The bulk and
        variety of Goldsmith's work and his interest in reaching
        the mass audience make him a useful author for studying
        these changes. During his Grub Street period he created
        warm and charming personas as his literary alter ego.
        Variations on these personas unify and help focus
        otherwise dull and skimpy material in the lives of Parnell
        and Bolingbroke. The persona in the Life of Nash is fairly
        suave with pretensions to accuracy to justify bringing in
        a mass of documentary "evidence." In Animated Nature he
        uses a genial, humorous persona. These techniques were
        vital elements in his masterpieces, the Citizen and the
        Vicar, where Lien Chi and Primrose are variously the
        naïve, the good man, and the public defender of morals.

3   JOEL, HELMUTH WULF, Jr. "The Theme of Education in the Works
        of Oliver Goldsmith." Ph.D. dissertation, University of
        Pennsylvania, 207 pp.
            The effects of Goldsmith's informal education came from
        his father, his uncle Contarine, and his travels, as well
        as his formal schooling, and were disastrous. The schools
        of the time were not fitted for a boy of his type.

Examination of the theme of education in his fiction shows
Goldsmith condemning the kind of education he himself had
had. In his nonfiction Goldsmith advocates that young
people stay home to go to college and avoid travel, but in
his fiction he stresses that travel alone brings a useful
education, the kind he most valued.

4   KIRK, CLARA M. Oliver Goldsmith. Twayne English Authors
    Series 47. New York: Twayne, 193 pp.
        Her five chapters consider Goldsmith as essayist, poet,
    novelist, playwright, and biographer, writing in these
    forms "not consecutively, but concurrently" (p. 1).
    Describes Goldsmith as having "Deistic views" (p. 116) and
    labors argument for 1764 as "the year when Johnson probably
    took the manuscript [of the Vicar] to the printer" (p. 86),
    despite the opinion of Crane, Friedman, and Quintana that
    the manuscript was probably finished about 1762, and surely
    before Boswell met Johnson in 1763. The space related
    to Goldsmith's biographies is unusual in such an introduc-
    tory study, but does reflect recent interest in these works,
    especially the Life of Nash. Much of this interpretation
    is rendered questionable by the view that "Part of the
    interest in Goldsmith's Life of Richard Nash lies in the
    fact that the author was composing an elaborate apologia
    pro vita sua, just as when he wrote the Memoirs of M.
    de Voltaire" (p. 173). Throughout the book, Kirk fails to
    distinguish between narrator or dramatic speaker and author
    speaking autobiographically. Citations are to Gibbs's
    edition, not Friedman's.

5   QUINTANA, RICARDO. Oliver Goldsmith, A Georgian Study.
    Masterpieces of World Literature Series. New York:
    Macmillan, 213 pp.
        In seven chapters he discusses Goldsmith's performance
    in each of the literary forms he practiced: the review
    and the Enquiry; the single essay and the Bee; the Citizen;
    Goldsmith among the Georgians, an account of his friendships
    and social life as he became famous, emphasizing his
    contemporaries' view of him as a writer of genius but a
    fool in society, as presented with different emphases in
    Boswell's Life of Johnson and Reynolds's character-sketch,
    first published in 1952; the Vicar, with all its attendant
    complexities and ambiguities; the poems as didactic,
    rhetorical works; and his two plays, especially She Stoops
    to Conquer, which Quintana regards as Goldsmith's most
    completely successful work. The study contains an appendix,
    "Notes on Some of Goldsmith's Miscellaneous Writings,"
    discussing what is commonly dismissed as "hack writing,"

1967

especially four groups: the pamphlet on the Cock Lane
Ghost; the biographical pieces, especially the Life of Nash;
the historical writings; and the popularizations of
scientific subjects, especially Animated Nature. The
"Bibliographical Notes" have comments on sources both old
and new.

B. Shorter Writings

1 DUSSINGER, JOHN A. "Oliver Goldsmith, Citizen of the World."
Studies on Voltaire and the Eighteenth Century [trans-
actions of the Second International Conference on the
Enlightenment, organized by the University of St. Andrews.]
55:445-61.
Goldsmith's writings show an interest in the empirical
philosophy of Bacon, Locke, and the philosophes, and his
Grub Street apprentice writing "evinces an intensive
search for a cohesive Weltanschauung, which is fulfilled at
last in his vocation as a poet" (p. 446). "Intellectual
cosmopolitanism is the ideal of Goldsmith's emulation, and
Voltaire is his model" (p. 447). Experience, as opposed to
fancy, as promulgated by Locke, Swift, Voltaire, and
Johnson, underlies Goldsmith's ironic view of the Man in
Black, Sir William Thornhill, Charles and George Primrose,
Sir William Honeywood, and young Marlow. "He found his
identity as a poet in Imlac's example of being 'contented
to be driven along the stream of life without directing
their course to any particular port'" (p. 450). "Goldsmith's empirical quest for identity . . . led progressively
to the role of the poet" (p. 460). "Finally, Goldsmith
believed in the utility of his poetic mission for society
as well as himself" (p. 461).

2 FERGUSON, OLIVER W. "Goldsmith." SAQ 66 (Summer):465-72.
A review-essay occasioned by Friedman's edition
(1966.A1). Pleads for the intrinsic interest of the "non-
literary" works like the histories and Animated Nature, as
well as the more widely read pieces. Praises Goldsmith's
prose as pliant and capable of both formal, rhetorical
effects and easy informality. Reminds us of such fundamental ideas as Goldsmith's belief in an unchanging human
nature and in the need to balance the claims of head and
heart to achieve the good life and finds Goldsmith
expressing interesting critical ideas such as his dislike
of Gray's odes. Finds Goldsmith hardly fits Thackeray's
sentimentalized description of him, but possessed of self-
knowledge and self-judgment, a sure comic sense, a proper
awareness of the emotional side of life, and an unillusioned
view of the world.

3   JACK, IAN. "The Deserted Village." New Rambler 3, ser. C
     (June):2-4.
         Johnson's preference for Traveller lies in its being a
     very Augustan poem, while the Deserted Village contains
     intimations of the poetic style of the future and may be
     seen as a development from the lines on rural depopulation
     in the Traveller, a passage, like the opening of Vicar,
     chapter four, perhaps inspired by Goldsmith's visit to the
     country described in Lloyd's Evening Post, 1762. Traveller
     presents spatial exile, Deserted Village temporal exile.
     A present/past contrast is very common in Augustan
     literature.

4   Le BRETON, MAURICE. "Goldsmith et l'Italie." Caliban 3
     (March):29-56.
         Discussion of Goldsmith's relationship to Italy, begin-
     ning with the possibility he got his medical degree there,
     but grants there is no factual evidence. Mainly compiles
     references to Italy in the writings, finding many in
     Animated Nature. In Traveller, the portrait of Italy is
     the least flattering. In other writings conventional
     references to Italian opera, generally refers to Italian
     painting as superior to French, but he was drawing on
     D'Alembert and difficult to tell how much is his own
     opinion. Recognized Italian greatness in the Renaissance,
     but finds decadence, futility, superstition in the
     eighteenth century.

5   LOWENTHAL, LEO. Literature, Popular Culture, and Society.
     Englewood Cliffs, N.J.: Prentice-Hall, A Spectrum Book,
     173 pp., passim.
         Examines Johnson's and Goldsmith's attitudes toward
     problem of writing for a mass public rather than for a
     more select group. Finds Goldsmith attacking booksellers
     forthrightly in the Enquiry for dubious practices and
     debating the problem of whether or not writer must write to
     the audience's taste, even if debasing his own genius, with
     success often largely a matter of luck. Similar opinions
     from Johnson. Goldsmith's views range from good-natured
     raillery at the magazines of the time to considerable
     pessimism about possible conflicts the author faced in
     writing for the public.

6   PAULSON, RONALD F. Satire and the Novel in the Eighteenth
     Century. New Haven: Yale University Press, pp. 269-75.
         Sees Vicar as "the step beyond Fielding in the
     exploitation of irony as a fictional device" (p. 269).
     Novel's critical reputation has suffered from its long

being a children's book. Popularity came from Goldsmith's
"building on fairy-tale motifs and archetypal patterns
that touched a sensitive chord in all readers and showed a
way toward introducing romance into the realistic novel
form" (p. 270). Uses myths of God searching for hospitality
among humans, the disguised ruler, Jack and the Beanstalk,
with Job the central myth. "Irony is part of his narrator's
temperament, creating a more complex as well as a wiser
person than was possible in Fielding's kind of narrative"
(p. 271). "The theme that emerges from this kind of central
character, however elemental in Dr. Primrose, is self-
knowledge and the growth to self-realization" (p. 272).
     In second half Goldsmith may have exhausted his ideas or
picked up his real interest, the Job myth. Reverts to
picaresque, and novel loses tight unity of family as
microcosm. Digressions, the sermon, political debates more
resemble Smollett's very loose structure. Romantic and
mythic elements become prominent; coincidence and interpo-
lated elements more frequent, and so by their unreality
help reader accept "preposterous reversals and recognitions"
(p. 274) of ending.

7   SHERBURN, GEORGE, and BOND, DONALD F. "The Restoration and
    Eighteenth Century." In A Literary History of England.
    2d ed. Edited by Albert C. Baugh. New York: Appleton-
    Century-Crofts, 3:1043-44, 1056-62. Bibliographical
    Supplement [by Donald F. Bond].
        Hardly any revision, and Bond's Bibliographical
    Supplement updates the scholarship and criticism cited to
    1966.

1968

A. Books

1   PETERSON, PATRICIA C. "Comic Unity in Oliver Goldsmith's The
    Vicar of Wakefield." Ph.D. dissertation, University of
    Wisconsin, 205 pp.
        The main plot presents two major themes, virtue triumphs
    over distress and happiness results from peace of mind, not
    material objects. Primroses' adventures imply the first
    and Vicar's didactic speeches the second. Each is touched
    by irony: the family wins because the deus ex machina, Sir
    William Thornhill, and even the Vicar cannot practice his
    own lessons. Novel establishes antitheses between inno-
    cence and experience, benevolence and selfishness, and
    authority and permissiveness. Goldsmith uses conventions

from Greek romance in first half, from romances of action
in second. These latter help explain quick reversals of
action. Organization has almost geometric precision, with
Olivia's elopements marking the division. Rhetorical
patterns of speech help unify and distinguish voices of
Vicar as narrator and Vicar as character and help establish
tone and unity. Dominant trait of both aspects of Vicar is
sententiousness. In first half the Vicar-narrator comments
ironically on Vicar-character's foibles; in second half
emotional exaggeration helps add comedy to sentimental
scenes. Thus Goldsmith gives serious perspective to comic
adventures and comic perspective to serious calamities and
keeps reader at proper aesthetic distance from both.

B. Shorter Writings

1   DUNCAN, JEFFREY L. "The Rural Ideal in Eighteenth-Century
    Fiction." SEL 8 (Summer):517-35.
        Discussion of Goldsmith pp. 524-27: The Vicar tells his
    own story, and we must remember he does not speak for
    Goldsmith necessarily. His interpretations are subject to
    correction, but the rural order is stable, using many
    elements present in Fielding and Smollett: "the golden
    mean between poverty and ostentation, microcosmic social
    structure . . . with attention devoted to duty and affec-
    tion subsisting between various members, and even in
    hospitality extended to good friends and neighbors of the
    family" (p. 524). Descriptions are far more general than
    Fielding's. Focuses on idyllic atmosphere--hardly anyone
    works. Aesthetic considerations important, with beauty of
    scenery emphasized. Tone is the complicating factor--the
    Vicar is outside most action, an observer, and this fact
    throws doubt on attaining this ideal, given ironic plot
    structure. Resolution lies in Vicar's belief in the ideal:
    "He learns, in fact, that his basic fault has been this
    very worldliness, which stems from vanity, an excessive
    concern with worldly fortune and happiness" (p. 562).

2   JAARSMA, RICHARD J. "Satiric Intent in The Vicar of Wake-
    field." Studies in Short Fiction 5 (Summer):331-41.
        Sees a distinction between Goldsmith's works that
    emphasize his "sentimentality and social awareness ('The
    Deserted Village'), and those works that are consciously
    satirical ('The Citizen of the World,' She Stoops to
    Conquer, and The Vicar of Wakefield)" (p. 332). Satire of
    Vicar has three objects: the ideal of rustic innocence,
    the sentimental novel, and the "belief in the innate good-
    ness and innocence of man" (p. 332). Primrose bears the

1968

brunt of Goldsmith's satire: pride his chief sin, though
he reiterates his lack of it. At end of novel, he has not
changed and his character "stands as one of the most
savage indictments of bourgeois values in eighteenth-
century literature" (p. 339). "Squire [sic] William
Thornhill (Mr. Burchell)," the moral norm against whom
Primrose is judged, is a man of rational prudence,
protects the Primroses against themselves, and offers
pronouncements on literature, art, and society remarkably
similar to Johnson's, in a rhetoric recalling rhythms of
Johnsonian prose.

3   ORWELL, GEORGE. Review of The Vicar of Wakefield. In
Collected Essays, Journalism, and Letters of George Orwell.
Edited by Sonia Orwell and Ian Angus. New York: Harcourt,
Brace & World, 3:268-71.
        Vicar is "essentially a period piece, and its charm
about equalled by its absurdity" (p. 269), but still
readable. Novel intended as a moral tale, "But the
confusion in Goldsmith's mind between simple goodness and
financial prudence gives the book, at this date, a strange
moral atmosphere" (p. 269). Endorsement of simple life is
not as absurd as it might seem, since Goldsmith attacking
the same moral evils as Swift and Fielding, and aware of
the rise of a new moneyed class with no sense of social
responsibility. Contains serious social criticism, but
enduring charm lies in manner, with story beautifully
constructed, even if absurd.

1969

A. Books

1   HOPKINS, ROBERT H. The True Genius of Oliver Goldsmith.
Baltimore: Johns Hopkins Press, 253 pp.
        A revision and enlargement of 1961.A1. Hopkins argues
that Vicar is consistently sustained satire of Primrose,
whom Hopkins cannot accept as an example of the amiable
humorist.

B. Shorter Writings

1   [BOSWELL, JAMES.] The Correspondence and Other Papers
Relating to the Making of the Life of Johnson. Edited with
an Introduction and Notes by Marshall Waingrow. Yale
Editions of the Private Papers of James Boswell (Research
Edition). New Haven: Yale University Press. Vol. 3,

Correspondence, 744 pp., passim.
Largely miscellaneous anecdotes and comments on
Goldsmith, including the controversy over Johnson's
epitaph, reappearing in the Life (1791.B1) in more polished
form. Virtually all the comments postdate Goldsmith's
death.

2   BRACK, O. M., Jr. "Goldsmith's A Survey of Experimental
    Philosophy." Book Collector 18, no. 4 (Winter):519-20.
    A bibliographical study: In gathering G, leaf eight
    was cancelled, though Temple Scott and Iolo Williams
    indicate otherwise. The book's compilation and printing
    extended over ten years, beginning as early as September,
    1765, but earliest advertisement of its publication appears
    in London Chronicle, 27 March 1776. Prior suggested need
    of revision occasioned delay. Inclusion of illustrations
    caused changes in printing. The pagination was continuous,
    and thus Williams and Scott could not explain gathering of
    only seven leaves.

3   FUSSELL, PAUL. The Rhetorical World of Augustan Humanism:
    Ethics and Imagery from Swift to Burke. New York: Oxford
    University Press, A Galaxy Book, pp. 22, 59, 188-89, 238,
    240-41, 262-63.
    A paperbound reprint of 1965.B3.

4   JAARSMA, RICHARD J. "The Deserted Village and 'Isaiah.'"
    N&Q, n.s. 16 (September):351-52.
    Important series of thematic parallels between the poem
    and Isaiah suggest it was a very possible source: the
    lament at the decadence of society concerned chiefly with
    wealth, supported by citations of particular sections of
    Isaiah such as 5:8 and 34:11. "Isaiah's habit of seeing
    man in terms of a plant or society as a garden is
    consistently imitated by Goldsmith" (p. 351), particularly
    in ll. 389-94. These parallels establish a symbolic
    substructure which by association reveals "an apocalyptic
    vision of existence in the poem" (p. 352).

5   LOUGHLIN, RICHARD L. "Lift Up Your Hearts: Oliver Goldsmith's
    Glory." Educational Forum 33 (March):337-41.
    For the general reader only, with praise for Goldsmith's
    many versatile accomplishments.

6   PIPER, WILLIAM B. The Heroic Couplet. Cleveland: Western
    Reserve-Case University Press, pp. 401-5.
    Goldsmith follows his great predecessors, especially
    Pope, by "infusing his poems with the impression of

1970

conversation" (p. 402). His main contribution is his
"tremendous variety of incidental lyric practices and its
pervasively lyrical appeal" (p. 403). Alliteration and
assonance recur in Deserted Village, as does frequent
elision. Also refrain-like echoes and repetition of
individual words, especially rather vague ones like "sweet,"
used only figuratively; "sport," any free and happy
activity; and "bower," suggesting sylvan comfort. "The
public listens passive and virtually ignored as the
speaker modulates his Orphic address, achieving a poetic
resolution merely between his two expressive urges--to
lecture and to sing" (p. 405).

1970

A. Books

1   ISAACS, DONNA A. "The Figure of the Outsider in Eighteenth-
    Century Satire." Ph.D. dissertation, Yale University,
    354 pp.
        Comparisons of Montesquieu and Voltaire with Swift and
    Goldsmith concentrate on examining the type of the
    traveller-character, with little or no reference to the
    fictive structure in which he occurs. A further problem,
    especially for the less experienced or hasty reader, is
    that while Montesquieu's and Voltaire's presuppositions
    about man, society, and the cosmos are generally critical
    of eighteenth-century French society, certainly Swift's
    and very probably Goldsmith's assumptions about similar
    matters were Christian and generally antirevolutionary.
    She assumes that Swift and Goldsmith shared the general
    assumptions of the philosophes. The eighteenth-century
    satirist did not need to attack vice in a savage,
    Juvenalian way, indecorously arousing anger in the attacked.
    Instead, his technique could be more subtle: he need only
    present those he was attacking from novel, ingenious angle
    to make them ridiculous and absurd. Condensed version:
    1973.B2.

2   LEVINE, PHILIP. "A Critical and Historical Study of Oliver
    Goldsmith's The Citizen of the World." Ph.D. dissertation,
    Princeton University, 235 pp.
        Six broad groups of subject matter: manners, politics,
    conduct, literary criticism, the mid-eighteenth-century
    man of letters, and contemporary interests. Concentrates
    on first three, with brief remarks on others. Goldsmith
    good-naturedly satirizes contemporary vices and follies

156

but also presents an extensive account of English manners.
Political letters set forth his Toryism, similar to
Johnson's, and argue that the current balanced English
system allows the middle group in society considerable
freedom. Associates decline of nations with colonial
expansion and argues for English self-sufficiency. Letters
on conduct reflect interest in ethics, taking both specula-
tive and prescriptive positions, discussing the problem
of happiness, uses of emotions, with advice to the young.
Skeptical note strong here, with emphasis on human
limitations as in Swift and Johnson. Diverse techniques
presenting subject matter make for artistic excellence and
include oriental tales, anecdotes, fables, biographies,
allegories, parodies, and some devices showing influence
of novel, especially characterization, setting, dialogue,
and concrete detail. By these techniques the letters
dramatize rather than explain ideas.

3 PONTHIEU, JUDY F. S. "Oliver Goldsmith as Social Critic in
The Citizen of the World." Ph.D. dissertation, Texas
Tech University, 163 pp.
    Analyzes Citizen papers as social criticism to define
borders of Goldsmith's social philosophy, noting such
critical devices as satire and models such as Marana and
Montesquieu. Letters follow light satirical style of
Spectator and differ from Johnson's sermonizing Rambler
style. Uses frame story of Lien Chi, his son Hing Po, and
his love affair with the beautiful Zelis to provide
narrative interest and literary continuity. Social
criticism generally aims at follies of society, pretensions
of lower-class people like the Tibbses to aristocratic
manners, and misguided aristocratic interests in cooking,
horseracing, and painting. Proposes cosmopolitanism as the
ideal.

B. Shorter Writings

1 ANDREWS, WILLIAM L. "Goldsmith and Freneau in 'The American
Village.'" Early American Literature 5 (Fall):14-23.
    Freneau's poem is an answer to Goldsmith's anticolonial-
ism, especially in his unflattering portrait of Georgia, ll.
341-362.

2 BURTON, DOLORES M. "Intonation Pattern of Sermons in Seven
Novels." Language and Style 3 (Summer):205-18.
    Analysis of Vicar's sermon in chapter twenty-nine,
pp. 210-12: "The sermon style is that of the "Senecan
amble, where every major proposition is immediately offset

by another that is similar in grammatical structure but
antithetical in meaning" (p. 210). The rhetorical
pattern--pitch contours--suggest irony: "All that comes
through here, however, is the tone of disappointment with
events and of philosophical resignation, although the
communication situation, involving as it does the Vicar's
unjust imprisonment, borders on irony." (pp. 211-12).

3   COLE, RICHARD C. "Oliver Goldsmith's Reputation in Ireland,
    1762-74." MP 68 (August):65-70.
        The comedies were the most widely known from the
    frequent advertisements of performances, and She Stoops to
    Conquer was published several times. The poems were read
    if not often reviewed. Faulkner did publish the Traveller,
    but the Deserted Village was more widely quoted and
    reviewed. In most cases, a Dublin edition followed soon
    after London publication, sometimes the same year, some-
    times the year following, although Essays, 1765, was not
    published in Dublin until 1767. The various histories
    also were published in at least one edition. Most Irish
    critics identified the Traveller and the Deserted Village
    as his finest literary achievements.

4   FRASER, G. S. "Johnson and Goldsmith: The Mid-Augustan
    Norm." Essays and Studies, n.s. 23:51-70.
        Johnson and Goldsmith are the only poets who add
    something to the heroic couplet after Pope: "Johnson has
    a weightiness and Goldsmith a mellowness, a tenderness, a
    musical flow . . ." (p. 51). Goldsmith had an ear for
    songs, which Johnson did not. The sense of spontaneity a
    key quality in Goldsmith's writing. "In this [the anti-
    thetical pattern of Augustan heroic couplets], Goldsmith
    looks forward, though unconsciously, to a new age, and
    Johnson consolidates the gains of an old one" (p. 69).

5   FRIEDMAN, ARTHUR. "Aspects of Sentimentalism in Eighteenth-
    Century Literature." In The Augustan Age: Essays
    Presented to Louis A. Landa. Edited by Henry Miller, Eric
    Rothstein, and G. S. Rousseau. Oxford: Clarendon Press,
    pp. 247-61.
        Begins with Goldsmith's remarks about two different
    features of sentimental comedy in his "Essay on the
    Theatre": the excessively good character and the effect
    this kind of drama has on the audience. Discusses the
    sentimental character and affective elements separately,
    accurately describes Goldsmith as antibenevolist throughout
    his writings, but speaking of Good Natur'd Man, finds him
    "attacking not the sentimental virtues but the faults that

resemble them" (p. 250). Plays Goldsmith called "Weeping Sentimental Comedy" limit themselves to very few sentimen- tal scenes. Friedman believes that the period produced comic novels with sentimental plots, unlike these plays, and uses the Vicar to develop ideas briefly. Concludes: "The sentimental plot, showing the sufferings of the virtuous, thus fits very well into the serious work with a happy ending" (p. 254). Mentions the importance of Primrose as narrator, but not the possibilities this technique offers for irony.

6   HART, PAXTON. "The Presentation of Oliver Goldsmith in Boswell's Life of Johnson." Re: Arts and Letters 3, no. 2:4-15.
   Prior, Forster, Scott, Irving, as Hilles noted in the Reynolds's Portraits (1952.B4) all see Boswell presenting an unflattering portrait of Goldsmith. Argues Boswell's portrait is just and that the Boswell Private Papers corroborate view presented by Reynolds. Boswell stressed Goldsmith's jealousy, vanity, and envy, usually qualified by granting his talents as a writer. Boswell balanced Goldsmith's personal failings against his writing talents. Johnson's remarks before Goldsmith's death more cutting than those made afterward, when he stressed Goldsmith's virtues as a writer and dwelt little on his personality. Boswell's attitude was at first cool, but warmed especially after She Stoops to Conquer. Reynolds was undoubtedly closer to Goldsmith than Johnson and understood him better, as his portrait-sketch shows.

7   QUINTANA, RICARDO. "Oliver Goldsmith, Ironist to the Geor- gians." In Eighteenth Century Studies in Honor of Donald F. Hyde. Edited by W. F. Bond. New York: Grolier Club, pp. 297-310.
   Argues Goldsmith's irony has assumed imaginative proportions in the Citizen, Vicar, and She Stoops to Conquer, an irony, he concludes, "which anticipates Jane Austen's" but is "not relentless like Swift's, not a constant reminder of incorrigible human folly, nor . . . defiant and skeptical like the irony of the romantics" (p. 310).

8   STORM, LEO F. "Literary Convention in Goldsmith's Deserted Village." HLQ 33 (May):243-56.
   Despite Prior's assertion to the contrary, Goldsmith's debt in the poem to classical and contemporary convention is great. Poem adapts two genres then current, the English version of the Virgilian georgic and the

1971

locodescriptive poem. Produces fresh effects from the
synthesis. Believes Thomson's influence important,
especially in his humanitarianism, but disagrees with
Miner (1959.B6) that the poem is a kind of redefined
pastoral, and sees it as more properly a georgic, as that
form was redefined by Dryden's translation of the Georgics.
Even though the locodescriptive or topographical poem was
not a classical genre, it had been a living English genre
since Denham's Cooper's Hill, with such various settings
as rivers, towns, and ruins. Deserted Village uses the
ruin convention. The poem is a general defense of the
traditional, complex system of the older order rather than
just an attack upon luxury, and certainly is not an
example of Romantic primitivism any more than Vergil's
poems are, rather an affirmation of Augustan values.

1971

A. Books

1 BACKMAN, SVEN. This Singular Tale: A Study of "The Vicar of
Wakefield" and Its Literary Background. Lund Studies in
English 40. Lund: G. W. K. Gleerup, 281 pp.
Surveys Goldsmith scholarship and the background
materials, in terms of traditional literary history.
Brings together materials generally familiar, summarizing
and assembling literary influences from the novel, periodical essay, and drama. Surveys relation to earlier
novelists, especially Fielding, discusses similarities between rogue literature and Goldsmith's handling of the
gulling of Primrose at the fair, the rural setting as a
later example of the classical and medieval "pleasant place."
Backman considers enthusiastically the contributions of the
periodical essay tradition, the incident-per-chapter method,
and suggests Goldsmith may have had serial publication in
mind. Concludes that Goldsmith's real originality consists
in his decision to have an unexciting, middle-aged clergyman tell the story.

2 FOYS, ROBERT M. "Narrative Strategy in the Major Prose and
Poetry of Oliver Goldsmith." Ph.D. dissertation,
University of Illinois–Urbana, 230 pp.
Argues that personas are not Goldsmith, even though
their experiences parallel his. Personas are not merely
techniques for Goldsmith to present themes but are his
major subjects. Lien Chi develops as character, testing
his idea of being a philosophical traveller working from
direct experience, not a priori assumptions. Traveller
primarily a philosophical prospect poem with stationary

speaker until latter portion where more emotional
involvement changes his detachment. Deserted Village shows
a different angle of perception, which accounts for stronger
emotional quality. Narrator's direct visual perception of
desolated Auburn leads to idealization of village of the
past. In Vicar, Primrose's unreliability changes novel
from didactic story Goldsmith seems to have intended.
Rejects view of novel as sustained satire for idea that
structure and characters are more similar to a comic play
than a novel of any variety. Sees novel as complex,
ironic, fictional comedy.

3   SCHANG, WILLIAM J. "Goldsmith's Development as a Comic
    Dramatist." Ph.D. dissertation, University of Michigan,
    193 pp.
        Goldsmith accepts two traditions in laughter, both
    amiable laughter and biting satire. Wants drama natural,
    lively, and original, but these qualities to be consistent
    with total dramatic tone. Understands practical needs of
    theatre and its mixed audience, and realizes audience wanted
    spectacle, stage business, novelty and may well have shared
    some of these preferences. Rejects entimental comedy as
    untrue to life and bad threatre, and contemporary audience
    shared some of these views. Vicar satirizes sentimentality
    but comic perspective is inconsistent and book shows im-
    balance between sympathy and detachment. Good Natur'd Man
    tries to satirize sentimental comedy, but by using both
    comic and sentimental techniques, he confuses audience.
    Satiric voice weak, but analysis of play shows he could
    control action on stage and audience response at particular
    times. She Stoops to Conquer moves audience to healthy,
    sanely comic view of life and love. Good stagecraft and
    clear idea of purpose lead to firm control.

B. Shorter Writings

1   F[RIEDMAN], A[RTHUR]. "Goldsmith." In The New Cambridge
    Bibliography of English Literature. Edited by George
    Watson. Cambridge: University Press, 2:1191-1210.
        Does not contain all the material Crane listed, but all
    listings of major importance are here through 1969.

2   FERGUSON, OLIVER W. "Goldsmith's Retaliation." SAQ 70
    (Spring):234-41 (Special Issue: Essays in Eighteenth-
    Century Literature in Honor of Benjamin Boyce).
        Poem's posthumous publication on 19 April 1774 caused
    much comment. "Its relaxed tone masks a good deal of
    anguish; behind its assured couplets are the complex,
    deeply personal relationships of Goldsmith and some of his
    most notable friends" (p. 149). Presents Lady Phillipina

1971

Knight's account of the genesis of the poem, written in
a letter now in the Farr Papers in the British Library
(Add. MS. 37060), adding some information about the probable
date of composition, but no substantial additional criticism.

3   FONG, DAVID. "Johnson, Goldsmith, and The Traveller." New
    Rambler (Autumn):22-30.
        Considers problem why Johnson thought so highly of the
    poem and points out Johnson contributed at least five
    couplets which form the conclusion and thus are more
    important than five couplets added at random; guided
    Goldsmith in revising and finishing the poem but vanity was
    surely not Johnson's motive; found the Toryism, the
    argument that excessive freedom leads to factionalism
    congenial, though Goldsmith had already expressed similar
    views in Citizen and Vicar, in which Johnson had no direct
    hand. Style much more Johnsonian than Popean, especially
    in use of balance and repetition.

4   HORNSBY, SAMUEL. "Utopia and Auburn." Moreana:31-32:197-98.
        Unlike satirists such as Swift and Twain, More and
    Goldsmith come from "Utopia and Auburn not indignant, not
    even sadly resigned, but aware of their moral obligations
    in the human community" (p. 197). Auburn's inhabitants
    favor "an idealized, unrealistic approach to life" (p. 197).
    Both More and Goldsmith say "in effect, the healing power
    of truth is in the heart of man himself" (p. 198). Change
    occurs when man accepts his place in his world and his
    time.

5   JAARSMA, RICHARD J. "Biography as Tragedy: Fictive Skill in
    Oliver Goldsmith's The Life of Richard Nash, Esq." Journal
    of Narrative Technique 1 (January):15-29.
        "The greatness of The Life of Nash does not lie in its
    stated theme, but in the much more subtle development of
    that theme through a species of near symbolism that forms
    the structural framework of the Life. The focus of this
    thematic development centers on the relationship between
    Nash's life and the life of society" (p. 18). Throughout
    the reader is often asked to identify himself with Nash and
    the narrator. Narrator uses a double standard, that of
    larger world and that of Nash's world to put Nash's world
    in its proper perspective. Considers whether Goldsmith's
    attitude is sympathetic and ironic as Quintana argued
    (1967.A5) or wholly ironic as Hopkins argues (1969.A1) and
    concludes Nash is seen as a tragic figure destroyed by his
    society.

6   _____. "Ethics in the Wasteland: Image and Structure in

The Deserted Village." Texas Studies in Language and Literature 13 (Fall):446-59.
Argues that "At the heart of The Deserted Village is a
lament for the dissolution of social order and the
destruction of the humanistic values on which, Goldsmith
feels, society ought to be based" (p. 449). Analyzes the
poem's structure, with idealized Auburn tending to become
symbolic of Miltonic and Biblical echoes of Eden. "Goldsmith's technique of describing society in terms of natural
images reinforces the structural principle of symbolic
contrasts on which the poem is built" (p. 453). Considers
it the kind of poetry that exercises deliberate control
over its material.

7 _____. "Satire, Theme, and Structure in The Traveller."
Tennessee Studies in Literature 6:46-66.
Though widely praised after publication, recent interpretations have distorted meaning by failing to treat the
poem as coherent and consistent. It is essentially
Augustan, exploring through "Juvenalian satire . . . the
relationship of the individual human soul to the collective
demands of society . . ." (p. 49). Goldsmith presents his
theme two ways: the famous satiric portraits of European
countries stress ephemeral human happiness, while, second,
the individual human effort to find happiness stresses
problems of the poem's speaker. Resolution of conflict
between individual and society occurs through realization
that human happiness is highly individual and not necessarily connected with societies that attempt to provide it.

8 McCARTHY, B. EUGENE. "The Theme of Liberty in She Stoops to
Conquer." University of Windsor Review 7, no. 1 (Fall):
1-8.
Sets out to examine the construction of the play "and to
suggest that analysis only shows how smoothly operates
under the effortless structure" (p. 1). Argues that the
theme of liberty draws the dualities of appearance and
reality together into a unity. Draws heavily upon Quintana
(1967.A5), but shows little familiarity with other recent
Goldsmith scholarship. Believes Goldsmith underrated as a
conceptual thinker, a view seldom found among recent
Goldsmith scholars.

9 PATRICK, MICHAEL D. "Oliver Goldsmith's Citizen of the World:
A Rational Accommodation of Human Existence." Enlightenment Essays 2:82-90.
Citizen illustrates Ernst Cassirer's distinction between
seventeenth- and eighteenth-century conceptions of reason
in that "eighteenth-century man looks upon reason not as a
static body of knowledge, principles, and truth, but a

1972

force that dissolves the dispersed parts of knowledge into a whole" (p. 82). Believes <u>Citizen</u> the best of the pseudo-letter series but also that "the letters are always individual essays" (p. 83). Finds Goldsmith "sometimes inconsistent in using the device of the persona when the Chinese Philosopher becomes more English than Chinese . . ." (p. 90). Finds The Man in Black more satisfactorily developed than Lien Chi, but does not see that the Chinese as principal character and principal narrator anticipates Goldsmith's technique in <u>Vicar</u>.

<u>1972</u>

A. Books

1   COHANE, CHRISTOPHER B. "More New Essays by Oliver Goldsmith: A Problem in Ascription." Ph.D. dissertation, New York University, 371 pp.
    Presents twenty-four essays published anonymously in the <u>Royal Magazine</u> between 1759 and 1771, a publication Goldsmith is known to have contributed to. Introduction presents arguments for Goldsmith's authorship as well as a description of the <u>Royal Magazine</u> and a discussion of its relation to essays of the period and to Goldsmith.

B. Shorter Writings

1   HUME, ROBERT D. "Goldsmith and Sheridan and the Supposed Revolution of 'Laughing' Against 'Sentimental' Comedy." In <u>Studies in Change and Revolution</u>. Edited by Paul Korshin. London and Menston: Scolar Press, pp. 237-76.
    Scholars have greatly overrated Goldsmith as a revolutionary against sentimental comedy. Closely analyzes the "Essay on the Theatre," finding it "essentially a puff for <u>She Stoops to Conquer</u>, first staged two months after the essay's appearance" (p. 238). Considers the essay brilliant polemical rhetoric, but an unreliable account of contemporary dramatic trends and not intended as such. Notes that the critical argument is marked by more rhetorical fire than careful use of the terms "laughing" and "sentimental." Laughing comedy was very far from disappearing from the theaters. "Despite the development of interest in various sorts of 'sentimental' plays during the 1760's, Goldsmith and Sheridan inherited a thriving comic tradition which continued around them" (p. 271).

2   LOUGHLIN, RICHARD L. "Laugh and Grow Wise with Oliver Goldsmith." <u>Costerus</u> 6, no. 1:59-92.

A very general essay, citing rather old scholarship.
Speculates whether a Goldsmith revival has been occurring
during the late 1960s and early 1970s. Stresses Goldsmith
as a comic writer emphasizing need for human happiness.
Considers Goldsmith's laughing comedies, his philosophy of
comedy, the comic spirit in life and literature with
superficial discussion of Freudian theory of wit and
comedy.

3   YEARLING, ELIZABETH M. "The Good-Natured Heroes of Cumberland,
     Goldsmith, and Sheridan." MLR 67 (July):490-500.
          Goldsmith and Sheridan attack sentimentalism by present-
     ing their versions of good-natured hero. Sees Good Natur'd
     Man as semisentimental; plot of Good Natur'd Man depends
     upon basically sentimental attitudes. "Goldsmith sets
     out to criticize the philosophy of benevolence directly,
     and he succeeds in most accurately stating the rational
     basis of such a philosophy--that altruism is best, but it
     must be a reasoned altruism. In other words, Goldsmith,
     perhaps unwittingly, is alone of the three in basing
     benevolence on true Shaftesburian principles" (p. 510).
     Concludes the distinction is "not between sentimentalism
     and something else that criticizes the sentimentalist
     philosophy but between sentimental drama and a drama which
     implicitly accepts the basic tenets of sentimental
     philosophy" (p. 510).

1973

A.   Books

1   BAILEY, EDWARD B. "The Conflict of Art and Nature in the
     Writings of Oliver Goldsmith." Ph.D. dissertation, New
     York University, 291 pp.
          Views works as an extended criticism of eighteenth-
     century civilization, declining according to Goldsmith.
     France and Italy decadent beyond hope, but England could
     still avoid decline. Goldsmith believes a major cause of
     decline is the assumption behind European civilization:
     that with art man may transform hostile nature into a man-
     dominated world. History of this idea sketched and its
     presence in Johnson's thought noted (a secondary purpose of
     this study is to show most recent Goldsmith scholarship
     does not stress differences between Johnson and Goldsmith
     enough). In Goldsmith's view, there is dominating role to
     art, causing an art-nature conflict from which nature
     suffers. Commercial nations gradually lose their rural

1973

part, but man is the real loser. To prevent decline in
England, Goldsmith proposes stopping further development
in civilization and remaining content with what nature
gives, not improving nature. His ideal is civilization in
harmonious balance, realized in fast-vanishing English
villages. Draws most from nonfictional writings, but the
art-nature conflict is major in Traveller, Deserted Village,
Vicar, and his two comedies.

2   DOBSON, AUSTIN. Life of Oliver Goldsmith. Port Washington,
N.Y.: Kennikat Press, 238 pp.
    Facsimile reprint of 1888.A1.

3   PITMAN, JAMES H. Goldsmith's "Animated Nature." Hamden,
Conn.: Archon Books, 159 pp.
    Facsimile reprint of 1924.A2.

B. Shorter Writings

1   DALNEKOFF, DONNA [A.] ISAACS. "A Familiar Stranger: The
Outsider of Eighteenth Century Satire." Neophilologus
57 (April):121-34.
    A condensed version of 1970.A1.

2   FERGUSON, OLIVER W. "An Early Goldsmith Reprint in the London
Chronicle." HLQ 36 (February):163-67.
    Friedman found Public Ledger texts for Citizen letters
101 and 103 missing in British Library file and so used
1762 Citizen texts. London Chronicle, 8-10 January 1761,
reprints without acknowledgment or introduction what
appears to be Public Ledger text of letter 101, under the
heading "A Tale." Shows typical revisions Goldsmith made
between newspaper text and 1762 Citizen text. London
Chronicle had reprinted at least six other Goldsmith items
previously and was then published by John Wilkie, who
published Goldsmith's Bee.

3   GOLDSTEIN, LAURENCE. "The Auburn Syndrome: Change and Loss
in The Deserted Village and Wordsworth's Grassmere." ELH
40 (Fall):352-71.
    Main discussion of Goldsmith, pp. 354-59. Disagrees
with Quintana (1967.A5) that depopulation is Goldsmith's
major subject because the personal element is introduced.
Role of persona as observer is important in the familiar
eighteenth-century contrast of pleasant youthful memory
contrasted with the dreadful present. Goldsmith emphasizes
that continuity of self depends on continuity of place.

The picture of the baneful influence of city life is another
anticipation of Wordsworth. "Goldsmith faces the physical
ruin and accepts the irreversible dislocation of his past
and present experience" (p. 359).

4   GRUDIS, PAUL J. "The Narrator and The Vicar of Wakefield."
    Essays in Criticism [Denver], 1 (January), 51–66.
        Understanding the Vicar is key to explaining the opposed
    interpretations and the novel itself. External evidence of
    Goldsmith's reviews and letters shows his dislike of
    sentimental fiction. Vicar is by no means perfect: vain
    and proud, but even so most readers find him sympathetic
    and he does reveal his own weaknesses. Does understand his
    family. Distinguishes Vicar as narrator (aware) and as
    central character (myopic). Sees Primrose as learning about
    reality through suffering of Olivia's abduction. "The
    Vicar might well be the instrument of Goldsmith's satire,
    but he is certainly not the butt" (p. 64).

5   HELGERSON, RICHARD. "The Two Worlds of Oliver Goldsmith."
    SEL 13 (Summer):516–34.
        Recognizes Goldsmith as a conscious craftsman and dis-
    cusses the irony of his work before 1770 arising from the
    opposition of the "static world of the Village home . . .
    and the active world . . ." (p. 517). Describes Goldsmith
    as a writer of comic satire, but somewhat weak in showing
    this quality in the Good Natur'd Man and the Vicar. Much
    of argument centers on defining the two worlds of his
    conceptual scheme, especially the static world of the
    village home in a discussion of the Traveller and the
    Deserted Village, contrasted with the larger world of the
    good-natured man (Honeywood, the Man in Black, and Sir
    William Thornhill), with Primrose "not of the same world as
    the good-natured man, nor . . . subject to its laws"
    (p. 529).

6   HUNTING, ROBERT. "The Poems in The Vicar of Wakefield."
    Criticism 15 (Summer):234–41.
        Allies himself with the revisionist critics who view the
    novel as primarily satirical. Follows Curtis Dahl (1958.B1)
    in finding patterns of disguise as the key to interpreting
    the novel, but argues for keeping the disguises, seeing
    the two long poems in the novel, "Edwin and Angelina" and
    "The Elegy on the Death of a Mad Dog" in relation to the
    scenes in which they occur and especially the two charac-
    ters who recite them, Burchell and Bill Primrose. Finds
    each poem satirizes Dr. Primrose and argues that "illusion,
    throughout the Vicar, has an appeal which reality lacks"

1973

(p. 240), and "these poems suggest that Thomas Gray's
argument is applicable to this book and is worth thinking
about: 'Where Ignorance is bliss, / Tis folly to be wise"
(p. 241). Hunting devotes only a single sentence to the
most famous poem in the book, Olivia's "When lovely woman
stoops to folly," but finds it too supports the same idea:
"Appearance attracts the lovely woman; reality hurts.
Avoid it, if you can" (p. 240).

7 ITZKOWITZ, MARTIN. "A Fielding Echo in She Stoops to Conquer."
   N&Q, n.s. 20 (January):22.
   The passage in Act II in which Marlow observes to
   Hastings that travellers always pay, but in good inns they
   pay dearly and in bad ones they are cheated or starved,
   probably reflects Goldsmith's personal experience, but also
   echoes a passage from Fielding's Journal of a Voyage to
   Lisbon, one of the books which Goldsmith owned at the time
   of his death.

8 KRISHNA BATTA, S. "Deserted City, Deserted Village." Indian
   Literature 16 (July-January):153-56.
   Comparison of Kalidasa's Raghuvasama, Canto 16, with
   Goldsmith's Deserted Village. Both excel in description.
   Comments on Goldsmith's poem rehash basic and obvious
   themes in poems, such as the superiority of agriculture to
   trade.

9 MUNBY, A. N. L., ed. Sale Catalogues of Libraries of Eminent
   Poets and Men of Letters. Vol. 7. Edited, with an
   Introduction, by Hugh Amory. London: Mansell with Sotheby
   Parke Bernet Publications, pp. 227-46.
   A facsimile reprint of 1774.B6, pp. 235-46. In introduction observes "in general, scholars seem to have started
   their investigations of Goldsmith's 'sources' by analyzing
   his printed references, rather than by reading the books
   in his library" (p. 230), and suggests they do more of the
   latter.

10 QUINTANA, RICARDO. "The Vicar of Wakefield: The Problem of
   the Critical Approach." MP 71 (August):59-65.
   Cannot accept view that the novel is consistently
   satirical, but adds, "It is possible, I think, to end up
   disagreeing with some of [Robert] Hopkins' conclusions,
   yet at the same time feeling that he has made an entirely
   legitimate effort. It is right to acknowledge that The
   Vicar means more than its background" (p. 64). In
   discussing other legitimate lines of investigation,
   Quintana considers structuralistic approaches to earlier

novels, noting especially J. J. Richetti's Popular Fiction
Before Richardson: Narrative Patterns 1730-1739, which
argues that eighteenth-century fiction is best understood
not as the rise of realism but an early stage in the
emergence of popular culture through "the establishment of
a 'fantasy machine' operating through the structures of
feeling comprising the characteristic ideological forces of
the age" (pp. 64-65). Notes Goldsmith's response to this
conflict, especially as a writer dependent on the booksellers, is in the Vicar comic.

11   STYAN, J. L. "Goldsmith's Comic Skills." Costerus 9, no. 2:
      195-217.
         In 1773, Goldsmith adapted into one act Sir Charles
      Sedley's three-act version of The Grumbler from de Brueys
      and de Palaprat's Le Grondeur. Goldsmith's version is
      colloquial, not epigrammatic, and his comic success "lies
      in the nimble dance of words, the range of vocal colour,
      the sense of broad gesture in character, and feeling for
      the regard in which the audience holds the action on the
      stage" (p. 197). Discusses various stage techniques, such
      as vocal acrobatics, with characters changing their voices
      like Kate in She Stoops to Conquer. The Good Natur'd Man
      suffers by comparison with the later play in plot,
      characterization, and consistency of style. In Goldsmith's
      first play, the characters all exist independently, not
      in relationship to one another as do the Hardcastles.
      The situation of She Stoops to Conquer allows for consis-
      tency from the start: most of Act I prepares us for
      Marlow's seeing Hardcastle as an innkeeper, setting outside
      London prepares us for barbs at London gentility. Tony and
      his mother both humours or types, but unlike Sheridan's
      characters, all remain consistent and lifelike to the end
      of the play. Kate's speeches to her father in their
      natural honesty exemplify the core of the British comic
      tradition.

12   WILLS, JACK C. "The Deserted Village, Ecclesiastes, and the
      Enlightenment." Enlightenment Essays 4:15-19.
         Argues persona is "an old, disillusioned, and . . .
      even embittered resident of the now-decaying village of
      Auburn . . . a true man of the Enlightenment, expressing
      his views in all sincerity but also seeing the relationship
      of what he observes to other men and times" (p. 15).
      Besides recently identified sources and parallels in
      Vergil's First Eclogue, Isaiah, the poem expresses
      Goldsmith's familiar idea of decay of civilization, as in
      Enquiry and Traveller. Argues for parallels with

1974

Ecclesiastes, both general and specific, in themes of
pessimism, isolation, vanity, and patterns of light-dark
imagery, especially association of darkness with the rich
man.

<u>1974</u>

A. Books

1   FRIEDMAN, ARTHUR, ed. <u>The Vicar of Wakefield by Goldsmith</u>.
     Oxford English Novels edition. London: Oxford University
     Press, 230 pp.
          Text is that of <u>Works</u> 4. Considers the sentimental
     plot, one "in a rather special kind of comic novel" (p. ix).
     Goldsmith's combination of his narrator and his central
     character causes problems: considers Primrose "the moral
     center of the book" and "a paragon; but . . . a very
     fallible paragon" (p. xv). Disagrees with Hopkins's view:
     "I doubt that any unprejudiced reader can fail to find the
     Vicar on many occasions a man of superlative virtue, any
     more than he can possibly read the novel as a consistent
     parody, where he can have no emotional involvement with
     the character" (p. xvi). Main evidence for rejecting the
     ironic or satirical interpretation is the "Advertisement"
     to the novel, which he believes is "completely unambiguous
     and free from guile" (p. xvii), a sincere statement of
     Goldsmith's intentions.

2   HARP, RICHARD L. "Thomas Percy's <u>Life of Oliver Goldsmith</u>:
     An Edition." Ph.D. dissertation, University of Kansas,
     272 pp.
          Percy did not use Goldsmith's fictions, and his bio-
     graphical standards are those prescribed by Johnson, who
     found anomalies between a man's behavior and writings a
     perfectly natural phenomenon. Later biographers found
     anomalies but Percy's <u>Life</u>, especially when illustrated by
     statements from Johnson and Reynolds, shows Goldsmith a
     man of his age, imperfect and human. The history of the
     <u>Life</u> is long and complex (see Balderston, 1926.A2). The
     Memorandum dictated by Goldsmith to Percy in 1773 was the
     basic document, but Percy shunted it and other materials
     to Johnson, and after his death in 1784, asked the Rev.
     Thomas Campbell to write the life, but Campbell died
     before Percy found a publisher. Percy revised Campbell's
     "Life" and submitted it to Cadell and Davies, the London
     publishers, but further delays occurred, and when published
     in 1801, Samuel Rose had replaced Percy as editor. The

present edition closely compares the text with Campbell's
unpublished "Life," unavailable to Balderston.
Printed 1976.A1.

3   HAYFORD, DONALD P. "Oliver Goldsmith's Prose Satire." Ph.D.
dissertation, State University of New York at Albany,
206 pp.
    Goldsmith's reviewing for Griffiths's Monthly Review
shows a disposition to satire, and his work for the Monthly
offered him enlarged scope for literary targets, especially
sentimental romances, but satire remains gentle and good-
natured. Bee and other periodical essays show more
complex satire, more individualized personas, some
satirical, some butts, others storytellers who relate
incongruous situations. His targets are often literary
and parody a frequent device. Citizen his best satiric
performance, in which he perfects earlier techniques.
Vicar, despite faulty construction, illustrates Goldsmith's
consistently mild satiric tone. First half is mainly
satire of self-deception of Primroses with unconscious
self-revelation of narrator. Second half predominantly
comic, but does use parody to satirize sentimental
romances, a favorite target of Goldsmith's.

4   LEHMANN, ELMAR. "Not Merely Sentimental": Studien zur
Goldsmiths Komoedien. Beihefte zu Poetica 21. Munich:
Wilhelm Fink, 193 pp.
    Jeremy Collier and the Spectator advocated the "new"
comedy, and Fielding and Goldsmith brought a new synthesis.
Discusses conventions of mid-eighteenth-century drama,
especially the pair(s) of lovers and parodies of this
convention of sentimental comedy, as well as humor
characters like Mrs. Hardcastle and Tony Lumpkin. Section
on the discovery of the comic hero and his relation to the
moral norm considers Honewood and Marlow, the latter as a
hero of the city mode. Lehmann considers the Good Natur'd
Man as representing a victory of common sense, She Stoops
to Conquer as comic play opposing city and country
forces.

5   LYTTON SELLS, ARTHUR. Oliver Goldsmith, His Life and Works.
New York: Barnes & Noble, 423 pp.
    Divided into two distinct sections, with little connec-
tion between the two, as the subtitle notes. The biographical section offers numerous problems, ranging from
using 1728 as Goldsmith's apparent birth date, despite
considerable research done almost forty years ago showing
it is the least likely of the probable dates. No mention

of Wardle's biography (1957.A1), and while Quintana's
study (1967.A5) is mentioned, little use was apparently
made of it. Opinions in the "Works" section represent a
taste almost untouched by recent criticism: finds
Deserted Village Goldsmith's best work, outstanding for
its sincerity, strongly dislikes Goldsmith's light verse,
and discussion of Vicar ignores virtually all recent
criticism. Lytton Sells has little sympathy with the
plays, apparently because he prefers the kind Goldsmith
attacks. Does add some information about Goldsmith's use
of French sources beyond his earlier study (1924.A1).

6 ROUSSEAU, G. S., ed. Goldsmith: The Critical Heritage.
London and Boston: Routledge & Kegan Paul, 409 pp.
An anthology of biographical and critical writing about
Goldsmith from 1762 to 1912. First half devoted to
discussions of The Traveller, the Vicar, The Good Natured
[sic] Man, The Deserted Village, She Stoops to Conquer,
Retaliation, and Animated Nature, with no critical
discussion of the Bee, miscellaneous essays, or the Citizen,
perhaps because published anonymously, but criticism of
the Citizen omitted because the essays "remain interesting
primarily to eighteenth-century specialists" (p. 21). The
second half is devoted to Goldsmith's life and works, with
many anecdotes and examples of the Goldsmith "legend."
Rousseau reprints a great deal of material not easily
available outside very large libraries. Introduction
(pp. 1-28) maintains three large problems have interfered
with critical writing about Goldsmith: greater interest in
Goldsmith-the-man than in Goldsmith-the-writer, the nineteenth-century dislike for and frequent misunderstanding of
eighteenth-century literature, and Goldsmith's having written in many genres rather than any predominant one.

B. Shorter Writings

1 BATTESTIN, MARTIN. "Goldsmith: The Comedy of Job." In The
Providence of Wit. Oxford: Clarendon Press, pp. 193-214.
Specifically rejects Hopkins's (1969.A1) interpretation
of the novel as consistently satirical but finds an irony
in Dr. Primrose. Believes Goldsmith's first-person
narration creates problems and finds novel far removed
from realistic tradition of Defoe and Richardson. "Like
Fielding--though without the advantage of Fielding's
'omniscient' narrator, a device which contributes much to
our sense of the artificial world of Joseph Andrews and
Tom Jones--Goldsmith in The Vicar of Wakefield manipulates
his style and plot in such a way as to parody the conventions of a whole range of literary modes" (p. 195).

Goldsmith relies on a "controlling analogy to unify and
universalize his theme" (p. 195), an analogy with the
Book of Job. By considerable reference to contemporary
theological arguments over the Book of Job, especially
its theme of unequal providence, argues that Goldsmith
followed the line of interpretation in which Job was
presented as "not at all a model of patience and humility
but rather a <u>negative</u> example of those virtues" (p. 203)
and agrees that recent critics have seen somewhat the same
effect in Goldsmith's presentation of his narrator-
protagonist, though he believes they overemphasize satire
of Primrose's flaws at the expense of his virtues. Finds
Vicar's sermon in chapter twenty-nine "the true climax
of Goldsmith's tale" (p. 211), but believes Vicar's
insight shown in his prison sermon is permanent, not
temporary as argued by Hopkins (1976.B4).

2   COHANE, CHRISTOPHER B. "A New Essay by Oliver Goldsmith."
     <u>N&Q</u>, n.s. 21 (July):262-64.
          "The Avaricious Persian," published in the <u>Royal</u>
     <u>Magazine</u>, January 1760, shows striking similarities to
     "Alcander and Septimus," published in the <u>Bee</u>, No. 6,
     three months earlier. Goldsmith probably wrote both
     papers, since he was writing for the <u>Royal Magazine</u> at the
     time, with "Asem" appearing in the December issue.
          A section of 1972.A1.

3   DUSSINGER, JOHN A. "<u>The Vicar of Wakefield</u>: A 'Sickly Sensi-
     bility' and the Rewards of Fortune." In <u>The Discourse of</u>
     <u>the Mind in Eighteenth-Century Fiction</u>. [Mouton] Studies
     in English Literature 80. The Hague: Mouton, pp. 148-72.
          Acknowledges well accepted debt to Fielding and the
     Cervantean tradition, but chiefly examines the book as
     a revelation of the narrator's sensibility of sentimen-
     tality. Generally grants irony directed against Primrose,
     but argues "the whole irony of the story which envelops
     everyone in an affirmation of God and country, the typical
     social affirmation of comedy" (p. 161, n. 15). Finds the
     probability of book flawed by the first-person narrative
     more appropriate to the longer novel. Grants the <u>Vicar</u>
     is a romance with heavy overtones of comic irony, yet
     the criteria he applies in judging it appear to derive
     from the Richardsonian novel. Appears unwilling to grant
     Goldsmith may have intended to write an ironically comic
     romance.

4   FERGUSON, OLIVER W. "Sir Fretful Plagiary and Goldsmith's
     'An Essay on the Theatre.'" In <u>Quick Springs of Sense</u>:

1974

Studies in the Eighteenth Century. Edited by Larry S.
Champion. Athens: University of Georgia Press, pp. 113–
20.
    Shows that Richard Cumberland in writing his "Dedication
to Detraction" did not know that Goldsmith was the author
of "An Essay on the Theatre" and believed it was an attack
on him. Convincingly shows that Goldsmith's authorship of
the essay was not generally known during his lifetime and
was first attributed to him in the 1798 collection
Essays and Criticisms, where Thomas Wright made the
attribution.

5   HASSERT, MARGARET. "Appraisals: The Plays of Oliver Gold-
    smith." Journal of Irish Literature 3, no. 3:39–48.
        "Essay on the Theatre" written after both plays [though
    She Stoops to Conquer underwent considerable revision
    before its production in 1774] and echoes ideas long held.
    In his first play Goldsmith "chose to use the sentimental
    comedy itself as a vehicle for an ironic criticism of the
    genre" (p. 40). Its virtues are its comic scenes and
    characters and sometimes verbally ingenious language. The
    chief fault is that the play "becomes a sentimental
    comedy instead of a satire of one" (p. 43) and suffers
    from too much moralizing and sententiousness not easily
    identifiable as ironic. She Stoops to Conquer triumphs
    as laughing comedy. Its problems, the improbabilities
    and the dullness of the lovers in the subplot, work within
    the play. The audience is caught up by laughter and
    overlooks the improbabilities, and the dullness of Hastings
    and Constance help set off Marlow and Kate and provide
    satiric comment on sentimental comedy.

6   SABINE, NATHAN. "The Place of The Vicar of Wakefield within
    the Realistic Tradition of the Eighteenth Century." Wissen-
    schaftliche Zeitschrift der Universität Rostock 23:413–20.
        A Marxist socialist-realist critique of the novel,
    emphasizing the impossibility of attaining the idyllic life
    described in the first half and thus sees the book as part
    of eighteenth-century critical realism. Sabine argues
    Goldsmith is not showing an idyll destroyed by urban
    corruption; rather the feudal outlook of Squire Thornhill,
    "conceived by Goldsmith realistically" (p. 415), expressing
    the logic of his class is the cause. The theme of social
    instability dominates the book despite the digressions,
    and the difficulty of restoring social harmony increases.
    The digressions nearly all stress disharmony occurring
    in the world of the novel and all foreshadow the destruc-
    tion of the pastoral ideal. The disasters are caused by

the corrupt social system. In his sermon, the Vicar really
renounces God's world and the attempt to reconcile the
divine and human systems, a cry of despair and defiance.
Happy ending is a mere convention of the age, and the
events of the main action are far more important for
showing Goldsmith's ideas.

7 WENZEL, MICHAEL J. "Re-Populating The Deserted Village."
   Rocky Mountain Modern Language Association Bulletin 28,
   no. 1:18-25.
        Follows recent views that the poem has a "definite
   structure, a pattern based on a clearly indicated attitude
   toward a specific sequence of events--the effects of
   enclosure on rustic life" (p. 19). Using John Crowe
   Ransom's notion of texture, Wenzel argues that "textual
   and individuating factors in 'The Deserted Village' play a
   crucial role in the effect of the poem and that, by
   threatening its local progress, actually assist in making
   the poem's assertions more acceptable" (p. 19). Much of
   the success of the poem depends on the poem's experience
   being conveyed to the reader through the mind of the
   speaker rather than being accepted as literal, factual
   account. The desolate village is sad, but Goldsmith
   "re-populate[s]" (p. 21) it with attractive portraits of
   former inhabitants and the poem thus describes a world the
   speaker has lost and "exploits one of the basic archetypes--
   the loss of community" (p. 21), evoking its strongest
   emotion. Thus the speaker is one of the displaced and the
   portraits are of "subjects that are institutions, of
   importance to the maintenance of community" (p. 23).
   The convention is pastoral, and even the apostrophe to
   poetry argues the power of the poet to defend truth and
   make our perception of it more intense.

1975

A. Books

1 DAVIS, TOM, ed. Poems and Plays. London: Dent; Totowa,
   N.J.: Rowman & Littlefield, 288 pp.
        Contains all Goldsmith's poems and plays, except the
   one-act adaptation of Sedley's Grumbler, and a glossary of
   eighteenth-century words and special eighteenth-century
   uses of words. Introduction summarizes Goldsmith's
   biography and "the current critical position on his plays
   and poems, with suggestions as to further, or different
   lines of exploration" (p. viii). Biographically, sees him

1975

as self-made and classless, and thus playing many roles
from the inept dandy to admirer of rural retreat, but also
the imprudent gambler, saved by his literary skill. Finds
three classes in his verse: the self-consciously serious
Traveller and Deserted Village; light verse, lyrics and
ballads, especially in Vicar, and conversation poems, of
which Retaliation is the masterpiece because speaker is not
dramatized persona but Goldsmith "directly there, confron-
ting these giants, Burke, Garrick, Reynolds, as equals"
(p. xxi). Poem does not attack subjects but is "satire of
judgment and balance" (p. xxi). Good Natur'd Man has
puzzled readers. She Stoops to Conquer is "one of the best
plays in our literature" (p. xxiii). Kate takes over part
of Toby's ruse and drives the play toward removing dis-
guises and bringing recognition of true love.

2 MacLENNAN, MUNRO. The Secret of Goldsmith. New York: Vantage,
   177 pp.
       Thinks Goldsmith was colorblind. Collects hundreds of
   references to colors from the works, even classifying them
   into chapters by particular color.

3 WILLIAMS, FRANKLIN C., Jr. "Oliver Goldsmith: Reactions to
   the Man and his Principal Literary Works, 1730-1970."
   Ph.D. dissertation, University of Wisconsin, 391 pp.
       Explains "Percy Memorandum" and includes reactions of
   reviewers and contemporaries to works. Despite the fame
   of the Traveller, 1764, Goldsmith's behavior and reluctance
   to speak of his past caused him to be identified with
   characters and situations in his works, especially the main
   literary works. Part two discusses memoirists and biographers from 1774 to 1801. In this period, Deserted Village
   thought best, though Retaliation was admired for its satire.
   Part three, 1801-1890, discusses the interpretations by
   Prior, Forster, and Irving, and shows the Vicar becoming
   widely popular. Forster's biography gains more popularity
   than Prior's because it stresses Goldsmith the troubled
   author working without patronage. Part four, 1890-1970,
   sees a gradual dissociation of Goldsmith from his works,
   increasingly stressing his work as part of the main
   eighteenth-century tradition. The desire to adjust past
   inequities threatens to distort current investigations.

B. Shorter Writings

1 BÄCKMAN, SVEN. "The Real Origin of One of the 'Manufactured
   Anecdotes' in Goldsmith's Life of Nash." MP 72 (February):
   277-79.

An anecdote is borrowed from Marivaux's Le Spectateur Français and occurs after the description of Nash as improvidently benevolent (Works 3:295-96).

2   FERGUSON, OLIVER W.   "Dr. Primrose and Goldsmith's Clerical Ideal." PQ 54 (Winter):322-32.
    Discusses his relationship with various clergymen, real and fictional: his brother Henry, to whom he dedicated The Traveller; the heroine's clergyman-father in The History of Miss Stanton; the preacher in The Deserted Village, and Dr. Primrose, in whom he sees an example of the amiable humorist. Notes many identical views that Primrose and William Whiston, a nearly contemporary actual eccentric Arian Clergyman, held in common. Rejects Hopkins's view that Primrose's Whistonianism is a repeated ironic signal to the knowledgeable contemporary reader of Primrose's possible religious unorthodoxy; "he [Whiston] was equally well known to eighteenth-century readers as a singular clergyman with whimsical eccentricities and an honest, forthright man with admirable courage of his convictions" (p. 328). View that "Primrose the Christian is never the object of comedy" (p. 329) already questioned implicitly by D. W. Jefferson (1950.B2 and 1964.B3), as Ferguson concedes in his note 11.

3   JEFFARES, A. NORMAN.   "Goldsmith: The Good Natured Man." Hermathena no. 119:5-19.
    Surveys life gracefully, emphasizing similarities of his college career to Swift's, his roots in Anglo-Irish professional class, his difficulties in finding himself, becoming a writer whose achievement is "the sum of the compulsion to write and the sacrifice of happiness" (p. 6). Both Traveller and Deserted Village reveal considerable amount of autobiographical feeling as well as expressing his conservative views of the dangers of social disruption.

4   VALLIANCE, ROSALIND.   "Forster's Goldsmith." Dickensian 71 (January):21-29.
    Forster believed Prior's Life accumulated details about Goldsmith but did not present a living picture of the man in his milieu. Admiration for Dickens led him to dedicate book to him. Bee was a kind of model for Sketches by Boz and The Uncommercial Traveller. Quotes Dickens's letter after reading book, showing his admiration and relief, he believed, that Forster did not use special pleading [though Forster and Irving are the principal purveyors of the Goldsmith "legend" of the neglected author exploited by publishers]. Especially in second edition, Forster

1975

increased the space devoted to the eighteenth-century
milieu, sometimes obscuring Goldsmith.

5   WILLS, JACK C. "The Narrator of The Deserted Village: A
    Reconsideration." West Virginia University Philological
    Papers 22:21-28.
        Believes the narrator is the primary device by which
    Goldsmith "broadens or universalizes his thesis: he
    helps dramatize, particularize, and personalize the human
    plight depicted in the poem; and he combines the various
    themes into a single, coherent statement" (p. 21).
    Besides ugly present, pleasant past contrast, the poem
    also contains universalized nostalgic lament for youthful
    golden age. All these elements do three things: concen-
    trate attention on narrator, "bring to the pre-Enclosure
    village a hint of memento mori" (p. 25), and support a
    duality in the whole poem important to the theme. Finds
    three movements in poem: the village before Enclosure,
    the replacement of village by isolation figures, and the
    exodus of villagers to corrupt London or unfriendly
    America. Poem is "broader and more objective than is
    generally recognized and the speaker plays a central part
    in Goldsmith's large design" (p. 28).

1976

A. Books

1   HARP, RICHARD L., ed. Thomas Percy's Life of Dr. Oliver
    Goldsmith. Salzburg Studies in English Literature, Roman-
    tic Reassessment, 52. Salzburg: Institut fur Englishsche
    Sprache und Literatur, 233 pp.
        Published version of 1974.A2.

B. Shorter Writings

1   BLIGH, JOHN. "Neglected Aspects of The Vicar of Wakefield."
    Dalhousie Review 56 (Spring):103-11.
        Three large patterns dominate the book, the similarity
    to Job, sexual morality illuminated by comparison to Tess
    of the d'Urbervilles, and social and political themes by
    comparison with Godwin's Caleb Williams. Finds the Vicar's
    argument that Christian life after death compensates for
    worldly injustice derived from Job. On sexual morality,
    argues that Primrose, like Angel Clare in Tess, believes
    sexual consummation makes Olivia and Squire Thornhill one
    flesh, but Primrose overlooks logical absurdity here,

since Thornhill would then be one flesh with first woman
he seduced. When marriage turns out to be legal, Primrose's response is equally illogical, since Thornhill's
intent to have a valid marriage was never there, but
Primrose's belief appears to dominate here as a similar
view does in Hardy's novel. Most of the social and
political issues in the novel are concealed by the happy
ending, which does show Squire Thornhill's outrageous
manipulation of the law corrected by his uncle. Caleb
Williams shows oppression of the poor leading to unhappy
ending, as does Deserted Village, but Goldsmith's Toryism
plus literary convention lead to happy ending novel.

2   BOOTH, WAYNE. "The Self-Portraiture of Genius: The Citizen
    of the World and Critical Method." MP 73 (May, Part 2:
    A Supplement to Honor Arthur Friedman):S85-96.
        Argues that "much of Goldsmith's art [in the Citizen]
    is obscured by any predetermined quest for 'intrinsic'
    harmonies" and is the "art of the miscellaneous" (p. S86)
    in its rhetorical variety. Finds recent critics have
    overstressed the ironic element as a unifying factor,
    though granting it is one of the pleasures. Concludes
    "there is in The Citizen at least as much artistic skill
    of the maker, and thus artistic pleasure for the receiver,
    as can be found in most novels, satires, plays, and poems
    of the period. I think a case can be made that it is
    Goldsmith's most important work, clearly outranking The
    Vicar, say, or She Stoops to Conquer, works that have had
    far more critical attention" (p. S96).

3   [BOSWELL, JAMES.] The Correspondence of James Boswell with
    Certain Members of the Club. Yale Editions of the Private
    Papers of James Boswell (Research Edition). Edited by
    Charles N. Fifer. New Haven: Yale University Press.
    Vol. 3, Correspondence, 552 pp., passim, especially pp. 8,
    24-25, 26.
        The first is an invitation to dinner, and the second a
    gracious note of congratulations from Boswell on the
    success of She Stoops to Conquer, the third Goldsmith's
    cordial reply, looking forward to Boswell's forthcoming
    London visit. Other references in other letters concern
    Johnson's epitaph, the Goldsmith-Percy friendship, and
    Goldsmith's various writings. Fifer comments on Boswell's
    relationship to Goldsmith: "No warmth of personal affec-
    tion [for Goldsmith] is reflected in the Life [of Johnson],
    which is a great pity. His strategy there is to charac-
    terize Goldsmith mainly through pronouncements that
    Goldsmith was a very great author and a very great man.

1976

But Johnson's utterances in fact consist of vivid and
unsparing disparagements of Goldsmith's oddities and
foibles; and Boswell refrains from providing the enveloping
personal appreciation by which he holds in proper scale the
unattractive details in his portrait of Johnson.
"The two men met fairly often in London when Boswell
was there, but neither made any attempt to maintain their
relationship by correspondence when they were separated.
There is no indication that Goldsmith ever wrote Boswell
more than the two letters published here."

4   HOPKINS, ROBERT H. "Social Stratification and the Obsequious
    Curve: Goldsmith and Rowlandson." In Studies in the
    Eighteenth Century III: Papers Presented at the Third
    David Nichol Smith Memorial Seminar, Canberra 1973. Edited
    by R. F. Brissenden and J. C. Eade. Canberra: Australian
    National University Press; Toronto: University of Toronto
    Press, pp. 55-71.
        Proposes that one of Goldsmith's motives in writing The
    Vicar may well have been to emphasize the shifting class
    relationships increasingly polarizing into rich and poor.
    Suggests that Rowlandson's illustration for the 1817
    edition of novel may intuitively reflect Goldsmith's
    preoccupation with these social changes. In a number of
    Rowlandson illustrations (six plates reproduced), he finds
    the figures of the poor bent over and slouching and
    describes this motif as "the obsequious curve." Uses
    obsequiousness as an organizing motif to focus on the
    integrity or lack of integrity in class relationships.
    Believes it is necessary to Goldsmith's purpose that the
    Vicar lose his tendency to judge other human beings in
    material terms. Finds Primrose at his best in person,
    where he can be believably human and truly Christian. But
    at the end of the novel, wealth brings back the critical
    attitude of the beginning of the novel, and in the end
    Primrose has learned nothing.

5   MIEHL, DIETER. "Oliver Goldsmith: She Stoops to Conquer; Or,
    The Mistakes of a Night." In Das Englische Drama im 18.
    und 19. Jahrhundert: Interpretationen. Edited by Heinz
    Kosok. Berlin: Schmidt, pp. 147-58.
        Begins by differentiating Goldsmith's comic mode from
    sentimental comedy, finding his roots primarily in
    Farquhar. Play belongs in the main line of the English
    comic tradition, having succeeded in the eighteenth century
    and continuing today to be a pleasing comedy.

6   ROTHSTEIN, ERIC, and WEINBROT, HOWARD D. "The Vicar of
    Wakefield, Mr. Wilmot, and the 'Whistonean Controversy.'"
    PQ 55 (Spring):225-40.
        Problem of why Vicar leaves Wakefield and his later
    unsatisfactory explanation, "the Whistonean controversy,
    my last pamphlet, the archdeacon's reply, and the hard
    measure that was dealt me" (Works 4:72). Suggestions of
    an earlier clearer version omitted from published versions
    "needlessly complicate the text and distort Goldsmith's
    intentions about moral responsibility" (p. 225). The
    authors do not believe Primrose was forced to resign;
    he has alienated his salary for widows and orphans of
    the diocese, and because George's engagement to Miss Wil-
    mot falls through, a new living becomes necessary. Prim-
    rose cannot reclaim funds without undermining his essential
    benevolence. Rothstein and Weinbrot argue that Primrose
    would not have knuckled under to the Archdeacon because
    no trial or threatened trial is mentioned, and Primrose
    never surrenders in matters of principle. Church of
    England tolerated great latitude, even Whiston's Arianism.
    In writings of the time only Goldsmith associates unusual
    ideas about marriage with Whiston: "the speaking silence
    of Whiston and others indicates that Primrose has indulged
    himself by inventing companions and green pastures for
    his hobbyhorse" (p. 230).

7   WOODS, SAMUEL H., Jr. "The Vicar of Wakefield and Recent
    Goldsmith Scholarship." Eighteenth-Century Studies 9
    (Spring):429-43.
        Surveys major scholarship 1970-74.

                            1977

A. Books

1   GINGER, JOHN. The Notable Man: The Life and Times of Oliver
    Goldsmith. London: Hamish Hamilton, 424 pp.
        A full-scale, documented biography, with great emphasis
    on the milieu. Disagrees with Friedman over probable
    dating of Vicar's composition, favoring 1764 rather than
    1761-62. Suggests Isaac Bickerstaffe's Love in a Village
    is principal source of many elements in She Stoops to
    Conquer. On Goldsmith's personality, does not present
    the paradox of the social fool and the literary genius,
    but in conclusion, stresses Goldsmith's loneliness late
    in life and somewhat tentatively attempts explanation
    of his personality: "Goldsmith, beneath his kindness, his

1977

reckless charity, and his desire to make people laugh,
suffered from a congenital and unnatural ability to feel"
(p. 360); "In a sense, the man who at the end of his life
rejected reason and gambled his life away was the real
Goldsmith. The other, the journalist who had given
graceful expression to the liberal ideals of his age, the
good natured man whom children never forgot, was his own
hard-won creation" (p. 362).

B. Shorter Writings

1   BATAILE, ROBERT A. "City and Country Life in The Vicar of
     Wakefield." Eighteenth-Century Life 3, No. 2: 112-14.
          "Although Goldsmith may very well idealize country life
     in his Tory elegy, The Deserted Village, in The Vicar of
     Wakefield he presents a more rounded realistic view of
     country life than in the Village, and at the same time
     manages to avoid the usual oversimplified moral view of
     the city" (p. 112). Recent criticism has stressed idyllic
     view of novel's first half, but Goldsmith presents country
     life as containing seeds of its own destruction. Analysis
     of city and country must rest on character of Sir William
     Thornhill, since he is the deus ex machina and, more
     important, the only character at home in both city and
     country. As Burchell he seems simple and primitivistic,
     but Primroses notice his wisdom and wit. The town ladies
     appear to offer stereotypes of town corruption, but Jenkin-
     son's duping both Moses and Vicar at country fair shows
     evil exists in country, too. Likewise, Sir William, the
     paragon of virtue, lives in the heart of London, as
     George's account reveals, and George's description of
     London not nearly so dreadful as might be expected after
     Vicar's praise of rural virtue.

2   DIRCKS, RICHARD J. "The Genesis and Date of Goldsmith's
     Retaliation." MP 75 (August):48-53.
          Summarizes known facts: Cumberland's account in his
     Memoirs is the most detailed, but Ferguson (1971.B2)
     considers Garrick's more authoritative. Dircks considers
     basic outline of events in Cumberland's Memoirs accurate:
     three meetings occurred: at first epitaphs centering on
     Goldsmith were composed by Garrick, Barnard, and Cumberland;
     at second Goldsmith read Retaliation, followed by Cumber-
     land and Whitefoord reading their efforts; and the final
     meeting after Goldsmith's death, where participants
     decided to publish Goldsmith's poem. A Cumberland letter
     confirms the account in Cumberland's Memoirs, establishing
     their general accuracy.

3   DURANT, DAVID. "The Vicar of Wakefield and the Sentimental
     Novel." SEL 17 (Summer):477-91.
          The novel is not sentimental because it demonstrates
     the failure of Vicar's basic idea and argues that experience
     teaches even if abstract moral instruction does not.
     Argues against recent efforts to show Primrose as wicked
     or worldly, though these efforts do reveal complexity of
     Goldsmith's achievement. Vicar's sententiousness follows
     a trait commonly found in sentimental drama. Primrose
     tries to fit his experience into patterned, schematic
     intelligibility as opposed to unruly experience, and
     life turns out to be different from Vicar's simplified
     view. His principles almost without exception fail and
     his other good principles, like suffering in adversity,
     cause problems--the loss of family fortune without trying
     to get it back. The Vicar's happy ending has come already
     in his realization that the man of principle's reward is
     in heaven. Burchell the superman replaces Vicar in the
     worldly happy ending and seems to disprove Vicar's idea
     of patience in adversity. Interpolated stories, in their
     artificiality, show that didactic fiction is impotent.
     Reader's pleasure comes from the distance from the
     characters, from not sharing the Vicar's experience.

4   GOLDEN, MORRIS. "Goldsmith, The Vicar of Wakefield, and the
     Periodicals." JEPG 76 (October):525-36.
          The Vicar was heavily excerpted in periodicals in
     spring of 1766 (cites nine examples), even though reviews
     were unenthusiastic. Argues magazines illumine Goldsmith's
     world and his interests in matters of topical concern like
     the penal system and process of justice. Likewise, the
     magazines in spring 1763 made much of the absconding broker
     John Rice in 1762, who forged a letter of attorney, fled,
     returned, confessed and returned some of the money he had
     embezzled. Believes topicality of Rice's absconding may
     well have provided suggestion for Vicar's loss of fortune
     and explain Goldsmith's failure to develop the Whistonian
     material in the novel. "Goldsmith may have started with
     a satire on the controversialist temperament but turned
     from psychological to more congenial social and moral
     interests" (p. 529).

5   HAMLYN, SUSAN. "A New Source for the Plot of She Stoops to
     Conquer." N&Q, n.s. 24 (May-June):278-79.
          Suggests anecdote in John Quick's Whim, a collection
     of humorous anecdotes may be a possible source, since
     Goldsmith knew Quick from his having acted in the Good
     Natur'd Man and later playing part of Tony Lumpkin.

1977

6   HOPKINS, ROBERT H. "Matrimony in The Vicar of Wakefield and
     the Marriage Act of 1753." SP 74 (July):322-39.
          Goldsmith had attacked the Marriage Act of 1753 in
     Citizen letters 114 and 172 and in his History of England
     in a Series of Letters, 1764. Argues that debates pre-
     ceding passage of the act may be one source of some of
     Goldsmith's political ideas in the early 1760s, and thus
     matrimony is not a contrived means of resolving Vicar's
     plot but a major theme of the novel. Goldsmith's, and
     Vicar's, position that the act would erode ecclesiastical
     sanctions of marriage by increasing secular authority
     over marriage are at one here. Jenkinson's having secured
     a true license and true priest ensured Olivia's marriage
     was sound. But the marriage of Sophia and Sir William
     represents Goldsmith's "ideal of union between the aristoc-
     racy and the middle class" (p. 328).

7   MAHONY, ROBERT. "Lyrical Antithesis: The Moral Style of The
     Deserted Village." Ariel 8 (April):33-47.
          Most recent criticism of the poem has stressed its
     elegaic quality with heavy emphasis on rhetorical
     techniques. "Lyrical elements of Goldsmith's style, while
     evocative of one man's pain, are employed to fit the moral
     dimensions of the speaker's arguments for traditional
     values which Auburn represents and which luxury threatens"
     (p. 34). Lyricism stresses the antithesis between past
     and present in a "combination of argumentative strength and
     simple verbal music" (p. 35). Most Latinate words used
     pejoratively and simple words suggest vigor. In the
     poem's "style lyrical simplicity and antithetical strength
     are integrated, at once projecting the moral dimension of
     the speaker's argument and appropriating his emotions to
     fit it . . ." (p. 46).

8   STORM, LEO [F.]. "Conventional Ethics in Goldsmith's The
     Traveller. SEL 17 (Summer):463-76.
          Argues Goldsmith worked with a traditional set of ideas:
     the theme of liberty, drawn from Addison's Letter from
     Italy; the old-fashioned political cosmology associated
     with Denham's Cooper's Hill; and the parallel concept of
     the great chain of being. Most imitations of Denham shift
     away from his political and social ideas to natural
     description and from couplet to blank verse. Prior recog-
     nized Goldsmith's debt to Addison, though Addison converted
     Denham's emphasis on political balance to praise of Whigs,
     but Goldsmith returned to Denham's original idea of
     political balance, reflecting the Wilkite disturbances of
     the early 1760s and the need to restore strength to the

monarchy. Goldsmith's combination of great chain idea with
balance also echoes Montesquieu's Esprit des Lois (1748),
in which the particular institutions of a country are
linked with customs and manners of its people. Shows that
each national culture has an equal potential for harmony,
depending on its own blessings. In England, Goldsmith
sees the threat of imbalance and of possible chaos.
"Goldsmith's great genius lay in his skillful organization
of descriptive details and secondarily in synthesis of old
ideas into new and memorable form" (p. 476).

9 ZACH, WOLFGANG. "Das Literarishe Filter Autoptischer Erfahrung: Dichtung und Wahrheit über Goldsmiths Grand Tour,
   1755." Arbeiten aus Anglistik und Amerikanistik 2, no. 1:
   99-122.
      Questions how accurate the details of Goldsmith's
   letter from Leyden are and agrees with Sells (1974.A5)
   that the anecdote of the shipwreck is probably fictional.
   The details about Holland are conventional information.
   Suggests already Goldsmith was writing to interest his
   recipient-audience rather than to report literal truth.
   His letters are generally quite reticent about personal
   matters, and usually when specific details appear,
   Goldsmith is borrowing from a literary source. In general,
   like Johnson, Goldsmith was committed to the theory of
   expressing large, general truths, not idiosyncratic personal
   experiences.
      Evidence for Goldsmith's personally having visited
   Germany is rather shaky, too. The confusion of the author
   with his use of first-person narrators has caused much
   of the problem. Goldsmith's experiences on his European
   journey nearly always are filtered through literature and
   shed little reliable biographical light.

1978

A. Books

1 IRVING, WASHINGTON. Oliver Goldsmith, A Biography. In The
   Complete Works of Washington Irving: Oliver Goldsmith, A
   Biography; Biography of the Late Margaret Miller Davidson.
   Vol. 17. Edited by Elsie Lee West. Boston: Twayne,
   pp. xv-xxxvii, 1-241.
      A critical edition of 1849.A1. West's discussion of
   the sources Irving used for his brief 1825 life and of the
   various reprintings of the 1825, 1840, and 1849 versions
   of the Life is by far the clearest and most reliable

available. See also Stanley T. Williams and Mary Allen
Edge, A Bibliography of the Writings of Washington Irving:
A Checklist (New York: Oxford University Press, 1936),
pp. 88-93.

B. Shorter Writings

1   DANZIGER, MARLIES K. Oliver Goldsmith and Richard Brinsley
    Sheridan. New York: Frederick Ungar, pp. 5-55.
        An introductory account, primarily for undergraduates.
    Describes both playwrights as following in the main English
    comic tradition, derived from Terence and Plautus, of
    Shakespeare, Jonson, and the Restoration writers, all
    using intricate plots and type characters. Good Natur'd
    Man is weakly plotted with some awkward scenes, sees it as
    mocking facile sentimentalism, though not sentimental as
    such. She Stoops to Conquer a masterpiece for its
    naturalness and for Kate Hardcastle, though Tony Lumpkin
    is vivid and energetic as well as cloddish.

2   DUSSINGER, JOHN A. "Philanthropy and the Selfish Reader in
    Goldsmith's Life of Nash." Studies in Burke and his Times
    19 (Autumn):197-207.
        Generally Goldsmith's strategy is to depict Nash and
    Bath as below the moral standard of the reader, but Gold-
    smith's irony undercuts sanctimonious judgments against
    the lowly subjects. Disagrees with Hopkins (1969.A1) over
    tone of some passages Hopkins identifies as ironic,
    especially those which stress Nash's positive acts in re-
    fining crude manners of newly wealthy and in bringing
    order to the motley society of Bath. Shows Nash helping
    unskilled gamblers as a reformed philanderer who helped
    found General Hospital at Bath. Goldsmith's biography
    avoids sentimental gush and heavy-handed moralizing while
    presenting Nash's benevolence to the reader to admire and
    emulate. Considerable satire of Nash, but also implied
    criticism of the selfish reader, the kind who spurned Nash
    after he was no longer useful to the Bath "establishment."

3   FERGUSON, OLIVER W. "Antisentimentalism in The Good Natur'd
    Man: The Limits of Parody." In The Dress of Words:
    Essays on Restoration and Eighteenth Century Literature
    in Honor of Richmond P. Bond. University of Kansas
    Publication, Library Series 42. Edited by Robert B. White,
    Jr. Lawrence: University of Kansas Libraries, pp. 105-16.
        Questions the usual view that the play is a satirical
    attack on sentimental drama, noting that contemporary
    reviewers were unable to understand the play. "In writing

the play Goldsmith was concerned not with parodying
sentimental drama but with treating in the form of a conventional comedy a subject of abiding interest to him: the
dangers of untutored benevolence" (p. 111). Traces view
that play is antisentimental to William Cooke, 1805, who
saw it as precursor of She Stoops to Conquer. Discusses
mixture of comic and sentimental elements in Kelly's
False Delicacy, produced just before Goldsmith's play,
and sees Goldsmith's preface to published play mainly as
justification of bailiff scene and low comedy, not attack
on sentimental drama. Finds the play's main fault is
"unredeemable dullness" (p. 114) of main characters, but
otherwise a conventional comedy.

4   LONSDALE, ROGER. "'A Garden and a Grave': The Poetry of
    Oliver Goldsmith." In The Author in His Work: Essays on
    a Problem in Criticism. Edited by Louis L. Martz and
    Aubrey Williams. New Haven and London: Yale University
    Press, pp. 3-30.
        Considers shift from the nineteenth-century view that
    The Traveller and The Deserted Village acquire their force
    from the autobiographical element to the more recent
    opinion that autobiography has no place in poems whose power
    derives from the interaction of rhetorical techniques.
    Possible to avoid equating poetic rendering of experience
    with direct experience as well as to avoid denying connec-
    tion between external elements of life and what the poet
    writes. In Deserted Village, unexpected image of Poetry
    departing England clarifies the emotional significance of
    other action. Rejects Hopkins's (1969.A1) detached,
    rhetorical interpretation of Traveller for a much more
    personal "I," more nearly related to Goldsmith. Sees much
    of the force of both poems coming from Goldsmith-Narrator's
    assertion of autobiographical authenticity in both dedica-
    tions, which connect the narrator of the poem with the
    Goldsmith who signed the dedications.

5   WOODS, SAMUEL H., Jr. "The Goldsmith 'Problem.'" Studies in
    Burke and His Times 19 (Winter):47-60.
        Discusses critical approaches and scholarly opportunities
    in Goldsmith studies.

Index

Abbot, Sister M. John Vianny, 1967.A1
Account of the Late Dr. Goldsmith's Illness, so far as Relates to the
    EXHIBITION of Dr. James's Powders, together with Remarks on the
    Use and Abuse of Powerful Medicines in the Beginning of Fevers
    and Other Acute Diseases, An, 1774.B7
Adelstein, Michael, 1961.B2
Aiken, John 1796.B1
"American Couplets in The Deserted Village, The," 1962.B5
Among My Books, Centenaries, Reviews, Memoirs, 1908.B3
Amory, Hugh, 1973.B9
"Ancestry of John Payne Collier (1789-1883), with a Reference to
    Oliver Goldsmith, The," 1925.B2
Andrews, William L., 1970.B1
"Anecdotes of Dr. Goldsmith" [European Magazine], 1792.B1
"Anecdotes of Dr. Goldsmith" [Evans], 1808.B1
"Anecdotes of the Late Dr. Goldsmith" [Universal Magazine], 1780.B1
Anecdotes of the Late Samuel Johnson, LL.D. during the Last Twenty
    Years of his Life [Piozzi], 1785.B2
Angus-Butterworth, Lionel M., 1949.B1; 1961.B2
Annals of the Club, The, 1914.B1
"Another Manufactured Anecdote in The Life of Richard Nash?" 1957.B3
Anson, Elizabeth, 1925.B1
Anson, Florence, 1925.B1
"Antisentimentalism in The Good Natur'd Man: The Limits of Parody,
    1978.B3
"Appraisals: The Plays of Oliver Goldsmith," 1974.B5
Arthos, John, 1962.B1
"Aspects of Sentimentalism in Eighteenth-Century Literature,"
    1970.B5
Atkinson, A. D., 1947.B1
Aubin, Robert C., 1936.B1
"Auburn Syndrome: Change and Loss in The Deserted Village and
    Wordsworth's Grassmere, The," 1973.B3
"Auerbachs Keller Scene and She Stoops to Conquer, The," 1955.B6
"Authentic Anecdotes of the Late Dr. Goldsmith" [Glover], 1774.B3
Authorship in the Days of Johnson: Being a Study of the Relation
    between Author, Patron, Publisher, and the Public, 1726-1780,
    1927.B5

Index

Autobiography [Dichtung und Wahrheit], 1822.B1
Autobiography, Letters and Literary Remains of Mrs. Piozzi, 1861.B1

Backman, Sven, 1971.A1; 1975.B1
Bailey, Edward B., 1973.A1
Baker, Ernest A., 1934.B3; 1964.B1
Balderston, Katharine C., 1926.A1-2; 1927.B1; 1928.A1; 1929.B1;
    1930.B1; 1964.B2
Barbauld, Anna, 1810.B1
Barbier, C. P., 1951.B1
Barnett, George L., 1945.B1; 1957.B1
Barnouw, A. J., 1913.B1
Bataile, Robert A., 1977.B1
Battestin, Martin, 1974.B1
Baudin, Maurice, 1930.B2
Before Jane Austen: The Shaping of the Novel in the Eighteenth
    Century, 1965.B7
Bell, Howard, Jr., 1942.B1; 1944.B1
"Bibliographical Notes: Goldsmith to Sir William Chambers," 1936.B3
"Biography as Tragedy: Fictive Skill in Oliver Goldsmith's The Life
    of Richard Nash," 1971.B5
"Birth of Goldsmith, The" [Balderston], 1929.B1; 1930.B4
"Birthplace of Oliver Goldsmith" [Henderson], 1901.B1
Blacam, Hugh de, 1934.B2
Black, William, 1878.A1; 1879.A1
Bligh, John, 1976.B1
Bohn, H. G., 1848.A1
Bond, Donald F., 1967.B7
Bookseller of the Last Century, A, 1885.B1
Booth, Wayne, 1976.B2
Boswell, James, 1791.B1; 1924.B1; 1928.B1; 1929.B2; 1930.B3;
    1931.B1-2; 1932.B1; 1933.B1; 1937.B2; 1950.B1; 1955.B1;
    1956.B1; 1959.B1; 1966.B4; 1969.B1; 1970.B6; 1976.B3
Boswell for the Defense, 1764-1774, 1959.B1
Boswell in Search of a Wife, 1766-1769, 1956.B1
Boswell on the Grand Tour, 1765-1766, 1955.B1
Boswell's London Journal, 1762-1763, 1950.B1
"Boswell's Portrait of Goldsmith," 1961.B6
Brack, O. M., Jr. 1969.B2
British Novelists with an Essay, and Prefaces, Biographical and
    Critical [Barbauld], 1810.B1
"Broken Dream of The Deserted Village, The," 1959.B3
Brown, Joseph E., 1926.B1; 1927.B2
Brown, Wallace C., 1948.B1
"Browning and Goldsmith," 1946.B6
Bulwer-Lytton, Edward, 1848.B2
Burton, Dolores M., 1970.B2
Butler, William A., 1836.B1

C., S. P., 1848.B3
Campbell, Thomas, 1777.B1; 1854.B1; 1947.B2

Index

Catalogue of the Household Furniture, with a Select Collection of
    Books, Late the Library of Dr. Goldsmith, 1774.B6; 1837.A1;
    1854.A2; 1973.B9
Caulfield, James, First Earl of Charlemont, 1891.B1; 1894.B1
Census of the Manuscripts of Oliver Goldsmith, A, 1926.A1
Chalmers, Alexander, 1810.B2
Chapman, R. W., 1928.B2; 1929.B3; 1953.B1
"Characters--Dr. Goldsmith" [Glover], 1774.B5
Charlemont, First Earl of. See Caulfield, James
Chen Shou-yi, 1939.B2
Church, Richard, 1929.B4; 1951.B2; 1957.B2; 1961.B3
Churchill, Irving L., 1935.B1
"Citizen of the World, The" [Dobson], 1892.B1
"City and Country Life in The Vicar of Wakefield," 1977.B1
Clarke, Ernest, 1914.B2-3
Cohane, Christopher B., 1972.A1; 1974.B2
Cole, Richard C., 1970.B3
Collected Letters of Oliver Goldsmith, 1928.A1
Collected Works of Oliver Goldsmith [Friedman], 1966.A1
Colman, George the Elder, 1820.B1
Colman, George the Younger, 1820.B1; 1830.B1
Colum, Padraic, 1929.B5
"Comic Unity in Oliver Goldsmith's The Vicar of Wakefield," 1968.A1
Conant, Martha P., 1908.B1; 1966.B1
Concordance to the Poems of Oliver Goldsmith, A, 1940.A1
"Conflict of Art and Nature in the Writings of Oliver Goldsmith, The,"
    1973.A1
Congleton, James E., 1952.B1
"Conventional Ethics in Goldsmith's The Traveller," 1977.B8
Conversations with James Northcote [Hazlitt], 1830.B2
Cooke, William, 1793.B1; 1805.B1.
Correspondence [Boswell], 1969.B1; 1976.B3
"Correspondence" [Schorer about She Stoops to Conquer], 1933.B11
Coulter, John Knox, 1965.A1
Courthope, W. J., 1905.B1; 1962.B2
Cowley, Patrick, 1947.B3
Craddock, Joseph, 1826.B1
Crane, Ronald S., 1921.B1; 1923.B1; 1927.A1,B3-4; 1930.B4-5;
    1933.B2-3; 1934.B4-5; 1941.B1
Crawfurd, Raymond, 1915.B1
"Creative Genius of Oliver Goldsmith, The," 1961.A1
"Critical and Historical Study of Oliver Goldsmith's The Citizen of
    the World," 1970.A2
"Critical Dissertation, A" [on The Deserted Village], 1796.B1
Critical History of English Poetry, A, 1960.B1
"Critical Observations" [Mudford on The Vicar of Wakefield], 1811.B1
Cross, Marian Evans, 1884.B1
Cumberland, Richard, 1806-1807.B1
Cunningham, Peter, 1854.A1; 1881.A1
Curtis, Henry, 1925.B2

191

Dahl, Curtis, 1958.B1
Daiches, David, 1960.B1
Dalnekoff, Donna Isaacs. See Isaacs, Donna
Danziger, Marlies K., 1978.B1
D'Arblay, Frances Burney, 1842.B1; 1889.B1
Davidson, L. J., 1921.B2
Davie, Donald, 1954.B1; 1958.B2
Davies, Thomas, 1780.B2
Davis, Tom, 1975.A1
De C., J. P., 1941.B2
"Definition of 'Berserk,'" 1958.B3
Demsbolton, John, 1958.3
"Deserted Village, Ecclesiastes, and the Enlightenment, The,"
    1973.B12
"Deserted City, Deserted Village," 1973.B8
"Deserted Village, The" [Durrand], 1878.B1
"Deserted Village, The" [Jack], 1967.B3
"Deserted Village, The" [Redway], 1878.B2
"Deserted Village and Goldsmith's Social Doctrines, The," 1944.B1
"Deserted Village and Isaiah, The," 1969.B4
"Deserted Village and Sir Robert Walpole, The," 1959.B2
"Deserted Village: Poem as Virtual History, The," 1954.B1
"Deserted Village in Prose, (1762), The," 1927.B4
Diary and Letters of Madame D'Arblay, The, 1842.B1
Diary of a Visit to England in 1775 by an Irishman, 1854.B1
Dichtung und Wahrheit, 1822.B1
Dircks, Richard J., 1977.B2
D'Israeli, Isaac, 1801.B1
Dix, E. R. McC., 1928.B3
Dobson, Austin, 1885.A1; 1888.A1; 1892.B1; 1898.B1; 1899.B1;
    1902.B1; 1903.B1; 1910.B1; 1913.B2; 1923.B2-3; 1924.B2;
    1925.B3; 1933.B4; 1973.A2
Dr. Campbell's Diary of a Visit to England in 1775, 1854.B1; 1947.B2
"Dr. Goldsmith" [Rider], 1762.B7
"Dr. James's Powders" [De C., J. P.], 1941.B2
"Dr. James's Powders" [Haggis], 1941.B3
"Dr. James's Powders" [Heal], 1941.B4
"Dr. James's Powders" [Powell], 1941.B6
"Dr. Johnson and the Life of Goldsmith," 1933.B13
"Dr. Primrose and Goldsmith's Clerical Ideal," 1975.B2
Doughty, Oswald, 1928.B4
Druid's Monument, The, 1774.B9
"Duality of Theme in The Vicar of Wakefield," 1961.B1
Duff, Sir M. E. Grant, 1914.B1
Dumeril, Edith, 1926.B2
Duncan, Jeffrey L., 1968.B1
Durant, David, 1977.B3
Durrand, Edmund, 1878.B1
Dussinger, John A., 1967.B1; 1974.B3; 1978.B2

Early Diary of Frances Burney, The, 1889.B1
"Early Goldsmith Reprint in the London Chronicle, An," 1973.B2
"Early Haunts of Oliver Goldsmith, The," 1879.B1; 1905.A1
"Editions of Percy's Memoir of Goldsmith," 1935.B1
Eichenberger, Karl, 1954.A1
"Eighteenth-Century Divine, The," 1947.B3
Eliot, George. See Cross, Marian Evans
Eliot, T. S. 1930.B6; 1933.B5; 1940.B1; 1942.B2; 1947.B4
Elton, Oliver, 1929.B6
Emery, John P., 1938.B1
Emslie, Macdonald, 1963.A1
English Humourists of the Eighteenth Century, The, 1853.B1
English Literary Periodicals and the Climate of Opinion During the
    Seven Years' War, 1966.B6
English Literature from Dryden to Burns, 1948.B2
English Novel, a Panorama, The 1960.B6
English Novel in the Magazines, 1740-1815, with a Catalogue of 1375
    Magazine Novels and Novelettes, The 1962.B3
English Village: A Literary Study, The, 1919.B1
Entstehungsgeschichte von Goldsmiths "Vicar of Wakefield," 1903.A1
"Essay by Goldsmith in the Lady's Magazine, A," 1933.B6
Essay on Light Reading, As It May be Supposed to Influence Moral
    Conduct and Literary Taste, An, 1808.B2
Essays and Criticisms, with an Account of the Author, 1798.A1
Essays and Leaves from a Notebook, 1884.B1
"Essays Erroneously Attributed to Goldsmith," 1924.B3
"Ethics in the Wasteland: Image and Structure in The Deserted
    Village," 1971.B6
Evans, John, 1804.B1; 1808.B1
Eversole, Richard, 1966.B2

"Familiar Stranger: The Outsider of Eighteenth Century Satire, A,"
    1973.B1
"Family-Wanderer Theme in Goldsmith, The," 1958.B5
Ferguson, Oliver W., 1965.B2; 1967.B2; 1971.B2; 1973.B2; 1974.B4;
    1975.B2; 1978.B3
Ferguson, Robert, 1902.B2
"Fielding Echo in She Stoops to Conquer, A," 1973.B7
Fielding, K. J., 1959.B2
"Figure of the Outsider in Eighteenth-Century Satire, The," 1970.A1
"Figures in a Dream," 1928.B5
"First Edition of Essays by Mr. Goldsmith, The," 1952.B2
"First Edition of Goldsmith's Bee, No. 1, The," 1958.B4
"First Editions of The Good Natur'd Man and She Stoops to Conquer,
    The," 1958.B10
"First French Translation of The Deserted Village, The," 1946.B5
Fischer, Willi, 1902.B3; 1904.B1
Fong, David, 1971.B3
Ford, Edward, 1883.B1
"Forerunners of Goldsmith's Citizen of the World, 1921.B2
Forster, John, 1848.A2,B1-2,4; 1854.A2; 1885.B1; 1975.B4

"Forster's Goldsmith," 1975.B4
Forsythe, R. S., 1912.B1
Foys, Robert M., 1971.A2
Fraser, G. S., 1970.B4
Fraser Harris, D. F., 1936.B2
Freeman, William, 1952.A1
Free Thoughts on Quacks and their Medicines Occasioned by the Death
    of Dr. Goldsmith and Mr. Scawen, 1776.B4
"French Influence on Goldsmith's Citizen of the World, A," 1921.B1
"French Sources of Goldsmith's The Good Natur'd Man," 1960.B4
Friedman, Arthur, 1933.B3,6; 1935.B2-3; 1938.B2-3; 1940.B2-3;
    1946.B1; 1951.B3-4; 1952.B2; 1955.B2; 1956,B2-3; 1958.B4;
    1960.B2-3; 1963.B1; 1966.A1; 1970.B5; 1971.B1; 1974.A1
Fussell, Paul, 1965.B3; 1969.B3

Gallery of Illustrious Irishmen: 1. Goldsmith," 1836.B1
Galloway, W. F., 1933.B7
Gannon, Susan R., 1967.A2
"'Garden and a Grave': The Poetry of Oliver Goldsmith, A," 1978.B4
Garrick, David, 1831.B1
Garrod, Heathcote William, 1963.B2
Gassman, Byron E., 1960.B4
Gaussen, Alice C. C., 1908.B2
"Genesis and Date of Goldsmith's Retaliation, The," 1977.B2
Gibbs, J. W. M., 1883.B2; 1884.A1
Ginger, John, 1977.A1
Glover,[?] Samuel, 1774.B3-5; 1777.B2; 1780.B1
Goethe, Johann Wolfgang von, 1822.B1; 1829.B1; 1945.B2; 1955.B6
"Goethe's Estimate of Goldsmith," 1945.B2
Goethe's Letters to Zeltner, 1829.B1
Golden, Morris, 1955.B3-5; 1956.B4-5; 1957.B3-4; 1958.B5-7; 1959.B3-5;
    1961.B4; 1977.B4
Goldsmith, Oliver
--Bibliographies, 1924.B3; 1928.B3; 1941.B1; 1971.B1
--Biographies, 1801.B2; 1825.B1; 1833.B1; 1835.B1; 1836.B2; 1837.A1,
    B2; 1840.A1,B1; 1848.B1; 1849.A1-2,B1; 1850.A1; 1854.A1; 1888.A1;
    1910.A1-2; 1935.A1; 1952.A1; 1957.A1; 1974.A1,5; 1977.A1
--Major Collected Editions, 1801.B2; 1837.A2; 1848.A1; 1854.A1;
    1881.A1; 1884.A1; 1966.A1
--Individual Works
--Bee, The, 1759.B3; 1760.B1; 1764.B7; 1913.B1; 1926.B1; 1929.B8;
    1939.B1,3; 1944.B2,6; 1955.B2,9; 1958.B4,6; 1966.B6; 1967.A5;
    1974.A3,6,B2; 1975.B4
--Citizen of the World, The, 1762.B1-2; 1764.B7; 1792.B1;
    1818.B1; 1819.B1; 1836.B1; 1878.A1; 1883.B2,3; 1892.B1; 1908.B1;
    1910.B1; 1913.B2; 1921.B1-2; 1924.A1; 1926.A3,B4; 1927.B1;
    1929.B10; 1933.B7; 1938.B3; 1939.B1-2; 1940.B3; 1946.B6;
    1948.B3; 1949.B2; 1951.B1,3; 1952.B2; 1953.B2; 1954.A1;
    1955.B2,7; 1956.A2; 1958.B3,5; 1961.A1; 1962.B3; 1965.A1;
    1967.A1-2,5,B1; 1968.B2; 1970.A2-3,B7; 1971.A2,B3,9; 1973,B2;
    1974.A6; 1976.B2

--Deserted Village, The,   1770.B1-4; 1777.B1; 1785.B1; 1796.B1;
     1820.B2; 1822.B2; 1829.B1; 1832.B1-2; 1837.A1,B1,3; 1856.B1;
     1865.B1; 1878.B1-2; 1879.B1; 1883.B2-3; 1902.B1; 1905.B1;
     1919.B1; 1927.B4; 1928.B5; 1933.B7; 1937.B3; 1940.A1; 1943.B2-3;
     1944.B1,3; 1945.B4; 1946.B5; 1947.B3; 1948.B1-2; 1949.B2;
     1951.B6; 1953-B3; 1954.B1-2; 1955.B7; 1958.A1,B2,5,9; 1959.B2-3,6;
     1960.A1,B1-2; 1962.B4-5; 1964.B4; 1965.A1-2,B4; 1966.B2; 1967.B3;
     1968.B2; 1969.B4-6; 1970.B1,3,8; 1971.A2,B4-6; 1973.A1,B3,5,8,12;
     1974.A5-6,B7; 1975.A1,3,B2-3,5; 1976.B1; 1977.B1,7; 1978.B4
--Enquiry into the Present State of Polite Learning in Europe, An,
     1759.B1-2,4; 1764.B7; 1913.B2; 1962.B1,4; 1964.B3; 1965.A1,B6;
     1967.A5,B5; 1973.B12
--Essays,   1798.A1; 1804.B2; 1927.B1,3; 1939.B3; 1951.B1; 1952.B2;
     1956.A2,B5; 1965.A3; 1970.B3
--Good Natur'd Man, The,   1768.B1-6; 1818.B1; 1819.B1; 1831.B1;
     1836.B1; 1842.B1; 1848.A1; 1885.B1; 1927.B6; 1934.B1; 1938.B4;
     1940.B5; 1941.B5; 1944.B5; 1958.B9-10; 1960.B4; 1965.B5;
     1966.B5; 1967.B1; 1970.B5; 1971.A3; 1972.B3; 1973.A1,B5,11;
     1974.A4,6,B5; 1975.A1; 1977.B5; 1978.B1,3
--History of the Earth and Animated Nature, A,   1924.A2; 1942.B3;
     1943.B1; 1944.B4; 1945.B3; 1946.B2-3; 1967.A2,5,B2,4; 1973.A3;
     1974.A6
--Life of Richard Nash, The, 1762.B3-6; 1947.B1; 1949.B2; 1955.B9;
     1956.B2; 1957.B3; 1961.A1; 1965.B3; 1967.A2,4-5; 1969.A1;
     1971.B5; 1975.B1; 1978.B2
--New Essays, 1927.A1,B3
--Retaliation,   1774.B1-2,4; 1780.B1; 1940.A1; 1967.B5; 1971.B2;
     1974.A6; 1975.A1,3; 1977.B2
--She Stoops to Conquer,   1773.B1-8; 1793.B1; 1806-1807.B1; 1818.B1;
     1819.B1; 1820.B1; 1826.B1; 1831.B1; 1836.B1; 1837.A1; 1848.A1;
     1885.B1; 1912.B1; 1927.B5; 1928.A1; 1929.B7; 1930.B1-2;
     1933.B10-11; 1938.B1; 1941.B5; 1942.B3; 1944.B5; 1948.B3;
     1954.A1,B1; 1955.B2,6; 1958.B9-10; 1960.B1; 1965.B5; 1966.B5;
     1967.A5,B1; 1968.B2; 1970.B3,7; 1971.A3,B8; 1972.B1;
     1973.A1,B7,11; 1974.A4,6,B5; 1975.A1; 1976.B2-3,5; 1977.A1,B5;
     1978.B1,3
--Traveller, The,   1764.B1-3; 1774.B4,9; 1765.B1-2; 1777.B1; 1792.B1;
     1837.A1,B1,3; 1856.B1; 1885.B1; 1902.B2; 1905.B1; 1926.B2;
     1932.B2; 1940.A1; 1944.B3; 1948.B1; 1949.B2; 1954.A2,B3;
     1955.B7; 1956.A1; 1958.B5; 1960.B3; 1961.A1; 1962.B4; 1965.A1-2;
     1967.B3-4; 1970.B3; 1971.A2,B3,7; 1973.A1,B5,12; 1974.A6;
     1975.A1,3,B2-3; 1977.B8; 1978.B4
--Vicar of Wakefield, The, 1766.B1-2; 1774.B4,9; 1776.B2; 1777.B1;
     1785.B1; 1806-1807,B1; 1810.B1; 1811.B1; 1818.B1; 1819.B1;
     1822.B1-2; 1829.B1; 1831.B1; 1832.B2; 1837.A1,B3; 1842.B1;
     1856.B1; 1878.A1,B1-2; 1879.B1; 1883.B1; 1884.B1; 1885.A1,B1;
     1888.A1; 1889.B1; 1900.B1; 1902.B1-3; 1903.A1,B1-2; 1904.A1,B1;
     1907.B1; 1910.A1; 1913.B2; 1919.B1; 1928.B4; 1932.B2; 1933.B7;
     1934.B3; 1944.B5; 1947.B3; 1948.B3-4; 1949.B2; 1950.B2;
     1951.B1-2,5; 1952.B3; 1954.A1; 1955.B7; 1956.A2; 1957.B13;
     1958.B1,5,8-9; 1959.B4; 1960.B1,6; 1961.A1,B1,4; 1962.B3;

1963.A1,B1,3; 1964.B3; 1965.A1-2,B4,7,8; 1966.B3;
1967.A2,4-5,B1,3,6; 1968.A1,B1-3; 1969.A1; 1970.B2,5,7;
1971.A1-3,B3,9; 1973.A1,B4,6,10; 1974.A1,3,5-6, B1,3,6;
1975.A3,B2; 1976.B1-2,4,6; 1977.A1,B1,3-4,6
"Goldsmith" [Crane], 1941.B1
"Goldsmith" [Ferguson], 1967.B2
"Goldsmith" [Friedman], 1971.B1
"Goldsmith" [Garrod], 1963.B2
"Goldsmith" [Macaulay], 1856.B1
"Goldsmith and A Concise History of England" 1927.B7
"Goldsmith and Franklin on Sheep's Tails," 1939.B3
"Goldsmith and Freneau in 'The American Village,'" 1970.B1
"Goldsmith and Hanway," 1951.B3
"Goldsmith and his Biographers," 1848.B2
Goldsmith and His Booksellers, 1933.A1
"Goldsmith and Jean Rousset de Missy," 1940.B2
"Goldsmith and Johnson on Biography," 1927.B2
"Goldsmith and Justus Van Effen," 1934.B4
"Goldsmith and 'National Concord,'" 1955.B4
"Goldsmith and Sheridan and the Supposed Revolution of 'Laughing'
    against 'Sentimental Comedy,'" 1972.B1
"Goldsmith and Sheridan: Satirists of Sentiment," 1966.B5
"Goldsmith and Steele's Englishman," 1940.B3
"Goldsmith and the Annual Register," 1933.B12
"Goldsmith and the Bee," 1944.B6
"Goldsmith and the Chain of Being" [Lovejoy], 1946.B3
"Goldsmith and the Chain of Being" [Lynskey], 1945.B3
"Goldsmith and 'The Distresses of a Hired Writer,'" 1955.B3
"Goldsmith and the Encyclopédie," 1933.B3
"Goldsmith and the 'English Lives,'" 1931.B3
"Goldsmith and the Gentleman who Signs S,'" 1930.B9
"Goldsmith and the Jest Books," 1955.B2
"Goldsmith and the Literary Magazine," 1929.B8
"Goldsmith and the Marquis d'Argens" [Friedman], 1938.B2
"Goldsmith and the Marquis d'Argens" [Harth], 1953.B2
"Goldsmith and the Notions Grille and Wandrer in Werthers Leiden,"
    1902.B2
"Goldsmith and the Pickle-Shop," 1942.B1
"Goldsmith and 'The Present State of Russia and France,'" 1955.B5
"Goldsmith and the Present State of the British Empire," 1930.B8
"Goldsmith and 'The Universal Museum and Complete Magazine,'"
    1957.B4
"Goldsmith and the Warfare in Nature," 1944.B4
"Goldsmith and the Weekly Magazine," 1935.B2
"Goldsmith and Voltaire's Essai sur les Moeurs," 1923.B1
"Goldsmith and Wood," 1956.B2
"Goldsmith Anecdote, A," [Chapman], 1929.B3
"Goldsmith as a Biographer," 1940.B4
"Goldsmith as a Social Philosopher," 1930.B7
Goldsmith as Historian," 1949.B1; 1961.B2
"Goldsmith Attributions in the Literary Magazine," 1956.B4

"Goldsmith Attributions in the Weekly Magazine," 1956.B5
"Goldsmith Borrows," 1947.B1
Goldsmith Collection, A, 1963.A2
"Goldsmith en France au xviii^e Siecle: Les Essays et le Vicar de Wakefield," 1951.B1
"Goldsmith Essay in the 'Complete Magazine,' A," 1958.B6
"Goldsmith et l'Italie," 1967.B4
"Goldsmith in Camouflage," 1947.B5
"Goldsmith in France," 1933.B8
"Goldsmith l'Eternal Vagabond," 1933.B9
"Goldsmith on his Teachers," 1936.B2
"Goldsmith 'Problem,' The," 1978.B5
"Goldsmith Repeating Himself at Length," 1939.B1
"Goldsmith's A Survey of Experimental Philosophy," 1969.B2
"Goldsmith's Achievement as a Dramatist," 1965.B5
"Goldsmith's American Tigers," 1945.B4
"Goldsmiths and their Villages, The," 1951.B6
Goldsmith's "Animated Nature," 1924.A2; 1973.A3
"Goldsmith's Augustanism: A Study of his Literary Works," 1965.A2
"Goldsmith's Birthplace," 1944.B6
"Goldsmith's Comic Skills," 1973.B11
"Goldsmith's Contributions to the Critical Review," 1946.B1
"Goldsmith's Critical Outlook," 1938.B5
"Goldsmith's Degenerate Song-Birds: An Eighteenth-Century Fallacy in Ornithology," 1943.B2
"Goldsmith's Development as a Comic Dramatist," 1971.A3
"Goldsmith's 'Essay on Friendship,'" 1956.B3
"Goldsmith's Essays: Dates of Original Publication," 1927.B3
"Goldsmith's Indebtedness to Justus Van Effen," 1913.B1
"Goldsmith's Indebtedness to Voltaire and Justus Van Effen," 1926.B1
"Goldsmith's Library," 1892.B1
Goldsmith's Life of Bolingbroke and the Biographica Britannica," 1935.B3
"Goldsmith's Lives of the Fathers," 1929.B9
"Goldsmith's 'Natural History'--A Plan," 1946.B2
"Goldsmith's Poems and Plays" [Dobson," 1898.B1; 1899.B1; 1923.B2; 1925.B3
"Goldsmith's Retaliation," 1971.B2
"Goldsmith's Supposed Attack on Fielding," 1927.B1
"Goldsmith's Translation of the Roman Comique," 1934.B8
"Goldsmith's Vicar of Wakefield" [Fischer], 1902.B3
"Goldsmith's Vicar of Wakefield: The Reunion of the Alienated Artist," 1965.B4
"Goldsmith: The Comedy of Job," 1974.B1
Goldsmith: The Critical Heritage, 1974.A6
"Goldsmith: The Didactic Lyric," 1948.B1
"Goldsmith: The Good Natured Man" [Jeffares], 1975.B3
"Goldsmith: The Good-Natured Man" [McAdam], 1949.B2
"Goldsmith: The Vicar of Wakefield" [Emslie], 1963.A1
"Goldsmith, The Vicar of Wakefield, and the Periodicals," 1977.B4
Goldstein, Laurence, 1973.B3

Goldy, 1961.A2
"Goldy's Ballad," 1965.B1
Good, [?], 1774.B6; 1837.A1; 1854.B2; 1973.B9
"Good-Natured Heroes of Cumberland, Goldsmith, and Sheridan, The,"
    1972.B3
Graham, W. H., 1952.B3
Griffin, Robert J., 1965.A2
Growth of the English Novel, The, 1951.B2; 1957.B2; 1961.B3
Grudis, Paul J., 1973.B4
Grumbler, an Adaptation by Oliver Goldsmith, The, 1931.A1; 1973.B11
Gute Pfarrer in der Englischen Literatur bis zu Goldsmiths "Vicar of
    Wakefield," Der, 1904.A1
Gwynn, Stephen, 1935.A1

Haggis, A. W., 1941.B3
Hamlyn, Susan, 1977.B5
Hammer, Carl, Jr., 1945.B2
Harp, Richard L., 1974.A2; 1976.A1
Harrison, Frederic, 1908.B3
Hart, Paxton, 1970.B6
Harth, Phillip, 1953.B2
Hassert, Margaret, 1974.B5
"Hau Kiou Choaan," 1926.B4
Haunch of Venison, a Poetical Epistle to Lord Clare, 1776.B1,3
Hawes, William, 1774.B7
Hawkesworth, John, 1770.B3-4
Hawkins, Marion E., 1965.A3
Hawkins, Sir John, 1787.B1; 1961.B5
Haydon, Francis M., 1940.B4
Hayford, Donald P., 1974.A3
Hazlitt, William, 1818.B1; 1819.B1; 1822.B2; 1830.B2
Heal, Ambrose, 1941.B4
Heilman, Robert B., 1940.B5
Helgerson, Richard, 1973.B5
Henderson, W. A., 1901.B1
Hennig, John, 1955.B6
Heroic Couplet, The, 1969.B6
Hilles, Frederick W., 1951.B5; 1952.B4; 1955.B7
History Sources of Percy's Memoir of Goldsmith, The, 1926.A2
History of English Drama, 1955.B8
History of English Poetry, 1905.B1; 1962.B2
History of Late Eighteenth Century Drama, 1927.B6; 1955.B8
History of the English Novel: The Novel of Sentiment and the Gothic
    Romance, The, 1934.B3; 1964.B1
Hoadley, J., 1831.B1
Holder, Arthur S., 1927.B5
Hopkins, Robert H., 1958.B8; 1961.A1; 1969.A1; 1976.B4; 1977.B6
Hornsby, Samuel, 1971.B4
Howarth, R. G., 1938.B4
Hume, Robert D., 1972.B1

Hunting, Robert, 1973.B6
Hyder, Clyde Kenneth, 1940.A1

Ignoto, 1939.B1
"Image Frequency and the Split in The Vicar of Wakefield, 1959.B4
"Immediate Occasion of Goldsmith's Citizen of the World, Letter
    XXXVIII, The," 1938.B3
"Inconsistency in the Thought of Goldsmith, An," 1937.B3
Index to the Private Papers from Malahide Castle in the Collection
    of Lt-Colonel Ralph Heyward Isham, 1937.B2
Ingalls, Gertrude Van Arsdale, 1929.B7
"Intellectual Background of Goldsmith's Deserted Village, The,"
    1960.A1
"Intonation and Pattern of Sermons in Seven Novels," 1970.B2
"Irish Background of Goldsmith's Social and Political Thought, The,"
    1937.B4
"Irony in Oliver Goldsmith's The Citizen of the World," 1967.A1
Irving, Washington, 1825.B1; 1833.B1; 1835.B1; 1836.B2; 1837.B2;
    1840.A1,B1; 1849.A1-2,B1; 1850.A1; 1978.A1
"Irving and His 'Favorite Author,'" 1962.B6
Isaacs, Donna A., 1970.A1; 1973.B1
Isaacs, J., 1928.A2
"Issues of the First Edition of The Vicar of Wakefield," 1948.B4
Itzkowitz, Martin, 1973.B7

Jaarsma, Richard J., 1968.B2; 1969.B4; 1971.B5-7
Jack, Ian, 1967.B3
Jackson, R. Wyse, 1947.B5; 1951.A1
James Boswell: The Earlier Years, 1740-1769, 1966.B4
James, Henry, 1900.B1
Jeffares, A. Norman, 1959.A1; 1963.A2; 1975.B3
Jefferson, D. W., 1950.B2; 1964.B3
Joel, Helmuth W., Jr., 1967.A3
"Johnson, Goldsmith, and 'The History of the Seven Years' War,'"
    1922.B1
"Johnson, Goldsmith, and The Traveller," 1971.B3
"Johnson and Goldsmith: The Mid-Augustan Norm," 1970.B4
Johnson, Samuel, 1764.B3; 1785.B2; 1787.B1; 1791.B1; 1861.B1;
    1922.B1; 1930.B6; 1933.B5; 1940.B1; 1942.B2,4; 1947.B4; 1961.B5;
    1970.B4; 1971.B3
Johnstone, Coragreene, 1952.A2
Jones, Claude E., 1946.B2

Kelly, J. J., 1879.B1; 1905.A1
Kenny, R. W., 1937.B1
Kenrick, William, 1759.B4; 1760.B1
Kent, Elizabeth E., 1933.A1
Kenyon, Sir F. G., 1914.B1
King, Richard Ashe, 1910.A1
Kirk, Clara M., 1967.A4
Knight, Douglas, 1944.B2

Krause, Gerd, 1944.B3
Krishna Batta, S., 1973.B8

Langhorne, John, 1765.B2; 1776.B3
"Laugh and Grow Wise with Oliver Goldsmith," 1972.B2
Le Breton, Maurice, 1967.B4
Lectures on the English Comic Writers, 1819.B1
Lectures on the English Poets, 1818.B1
Lehmann, Elmar, 1974.A4
"L'Element Autobiographique dans The Traveller," 1926.B2
Leslie, Charles Robert, 1865.B1
Letters of James Boswell, The, 1924.B1
Levine, Philip, 1970.A2
Lewes, George Henry, 1848.B4
Life and Adventures of Oliver Goldsmith, The [Forster], 1848.A1,
    B1-2.4
"Life and Critique" [Mudford], 1804.B2
Life and Times of Oliver Goldsmith, The [Forster], 1854.A2
Life and Times of Sir Joshua Reynolds, with Notices of Some of His
    Contemporaries, The, 1865.B1
"Life of Dr. Oliver Goldsmith," [Percy], 1801.B2; 1935.B1; 1974.A2,
    1976.A1
Life of Dr. Oliver Goldsmith, written from Personal Knowledge,
    Authentic Papers, and Other Indubitable Authorities [Glover],
    1774.B4
"Life of Goldsmith" [Chalmers], 1810.B2
"Life of Goldsmith" [Irving], 1825.B1, 1833.B1, 1835.B1, 1836.B2,
    1837.B2; 1840.B1, 1849.B1
Life of Oliver Goldsmith [Dobson], 1888.A1; 1973.A2
Life of Oliver Goldsmith, A Biography [Irving], 1849.A1-2; 1850.A1,
    1978.A1
"Life of Oliver Goldsmith, M. B." [Malone], 1777.B2
Life of Oliver Goldsmith, M.B., from a Variety of Original Sources,
    The [Prior], 1837.A1, B1,3
Life of Oliver Goldsmith, The [Moore], 1910.A2
Life of Oliver Goldsmith, with Selections from his Writings [Irving],
    1840.A1
Life of Samuel Johnson, LL.D., The [Boswell], 1791.B1
Life of Samuel Johnson, LL.D., The [Hawkins], 1787.B1; 1961.B5
"Lift Up Your Hearts: Oliver Goldsmith's Glory," 1969.B5
"Literarische Filter Autoptischer Erfahrung: Dichtung und
    Wahrheit über Goldsmiths Grand Tour, 1775, Das," 1977.B9
"Literary Mode of Goldsmith's Essays and of The Vicar of Wakefield,"
    1956.A2
Literary and Miscellaneous Memoirs [Craddock], 1826.B1
"Literary Convention in Goldsmith's Deserted Village," 1970.B8
Literary Miscellanies, Including a Dissertation on Anecdotes
    [D'Israeli], 1801.B2
"Literary Views of Oliver Goldsmith, The," 1952.A2
Literature, Popular Culture, and Society, 1965.B5
Lives of the Novelists [Sir Walter Scott], 1823.B1; 1825.B2

"Logical and Rhetorical Elements in The Deserted Village," 1964.B4
London: A Poem and The Vanity of Human Wishes. . . ., 1930.B6;
    1933.B5; 1940.B1; 1942.B2; 1947.B4
Lonsdale, Roger, 1978.B4
Loughlin, Richard L., 1969.B5; 1972.B2
Lovejoy, Arthur O., 1946.B3
Lowenthal, Leo, 1967.B5
Lowes, John Livingston, 1911.B1
Lucas, F. L., 1958.B9
Lynskey, Winifred, 1942.B3; 1943.B1; 1944.B4; 1945.B3
"Lyrical Antithesis: The Moral Style of The Deserted Village,"
    1977.B7
Lytton Sells, Arthur, 1924.A1; 1941.B5; 1974.A5

Macaulay, Thomas Babington, 1856.B1
MacLennan, Munro, 1975.A2
"Madan Family and Goldsmith, The," 1934.B2
Magazine Serials and the Essay Tradition, 1956.B6
Mahony, Robert, 1977.B7
"Making of The Deserted Village, The," 1959.B6
Malone, Edmond, 1777.B2; 1780.B2
Mangin, Edward, 1808.B2
Manlove, George K., 1960.A1
"Manufactured Anecdote in Goldsmith's Life of Richard Nash, A,"
    1955.B9
"Manuscript Version of She Stoops to Conquer, A," 1930.B1
Manuscripts and Correspondence, 1891.B1; 1894.B1
Mary Hamilton, afterwards Mrs. John Dickenson, at Court and Home,
    from Letters and Diaries, 1756 to 1816, 1925.B1
Masson, David, 1869.B1
"Materials of History: Goldsmith's Life of Nash, The," 1965.B2
"Matrimony in The Vicar of Wakefield and the Marriage Act of 1753,"
    1977.B6
Mayo, Robert D., 1962.B3
McAdam, Edward L., 1949.B2
McCarthy, B. Eugene, 1971.B8
McDonald, Daniel, 1966.B3
McKillop, Alan D., 1948.B2
"Medical Education and Qualifications of Oliver Goldsmith, The,"
    1914.B2
"Melange of Literary Type and Idea in Goldsmith's Deserted Village,"
    1958.A1
Melmoth, Courtney. See Pratt, Samuel Jackson
"Memoir of Goldsmith" [Scott], 1823.B1
Memoirs [Cumberland], 1806-1807.B1
Memoirs of Samuel Foote, 1805.B1
Memoirs of Sir Joshua Reynolds, Kt., Comprising Original Anecdotes
    of Many Distinguished Persons, his Contemporaries, and a
    Brief Analysis of his Discourses, to which Are Added Varieties
    on Art, 1813.B1
Memoirs of the Life of David Garrick, 1780.B2

"Memorials of Literary Characters, No. XVIII: Pedigree of the Poet
    Goldsmith," 1848.B3
Miehl, Dieter, 1976.B5
Milner-Barry, Alda, 1926.B3
Miner, Earl, 1959.B6
Miscellaneous Works of Oliver Goldsmith, M.B., including a Variety
    of Pieces now first collected, The [Prior], 1837.A2
Montague, John, 1960.B5; 1962.B4
Moore, Frank Frankfort, 1910.A2
Moore, John Robert, 1943.B2
"More New Essays by Oliver Goldsmith: A Problem in Ascription,"
    1972.A1
Morgan, Lee, 1961.B5
"Mr. Tattler [sic] of Pekin: A Venture in Journalism," 1929.B10
Mudford, William, 1804.B2; 1811.B1
Munby, A. N. L., 1973.B9

"Names and Characters in The Vicar of Wakefield," 1883.B1
"Narrative Strategy in the Major Prose and Poetry of Oliver Goldsmith,"
    1970.A2
"Narrator and The Vicar of Wakefield, The," 1973.B4
"Narrator of The Deserted Village: A Reconsideration, The," 1975.B5
"Neglected Aspects of The Vicar of Wakefield," 1976.B1
"Neglected Mid-Eighteenth Century Plea for Originality and Its
    Author, A," 1934.B5
Neuendorff, Bernard, 1903.A1
Neveu, Raymond, 1946.B4
Newell, R. H., 1820.B2
"New Essay by Oliver Goldsmith, A," 1974.B2
New Essays by Oliver Goldsmith [Crane], 1927.A1
"New Goldsmith Letters," 1964.B2
"New Source for She Stoops to Conquer, A," 1977.B5
Nicoll, Allardyce, 1927.B6; 1955.B8
Northcote, James, 1813.B1; 1830.B2
Notable Man: The Life and Times of Oliver Goldsmith, The, 1977.A1
"Note on the Early Literary Relations of Oliver Goldsmith and
    Thomas Percy, A," 1926.B3
"Notes on Goldsmith," 1907.B1
"Notes on Three Goldsmith Attributions," 1958.B7
"'Not Merely Sentimental'" Studien zur Goldsmiths Komoedien,
    1974.A4

O., W. H., 1883.B3
"Observations on The Vicar of Wakefield," 1950.B2
Oliver Goldsmith [Black], 1878.A1; 1879.A1
"Oliver Goldsmith" [Church], 1929.B4
"Oliver Goldsmith" [Dobson], 1913.B2; 1933.B4
Oliver Goldsmith [Freeman], 1952.A1
"Oliver Goldsmith" [Graham], 1952.B3
Oliver Goldsmith [Gwynn], 1935.A1
Oliver Goldsmith [Jeffares], 1959.A1
Oliver Goldsmith [King], 1910.A1

Oliver Goldsmith [Kirk], 1967.A4
"Oliver Goldsmith" [Masson], 1869.B1
"Oliver Goldsmith" [Ritchie], 1934.B6
"Oliver Goldsmith" [Roberts], 1934.B7
"Oliver Goldsmith" [Stephen], 1890.B1
"Oliver Goldsmith" [Templar], 1934.B1
Oliver Goldsmith [Wardle], 1957.A1
"Oliver Goldsmith" [Woolf], 1934.B9; 1950.B3
Oliver Goldsmith, A Biography [Irving], 1849.A1-2; 1850.A1; 1978.A1
Oliver Goldsmith, A Georgian Study [Quintana], 1967.A5
"Oliver Goldsmith and Goethe's Werther," 1903.B2
"Oliver Goldsmith and his Chinese Letters," 1939.B2
"Oliver Goldsmith and Medicine," 1915.B1
"Oliver Goldsmith and Music," 1951.B7
Oliver Goldsmith and Richard Brinsley Sheridan, 1978.B1
"Oliver Goldsmith and The Vicar of Wakefield" [Plumb], 1963.B3
"Oliver Goldsmith as a Critic of the Drama," 1965.B5
"Oliver Goldsmith as a Medical Man," 1914.B3
"Oliver Goldsmith as Social Critic in The Citizen of the World,"
    1970.A3
Oliver Goldsmith, Bibliographically and Biographically Considered,
    1928.A2
"Oliver Goldsmith, Citizen of the World," [Dussinger], 1967.B1
Oliver Goldsmith: Das Komische in den Werken seiner Reifeperiode,
    1954.A1
Oliver Goldsmith: Essays toward an Interpretation, 1951.A1
Oliver Goldsmith, His Life and Works [Lytton Sells], 1974.A5
"Oliver Goldsmith, Ironist to the Georgians," 1970.B7
"'Oliver Goldsmith, M.B.'" [Crane], 1933.B2
"Oliver Goldsmith, Poète et Médicin," 1946,B4
"Oliver Goldsmith: Reactions to the Man and his Principal Literary
    Works, 1730-1970," 1975.A3
"Oliver Goldsmith's "Citizen of the World" [Smith], 1926.A3
"Oliver Goldsmith's Citizen of the World: A Rational Accommodation
    of Human Existence," 1971.B9
"Oliver Goldsmith, 1728(?)-1774" [Chapman], 1928.B2; 1953.B1
"Oliver Goldsmith: She Stoops to Conquer: Or, The Mistakes of a
    Night" [Miehl], 1976.B5
"Oliver Goldsmith's Influence on the French Stage," 1941.B5
Oliver Goldsmith's Literary Reputation, 1757-1801," 1965.A1
"Oliver Goldsmith's Prose Satire," 1974.A3
"Oliver Goldsmith's Reputation in Ireland, 1762-74," 1970.B3
"Oliver Goldsmiths Stellung zum Bauerntum in Zuzammenhang seines
    Dichterisches Werkes," 1944.B3
"Oliver Goldsmith the Essayist," 1965.A3
Oliver, John W., 1922.B1
"On Goldsmith's Deserted Village," 1785.B1
"Oratorical Design of The Deserted Village, The," 1966.B2
Oriental Tale in England in the Eighteenth Century, The,
    1908.B1; 1966.B1
"Original Anecdotes of Goldsmith" [Evans], 1804.B1

Orwell, George, 1968.B3
Osgood, Charles G., Jr. 1907.B1
O'Sullivan, Seumas. See Starkey, James.

Pacey, Desmond, 1951.B6
Paden, William D., 1940.A1
Paschal, The Rev. Father, 1930.B7
Patrick, Michael D., 1971.B9
"Patterns of Disguise in The Vicar of Wakefield," 1958.B1
Patton, Julia, 1919.B1
Paulson, Ronald F., 1967.B6
"Percy and Goldsmith" [Chapman], 1953.B1
"Percy and Goldsmith" [Dobson], 1910.B1
Percy: Prelate and Poet, 1908.B2
Percy, Thomas, 1801.B2; 1908.B2; 1910.B1; 1926.A2;,B3; 1935.B1;
    1974.A2; 1976.A1
Peterson, Patricia C., 1968.A1
"Philanthropy and the Selfish Reader in Goldsmith's Life of Nash,"
    1978.B2
Philosophical Survey of the South of Ireland in a Series of Letters
    to John Watkinson, M. D., A., 1777.B1
Piozzi, Hester Lynch Thrale, 1785.B2; 1861.B1; 1942.B4
Piper, William B., 1969.B6
Pitman, James H., 1924.A2; 1973.A3
"Place of The Vicar of Wakefield within the Realistic Tradition of
    the Eighteenth Century," 1974.B6
"Plagiarism of Goldsmith's, A" [O., W. H.], 1883.B3
"Plagiarism of Goldsmith's, A" [Gibbs], 1833.B2
"Pluche and Derham: New Sources of Goldsmith," 1942.B3
Plumb, John Harold, 1963.B3
Poems and Plays [Davis], 1975.A1
"Poems in The Vicar of Wakefield, The," 1973.B6
Ponthieu, Judy F., 1970.A3
Portraits by Sir Joshua Reynolds. Character Sketches of Oliver
    Goldsmith, Samuel Johnson, and David Garrick, together with
    Other Manuscripts of Reynolds discovered among the Boswell
    Papers and Now First Published, 1952.B4
Posthumous Letters from Various Celebrated Men; Addressed to
    Francis Colman, and George Colman the Elder, 1820.B1
Pottle, Frederick A., 1931.B2; 1937.B2; 1966.B4
Pottle, Marion S., 1931.B2
Powell, L. F., 1926.B4; 1941.B6
Pratt, Samuel Jackson, 1744.B8
"Presentation of Oliver Goldsmith in Boswell's Life of Johnson, The,"
    1970.B6
Price, Lawrence M., 1932.B2; 1944.B5
Prior, Sir James, 1837.A1-2,B1,3; 1848.B2-3; 1849.A1; 1885.B1
Private Correspondence of David Garrick with the Most Celebrated
    Persons of his Time, The, 1831.B1
Privateer, Paul, 1965.B4
"'Private Issues' of The Deserted Village, The," 1953.B3; 1954.B2
Private Papers of James Boswell from Malahide Castle in the
    Collection of Lieut.-Colonel Ralph Heyward Isham, The,

1928.B1; 1929.B2; 1930.B3; 1931.B1-2; 1932.B1; 1933.B1; 1937.B2
"Problem of Indifferent Readings in the Eighteenth Century, with a
    Solution from The Deserted Village, The,"   1960.B2
"Prose of Goldsmith, The,"   1962.B1
Prospect of Society, A,   1954.A2; 1956.A1
Prothero, G. W.,   1914.B1
"Proverbs in The Good Natur'd Man,"   1938.B4

Q. in the Corner,   1768.B6
"Quadruple Imposition: An Account of Goldsmith's Traveller,"
    1954.B3
Quintana, Ricardo,   1964.B4; 1965.B5-6; 1967.A5; 1970.B7; 1973.B10

"Ralph's Case of Authors: Its Influence on Goldsmith and DiIsraeli,"
    1937.B1
Random Records,   1830.B1
"Rasselas and The Vicar of Wakefield,"   1957.B1
Rawson, C. J.,   1959.B7
"Real Origin of One of the 'Manufactured Anecdotes" in Goldsmith's
    Life of Nash, The,"   1975.B1
Reception of English Literature in Germany, The, 1932.B2
Records of My Life,   1832.B1
Redway, George,   1878.B2
Remak, Henry H.,   1946.B5
"Remarks" [on The Deserted Village][Newell],   1820.B2
"Re-Populating The Deserted Village,"   1974.B7
"Restoration and Eighteenth Century, The,"   1948.B3; 1967.B7
Reynolds, Sir Joshua,   1813.B1; 1865.B1; 1952.B4
Reynolds, W. Vaughan,   1938.B5
"Rhetorical Strategy of Oliver Goldsmith, The,"   1967.A2
Rhetorical World of Augustan Humanism, The, 1965.B3; 1969.B3
Riccoboni, Marie Jeanne,   1831.B1
Rider, William,   1762.B7
Ritchie, G. S.,   1934.B6
Roberts, S. C.,   1934.B7
Roberts, W.,   1933.B8
Rocher, M. L.,   1933.B9
Rodway, Allan,   1966.B5
Rothstein, Eric,   1976.B6
Rousseau, G. S.,   1974.A6
"Rural Ideal in Eighteenth-Century Fiction, The,"   1968.B1

Sabine, Nathan,   1974.B6
Sale Catalogues of Libraries of Eminent Persons: Poets and Men of
    Letters,   1973.B9
Sands, Mollie,   1951.B7
Satire and the Novel in the Eighteenth Century,   1967.B6
"Satire, Theme, and Structure in The Traveller,"   1971.B7
"Satiric Ambiguity: The Vicar of Wakefield and the Kindly Satirist,"
    1965.B8

"Satiric Intent in The Vicar of Wakefield," 1968.B2
Schacht, Heinrich, 1904.A1
Schang, William J., 1971.A3
Schorer, Mark, 1933.B10-11
Schultze, Irving L., 1937.B3
Schwegel, Douglas M., 1962.B5
"Scientific Sources of Goldsmith's Animated Nature, The," 1943.B1
Scott, John, 1785.B1
Scott, Temple. See Isaacs, J.
Scott, Sir Walter, 1823.B1; 1825.B2
Search for Good Sense: Four Eighteenth-Century Characters: Johnson,
    Chesterfield, Boswell, Goldsmith, The, 1958.B9
Secret of Goldsmith, The, 1975.A2
Seeber, Edward D., 1945.B4; 1946.B5
Seitz, R. W., 1927.B6; 1929.B8-9; 1930.B8; 1931.B3; 1933.B12;
    1936.B3, 1937.B4; 1938.B6
"Self-Portraiture of Genius: The Citizen of the World, The,"
    1976.B2
"Sentimentalism of Goldsmith, The," 1933.B7
"Sentimentalism of Goldsmith's The Good-Natur'd Man," 1940.B5
"Sentimental Prophecy: A Study of The Deserted Village," 1962.B4
Seven XVIIIth Century Bibliographies, 1924.B3
"Shadwell's Contributions to She Stoops to Conquer and to The Tender
    Husband," 1912.B1
Sherbo, Arthur, 1955.B9
Sherburn, George, 1948.B3; 1967.B7
Sherman, Oscar, 1961.A2
"She Stoops to Conquer: A Parallel," 1933.B10
"Sir Fretful Plagiary and Goldsmith's 'An Essay on the Theatre,'"
    1974.B4
Smith, Hamilton Jewett, 1921.B1; 1926.A3; 1929.B10
Smith, John H., 1943.B3
"Social Stratification and the Obsequious Curve: Goldsmith and
    Rowlandson," 1976.B4
"Some of Goldsmith's Second Thoughts on English History," 1938.B6
"Some Sources of She Stoops to Conquer," 1929.B7
"Some Unpublished Letters of Pope and Gay and Some Manuscript Sources
    of Goldsmith's Life of Parnell," 1959.B7
"Source de She Stoops to Conquer, Une," 1930.B2
Sources Françaises de Goldsmith, Les, 1924.A1
Spector, Robert D., 1966.B6
"Speculations on Three Eighteenth-Century Writers," 1964.B3
Spilsbury, Francis, 1776.B4
Starkey, James, 1944.B6
Statistical Survey of the County of Roscommon, 1832.B2
Steeves, Harrison R., 1965.B7
Stein, Harold, 1934.B8
Stephen, Leslie, 1890.B1
Stevenson, Lionel, 1960.B6
Storm, Leo F., 1958.A1; 1970.B8; 1977.B8
Styan, J. L., 1973.B11
Survey of English Literature, 1730-1789, A, 1929.B6

Sutherland, W. O. S., Jr., 1965.B8

"Table Talk" [Cooke], 1793.B1
Table-Talk; or Original Essays [Hazlitt], 1822.B2
Tait, John, 1774.B9
Taylor, John, 1832.B1
Taylor, Tom, 1865.B1
Tears of Genius, Occasioned by the Death of Dr. Goldsmith, The,
     1774.B8
Templar, 1934.B1
Ten Master Historians, 1961.B2
"Text of Goldsmith's Memoirs of M. de Voltaire, The," 1930.B5
Thackeray, William Makepeace, 1853.B1
"Theme of Education in the Works of Oliver Goldsmith, The," 1967.A3
"Theme of Liberty in She Stoops to Conquer, The," 1971.B8
Theories of Pastoral Poetry in England, 1648-1798, 1952.B1
This Singular Tale: A Study of "The Vicar of Wakefield" and its
     Literary Background, 1971.A1
"Thomas Percy's Life of Oliver Goldsmith: An Edition," 1974.A2; 1976.A1
Thorpe, James, 1948.B4
Thraliana: The Diary of Mrs. Hester Lynch Thrale (Later Mrs. Piozzi),
     1776-1809, 1942.B4
Tillotson, Arthur, 1933.B13
"Time of Composition of Goldsmith's Edwin and Angelina, The," 1963.B1
"Time of Writing of The Vicar of Wakefield, The," 1961.B4
Tinker, Chauncey Brewster, 1928.B5
Todd, William B., 1953.B3; 1954.A2,B2-3; 1956.A1; 1958.B10
"Tony Lumpkin and the English Booby Type in Antecedent English
     Drama," 1943.B3
Topographical Poetry in XVIII-Century England, 1936.B1
Tracy, C. R., 1946.B6
"Tragic Picaresque: Oliver Goldsmith, the Biographical Aspect,"
     1960.B5
True Genius of Oliver Goldsmith, The, 1969.A1
Tupper, Carolyn F., 1924.B3; 1930.B9
"Two Essays Erroneously Attributed to Goldsmith," 1959.B5
"Two Issues of Goldsmith's Bee," 1944.B2
"Two Notes on Goldsmith," 1960.B3
"Two Unacknowledged Adaptations from Goldsmith," 1945.B1
"Two Worlds of Oliver Goldsmith, The," 1973.B5

"Unpublished Letter from Arthur Murphy to Goldsmith concerning She
     Stoops to Conquer, An," 1938.B1
"Utopia and Auburn," 1971.B4

Valliance, Rosalind, 1975.B4
"Vicar of Wakefield and Its Illustrators, The," 1902.B1; 1903.B1;
     1923.B3; 1924.B2
"Vicar of Wakefield and Recent Goldsmith Scholarship, The," 1976.B7
"Vicar of Wakefield and the Sentimental Novel, The," 1977.B3
"Vicar of Wakefield: A Paradox, The," 1966.B3

"Vicar of Wakefield, A Puzzler to the Critics, The," 1958.B8
"Vicar of Wakefield: A 'Sickly Sensibility' and the Rewards of
     Fortune, The," 1974.B3
"Vicar of Wakefield, Mr. Wilmot, and the 'Whistonean Controversy,'
     The," 1976.B6
"Vicar of Wakefield: The Problem of the Critical Approach, The,"
     1973.B10

Walcutt, Charles C., 1939.B3
Walz, John A., 1903.B2
Ward, Wildred, 1914.B1
Wardle, Ralph M., 1957.A1
Warner, James H., 1923.B1
Watson, Melvin R., 1956.B6
Webb, James W., 1962.B6
Weinbrot, Howard, 1976.B6
Welby, Lord, 1914.B1
Weld, Isaac, 1832.B2
Welsh, Charles A., 1885.B1
Wenzel, Michael J., 1974.B7
Williams, Franklin C., Jr., 1975.A3
Williams, Iolo, 1924.B3
Wills, Jack C., 1973.B12; 1975.B5
Wilmott, R. A., 1837.B3
Wood, Alice I. Perry, 1931.A1
Woodfall, William, 1773.B8
Woods, Samuel H., Jr., 1956.A2; 1976.B7; 1978.B5
Woolf, Virginia, 1934.B9; 1950.B3
"Wordsworth and Goldsmith," 1911.B1
Works of Oliver Goldsmith, The [Cunningham], 1854.A1; 1881.A1
Works of Oliver Goldsmith, The [Gibbs], 1884.A1
"Works of Oliver Goldsmith, a Hand-List of Dublin Editions before
     1801, The," 1928.B3
"Works of Oliver Goldsmith on the German Stage, 1765-1795, The,"
     1944.B5
Works of Oliver Goldsmith, with a Life and Notes, The [Bohn], 1848.A1
Woty, William, 1774.B9

Yearling, Elizabeth M., 1972.B3
"Year of Goldsmith's Birth, The," 1951.B4
"Young Goldsmith," 1929.B5

Zach, Wolfgang, 1977.B9
"Zu Goldsmiths Vicar of Wakefield," 1904.B1